THE FIVE

THE FIVE

The Evolution of the
Russian School of Music

BY MIKHAIL ZETLIN

TRANSLATED AND EDITED BY GEORGE PANIN

INTERNATIONAL UNIVERSITIES PRESS, INC.

NEW YORK NEW YORK

To

ALEXANDRA PREGEL

CONTENTS

THE FIVE

CHAPTER ONE

STASSOV

> *"Pound the drums and never fear,*
> *Kiss and hold the sutler near! ..."*
> HEINE

I

Vladimir Stassov was twelve years of age when he entered the Imperial Institute of Jurisprudence—an exclusive establishment for young gentlemen of good family which specialized in the training of future civil servants. His father, though an architect of but indifferent talent, was, in terms of erudition and moral qualities, an outstanding representative of his generation. While he belonged to the "upper-middle" income group of the capital and thus could frequent St. Petersburg "society" (which provided him with most of his clients) he had stayed in touch with the world of arts and letters and had taught his children to appreciate these things at an early age and aroused their intellectual curiosity. Vladimir (or *"Volodia"* as he was known to his friends and family) was thus far better read than most of his future classmates.

He was a good-natured, cheerful and gregarious boy and yet that first evening at school he felt sad and homesick. True, there was one consolation: he was now virtually grown-up, he was a student of jurisprudence—a *pravovied*—and from time to time he would glance surreptitiously and with a feeling of pride at the green piping of his uniform jacket even though, being unaccustomed to it, it chafed his neck.

After dinner a classmate mentioned that one of the senior boys was about to play the piano. Volodia was delighted for he loved music and he hastened downstairs to a small green-painted room where the performer sat before a box-shaped

spinet. Some forty boys from various classes sat or stood
around listening. The pianist was short and stocky, with a
bulging chest, a huge head and tiny feet and hands. His
crooked stumpy fingers could barely reach an octave, but he
played a transcription of the *trio* and *finale* from Weber's
Freischütz beautifully and was warmly applauded. Volodia
had noticed him earlier in the day, he knew that his name
was Aleksander Serov and so he now walked up to him, introduced himself, shook hands with him and informed him that
he, too, was a musician. Though Serov was nearly four years
his senior and their characters were very different, they soon
became bosom friends.

Volodia loved gymnastics and outdoor sports; his masters
were kind to him; the director addressed him by his first
name; he was loyal to and popular with his friends who
thought of him as a "regular fellow." About Serov, on the
other hand, there was something peculiar, repelling even.
Perhaps because he felt lonely among his own classmates, he
took an immediate liking to this young and enthusiastic boy
who seemed to love books and music just as ardently as he
himself did and who looked up to him with an air of adoration and never jeered at him or taunted him.

The friendship of the young possesses a charming quality
all its own that remains unforgettable to those who have
once experienced it. For the heart is as receptive as it is
vulnerable. There is an acute feeling of loneliness, a need
to share with someone the awakening and growth of one's
spiritual life. At times, this sensation is so acute that it is as
if the fibers and ligaments of one's innermost being, still so
sensitive, so very delicate, are about to break. But with a
friend at hand to share it all, this tension gradually eases,
one's trust in the world grows, one's feeling of identification
with the world at large is enhanced and this first exhilarating
friendship becomes something closely resembling a first love.

When the boys met, *"Sasha"* Serov was an indolent, colorless youth. Only when the conversation veered to art and

especially music, did he seem to come to life. Indeed it was
music that constituted the main bond between them. They
also loved painting, though in the beginning their knowledge of it was confined mainly to the reproductions in the
huge folios of the *Annales des Musées,* a French periodical
which they discovered in Volodia's father's library. They had
both begun to devour books at an early age. As a child, Sasha
was fascinated by the natural sciences and "adored" Buffon
(for in those romantic days, you didn't just love something—
you "adored" it and you positively "hated" that which you
happened merely to dislike). His father owned a complete
collection of the great French naturalist's works and Sasha
would copy Buffon's illustrations with loving care and considerable proficiency. He used to relate laughingly that when
he had an argument with his friends and wished to silence
them, he would announce sententiously: "Papa, Buffon and
I consider that . . ." (to which there obviously could be no
rejoinder). He was also quite a talented actor with a particular gift for reading comic skits out aloud, but then in this
Stassov was just as good. Besides the piano, Serov also played
the cello, but his fingers were too weak and stubby. Volodia
Stassov played the piano quite nicely too, taking lessons with
the famous Professor Herke and performing at school concerts. Their repertoire was typical for those days: Henselt,
Hummel, Thalberg (who ranked as a rival of Liszt—both as
pianist and composer).

Their friendship continued even after Serov had graduated
from school and gone to work for the Senate of the Empire
(his father, a high official in the Czarist administration, hoped
that his son would make a brilliant career for himself in the
Civil Service). Now, however, the two friends could not see
each other as frequently as before. Instead, they wrote each
other daily endless letters, so detailed that Volodia's studies
suffered. This correspondence was carried on in a conspiratorial manner: once a week, a schoolmate who spent Sundays
with the Serov family would bring with him Stassov's letter,

which was in the form of a diary covering the events of the previous week, and he would return in the evening with a reply equally extensive. This correspondence is concerned with the world of art, of ideas, of ideals and though it tells us nothing of their everyday life, it enables us to follow the gradual broadening of their outlook and to observe the process of maturation and refinement of their tastes.

Serov changed considerably with the years; his indolence vanished, giving way to an exceptional physical vitality. He became a remarkable *causeur,* seizing upon every random thought and elaborating upon it just as a virtuoso develops a musical theme through its many variations. No implicit meaning, no undercurrent of thought, no *nuance* however subtle escaped his vigilant mind and this slightly irritated Stassov, for it occurred to him that Serov was perhaps merely a "glove that fitted every hand" and that all this outward brio masked a lack of character, perhaps even a lack of convictions.

Serov liked to give dances, jointly with his sister Sofia, which were very popular with the younger set of the St. Petersburg *intelligentsia* and which the host himself enjoyed immensely, skipping around with his mincing gait and strumming improvisations on the piano until all hours of the night. On one of these chance visits to the Serov home, Stassov was somewhat taken aback to find brother and sister romping around the piano, clapping their hands and chanting gaily: "We are Yids! Just think of it, Voldemar, what a break! We are talented! We are Yids!" Their mother had apparently just informed them that one of their grandfathers, a Senator of Catherine the Great's days named Hablitz had been a converted Jew and this Semitic background seemed to them a sure token of talent.

Actually, Serov required no such proof. Even though both he and his friend had little concern for the material blessings of life, they were nevertheless convinced that theirs would be a glorious destiny. "A swarm of mediocrities is cluttering up the world," he proclaimed in one of his letters, "thereby

barring the way to the sovereign rule of the Muse of Art.
Roaming about incognito, she has perforce to pick her favorites from among those few individuals to whom beauty is
the ultimate and absolute *raison d'être* of man's existence."

It goes without saying that they regarded themselves as
belonging to these chosen few. And yet at times even Serov
went through moments of despondency to which alone Stassov knew the remedy. Alternating praise and reproach (he
had even coined an expression to describe this method: "he
jacked people up") he seemed already then to be practicing
the unique role he was to play later in the development of a
Russian school of music.

II

One spring day in 1847, the two friends learned that the
great Liszt himself was due to arrive in Russia on his first
tour of the country. They were, of course, terribly excited.
It was said of Liszt that as a pianist he excelled even Field
and Thalberg. He was, moreover, "divinely handsome," with
a profile resembling Dante and women simply raved about
him. For now, for the first time in their history, Russians
were beginning to succumb to the fad of lion-hunting—a fad
long fashionable in Western Europe and which seemed to be
in keeping with the romantic spirit of the age, along with
long hair, students' *berets,* Secret Societies and vague expectations of Freedom (with a capital "F"). In those early days,
however, this fad was still relatively free of the stamp of cheap
vulgarity which was to characterize it in later years.

On the day of Liszt's first concert, Serov and Stassov arrived at the Assembly of the Nobility (which boasted the
finest hall in town) far ahead of time. Stassov felt rather
conspicuous in his school uniform; Serov, however, looked
already quite grown-up in his pale-brown frock-coat, open at
the front and adorned by brightly-polished buttons. As they
waited, they carefully studied the program which seemed to

them unusually long. For Liszt was the first artist to introduce the concept of the so-called "historic concert" which offered a program of music from Bach through to the fashionable Chopin. This time, also, he was to perform alone, unaccompanied by an orchestra or even a singer—and this too was quite an innovation. The very appearance of the hall was unusual: a small dais had been raised in the center of the floor, upon which there stood two pianos—facing outwards—and two stools—back to back.

Gradually the hall began to fill. Stassov, of course, knew no one. Serov, however, kept greeting acquaintances, smiling and shaking hands. One of the people he hailed was a stoutish gentleman with a lock of hair curled rakishly on the top of his head, side-burns and a black frock-coat buttoned up to his very chin. He kept craning his neck and scanning the room with lively little eyes. This was Mikhail Glinka, the famous Russian composer (whose best-known opera, *A Life for the Czar,* Stassov, incidentally, disliked). Glinka was apologizing nervously to a lady for not having been to see her, he had been so busy working on another opera. *"Ah!"* the lady exclaimed, *"Ce sera certainement délicieux!* I shall never forget how you sang that lovely *romance* . . . Now which one was it? . . . Ah yes! 'Finn's song'! . . ."

Just then there was a stir and Stassov suddenly perceived Liszt behind a column, making his way through the hall at the arm of Count Vielgorski. The latter wore a frock-coat with a huge white cravat and a curly blond wig. Liszt also wore a frock-coat, a decoration dangled prominently over his white cravat and countless other medals and crosses hung from tiny chains across both lapels. The two young men noted this with distaste; they sensed in him a lack of simplicity, a sort of affectation, even in the tilt of his head.

Glinka explained to the lady at his side that he had already heard Liszt, the night before, at Vielgorski's. "Well? And how was it?" But Glinka was not an admirer of Liszt. Of course, the fellow played excellently, he said, but he had an unbearable way of dragging out his *tempi* and "mincing meat," as it were, with his fingers; moreover, even when he played Beethoven, he seemed unable to resist the temptation of dubbing in bits and snippets of music of his own; now take old Field or even Hummel . . .

All of a sudden, ignoring the steps, Liszt skipped up on to the dais, peeled off his white gloves, hurled them under the piano and after bowing in all four directions, sat down to play, starting off with the introduction to Rossini's *William Tell*. When the first number came to an end and the audience roared their applause, he switched pianos (as he was to do after each successive number on the program). The two friends sat as if transfixed. When he had finished, the hall went absolutely wild, the ladies tearing the virtuoso's gloves to shreds. But the two boys continued to sit speechless. Then, still in silence, for fear of spilling a single drop of the emotion that had welled up within them, they got up and went each his own way. Only later, when they were alone, did they proceed to exchange impressions, in writing. They assured one another that this day would remain forever enshrined in their memory. They were in love with Liszt.

They attended Liszt's other concerts with the same feeling of elation. The third time, he performed to the accompaniment of an orchestra which played the entire first part of Weber's *Konzertstück* alone, at first *piano* and then *fortissimo,* while Liszt himself sat absolutely motionless, as if engrossed in thought. Then, coming to life suddenly and, as Stassov described it later, "wrenching the instruments from out of the orchestra's hands and marching, as it were, over their bodies," he plunged into the *tutti* with such shattering power that the other musicians were drowned out altogether.

Stassov nearly missed this concert, having received his director's permission to attend only at the very last minute. He was already in the street when he realized that he hadn't any money either for his ticket or for his cab fare, but he went on running all the way to the concert hall anyway in the hope of meeting an acquaintance in the entrance. What with the rush and the fear of being late, his nerves were on edge and as Liszt started to play Beethoven's *Sonata quasi una Fantasia,* he was unable to hold back his tears and his neighbors were treated to the somewhat unusual spectacle of a lanky student of jurisprudence sobbing silently, his face burrowed in the velvet-covered ramp of the balcony.

After this concert, the friends summoned up their courage and both wrote Liszt a letter which Serov, being the bolder of the two, took to the maestro in person. Liszt couldn't help smiling as he read them. He realized that these were no ordinary "lion-hunters." In Hungarian, his mother-tongue, a young boy is known as a *"remèny"* or "one who gives hope." Calling in his youthful admirer, he sat down at his piano and then and there played to him his *Fantasy on a Theme from "Don Juan."* Serov emerged completely bewitched.

III

The years sped by. The two friends grew up, their respective lives following different courses, somewhat unusual for their times. Despite his father's inducements and even threats, Serov soon gave up his job with the Senate and embarked upon a career hitherto unknown in Russia—he became a music critic. To most of his contemporaries, it seemed sheer madness to choose to live by music, for the sake of music, when one was not oneself a musician and when one had, moreover, no private income of one's own particularly at a time when nobody in Russia seemed seriously interested either in music or in criticism. But Serov was sustained in his determination by the idealism inherent in youth and by his natural cheerfulness and perhaps also by that strain of Jewish blood over which he had been wont to rejoice as a youngster and which may well have accounted for the violence of his passions and for the fanatical tenacity with which he was to struggle through life.

Stassov, for his part, lacked the courage required to embrace the free career of an artist. Upon graduating, therefore, he entered Government service with the Department of Heraldry. He saw Serov nowadays but rarely. Their estrangement was due partly, perhaps, to the fact that Volodia had had a brief but passionate affair with Sofia Serova, his friend's sister, who had then transferred her affections to Dimitri Stassov, his younger brother. After which, again disappointed, the young lady had lapsed into a sort of obsessive hatred for the whole Stassov "tribe" (as she derisively called them), using probably the considerable influence she had over her brother against them.

Stassov lived all these years at home. Theirs was a typical pre-revolution Russian household: a *samovar* bubbled cozily twenty-four hours a day; guests wandered in and out; all day long there was music and laughter as the hosts and their friends played four hands on the piano or read to one another aloud or danced, sang songs and flirted. In the evenings, games were played, then dinner was served, followed by charades and amateur theatricals. The brothers were popular with their friends, especially Volodia. He kept falling in and out of love and was loved in his turn by many. He had borrowed a motto from Heine, his favorite poet:

> "Pound the drums and never fear,
> Kiss and hold the sutler near! . . ."

Unfortunately, however, these "sutlers" were apt to proliferate. A first illegitimate daughter died; another was now living with her mother, Elisaveta Klimentievna Serbina—a good, intelligent and cultivated woman. For Stassov objected to marriage on principle and especially in the case of two categories of persons: those endowed with an artistic or otherwise creative temperament and all the Stassovs generally. These, he claimed, should remain true to their bachelor's creed, to their Cossack community or *Sietch,* even if this meant that their countless illegitimate offspring were thereafter condemned to roam the world without a proper name. So strongly did he feel about this, that when his brother Dimitri took it into his head to get married and left the family abode, Volodia carried on and fumed and grieved as if this were a real calamity.

But presently he too was faced with a crisis. Like the hero of Heine's *Old Story,* he had fallen once again in love, only this time he encountered no response and merely inflicted further suffering upon another woman—the mother of his child. At one time he felt so despondent that he even contemplated suicide and bought a pistol. But he was far too attached to life, far too optimistic a man to ever go through with such an idea and so presently he did something else, he decided to go abroad and to forget all about it.

This, of course, involved giving up his job and now that his father was dead, leaving very little money, this was easier said than done. Just then something quite providential came to his notice. He learnt that Prince Demidov-San Donato, the descendant of Peter the Great's famous steelmaker and one of Russia's wealthiest men, was looking for a secretary to reorganize his fabulous library and collections. Stassov applied for the job and, having successfully passed a gruelling test, got it. For despite the many temptations of an outwardly fickle and carefree life, he had not wasted his time. Reading his beloved Heine and Diderot's *Les Salons,* he had been profoundly impressed with the novel type of literary and art criticism they had started; moreover he had studied much and earnestly and his first articles were even now beginning to appear in *The Fatherland's Transactions,* a much-read Russian periodical of the time. Deep down in his heart, he hoped one day to become the leading art critic of his day— the Bielinsky of the arts.

IV

Abroad Stassov "discovered himself." In his official capacity he came in close contact with some of the outstanding Europeans of his day and spent much time in their company. He was also able to continue his research work and read more than ever.

There exists a story about the impression his appearance made upon strangers in those days. Demidov was giving in his Tuscan castle of San Donato a fancy-dress ball which "all Florence" had been invited to attend in masks and period costumes. The climax of the evening came when the doors of the minstrels' gallery swung open and a knight appeared in shining armor and with lowered vizor. Judging by his gigantic size, it seemed quite impossible that the armor could be real or the man within—human. More likely as not, thought the guests, this must be merely another of Demidov's proverbial whims—a cleverly constructed robot. But presently the knight raised his vizor, revealing the handsome features of . . . Stassov. A stir of surprise and admiration ran through the throng of guests as the women whispered: *"E vero! Oh che bel uomo!"*

Though he followed his employer wherever he went, living in turn in Rome, Florence, London and Paris, Stassov was no ordinary tourist. Indeed, each of these cities became eventually a sort of spiritual home to him.

Italy, for all its great and glorious past, was in those days also the land of beggarly *lazzaroni,* of artists and artists' models, the land of song and painting. Stassov inhaled it all, drinking in the sun, the color, the beauty avidly, as if he wished to store it up for future consumption in drab, grey, gloomy Russia. Like Gogol before him, he enthused not only about the museums, but also about the merry, picturesque, vivacious Italian crowd, in the everyday existence of the man in the street. A letter, which he wrote during Easter week to an aunt, reads:

Saturday evening I dropped in at Nozzari's coffee shop (which is the best in Rome and is situated on the *Piazza di Spagna*) and ordering some ice-cream, sat down to talk with Botkin (the writer's brother) and two other Russians . . . about Gogol's death and Nekrassov's poetry. All of a sudden Ivanov, the painter, rushed in to tell us that we should get up immediately and start off on a tour of the city to watch the celebrations of "sausage day." We hired a hack, piled in all four of us, and proceeded to drive along the streets where the sausage-mongers have their shops.

On Good Friday and Holy Saturday, the streets look exactly like a benefit performance at the theatre: the doors are flanked with stout columns of piled-up parmesan cheeses, dark green and adorned with garlands of foliage; the ceiling looks as if it were sculptured, for it bulges with hundreds of small hams and Bologna sausages . . . The sculptors seem also to have been at work on the butter, cutting it, chiselling it, shaping it into a variety of groups, decorative patterns and statues. And everywhere there is foliage, fresh, bright-green and inter-woven with festoons of sausages. And everywhere too there are burning candles, hundreds of them, lighting everything up like a ball-room. Best of all, however, is the display of eggs, just opposite the doorway. A yard or so above the floor there is a sort of square little niche, in which countless eggs are lined up in a single row; at the far end of the niche a small mirror has been installed, so cleverly that you hardly notice it and the row of eggs appears to be a mile long and each one of them is lit up and sparkling. You catch a first sight of this delightful picture from the street and you just can't help stopping in the doorway, together with dozens of little boys and girls and especially those charm-ing Italian women. That night I stepped out of the hack some fifty times, I think, so as to look at every shop and particularly so as to watch all those faces and eyes feasting on the sight . . . I didn't even get to kiss anybody three times, as we Russians do traditionally at Easter! But then, if only you knew Rome, you would realize that I was not to blame for that! Had I had the opportunity, I would be kissing those Roman girls still! . . ."

Actually, this last complaint is quite unjustified, for he got to kiss at least one Roman girl and not only at Easter. He was, in fact, so much in love with this girl, a sultry beauty called Nina, that his passion for Rome and for her seems to have merged temporarily in a state of joyful ecstasy.

But time was passing and Stassov was beginning to feel more and more homesick. He sensed that the moment was fast approaching when he would have to put an end to this life of wandering and study. By now he had worked out his own views on art, his own concepts of that which he wished to teach and propound. The time had come to pass these views and concepts on to others. By now also the Crimean war had started, threatening to cut him off from Russia indefinitely. Lastly, the capricious if friendly despotism of his employer was also beginning to irk him.

Before leaving Florence, he went to have a last glimpse of the many things he had learned to know so well, the bluish Tuscan hills, his beloved San Mignato and his favorite churches. After which he returned to the tiny *Vicolo degli Agli* where he had rented a room in the ancient Palazzo Ricci-Aldovisi and where he used to stay overnight when loath to return to suburban San Donato. At first, the very name of this alleyway had scared him, for he couldn't stand garlic. But despite its name, the street smelled not of garlic but of cypress trees and this delicate fragrance, which seemed to pervade the whole town, was even stronger up in his room where the pictures on the walls were framed in cypress wood. He felt a sudden pang of regret as he realized that he was about to exchange this delicious perfume for the stench of onion and fusel of his homeland.

He stopped off in Vienna to hear Wagner's *Lohengrin*. He had never heard it before and something about the music immediately rubbed him the wrong way. And to think that his friend Serov had become one of the foremost champions of Wagner in Russia! But Serov too was now merely a part of his past. His heart missed a beat as he realized that someone else, someone so very much more important was awaiting him in St. Petersburg, the dean of Russian composers himself —Mikhail Ivanovich Glinka.

CHAPTER TWO

GLINKA

"Music is my soul!"
"Life is a counterpoint, a
symbiosis of opposites..."
GLINKA, *Reminiscences*

I

In exploring the human skull for the location of man's distinctive traits and faculties, Lavater—the founder of the science of phrenology—is said to have discovered, among others, a "bump of respect." If this is the case, Stassov must surely have been graced at this spot with a veritable tumor. For his was a religious temperament, requiring a human object of reverence. Though this was contrary to the second commandment, it was specifically an idol that he invariably looked for among the people who crossed his path.

He had been introduced to Glinka by Serov. By this time Glinka no longer led the life of dissipation that had so taxed his strength and leisures in earlier years. Upon returning to Russia after a prolonged stay abroad, he found himself the center of a group of amateur musicians which, besides Serov and Stassov's younger brother Dimitri, included a wealthy Smolensk landowner by the name of Engelhardt. Glinka, though many years their senior, treated them all as equals. He felt thoroughly relaxed in their company and referred to them affectionately as "our brotherhood."

Occasionally, Stassov would be invited to attend their gatherings at which they played four or even eight hands on the piano. Once or twice, he had heard Glinka sing in his small, ugly, peculiar voice.

Presently Glinka left St. Petersburg for Warsaw. He claimed that the climate of Warsaw was milder than that of

St. Petersburg, but there was another reason for which Warsaw was more congenial to him. "Polish women," he used to say, "are the Frenchwomen of the North. They are sweeter, kinder and more subtle than our Russian women. Polish women! What a paradise for an old man!" Shortly after his departure for that paradise, Stassov himself had left for Italy to work for Prince Demidov.

They occasionally corresponded. Glinka had toyed with the idea of going to Spain and when he learned that Stassov was also planning to go there, he wrote him a note saying: "I'm looking forward to meeting you on the banks of the Guadalquivir." But nothing came of this project.

In 1853 Stassov was in Rome when a mutual friend brought him a visiting card inscribed in French "Michel de Glinka" with a footnote in Russian in Glinka's own hand: "To Stassov, in Florence." All of a sudden Stassov felt a burning wish to meet with Glinka in Italy and he wrote him a long letter:

Dear Sir, Mikhail Ivanovich. You cannot imagine how much pleasure I derived from that little piece of glazed cardboard bearing your name. But chance (or is it fate?) is far more omniscient and all-powerful than we are in these matters. It knows that major joys become still greater when they drop in on you out of a blue sky, or wherever God knows they come from, and specifically in those places which are the most wonderful or the dearest to one's heart. It knows that ever since I left Russia and began to roam around Europe, I have never liked or enjoyed anything quite so much as I do Rome. It knows also how glad I was, after such a long silence, to note that you have not forgotten me, even after Paris. And thus it has gathered together in a sort of powder keg all that I like most and has set off the most wonderful fireworks. You should have seen how eagerly I questioned Zheleznov about you as we sat in that tiny grubby dimly-lit Cafe Greco, where you too must have sat out many an evening in the company of other Russians.

Incidentally, Gedeonov told me that you too were planning to come to Rome. Why don't you? In Rome you would feel wonderfully well; the air one breathes here is so genuinely an artist's air, it is so heartwarming and you would find yourself the object of that wholesome Russian hero-worship amidst which, I believe, you grew up in St. Petersburg. Nowadays Rome is a widow, bereft of powerful creative personalities. Briulov is gone, so is Gogol, after having swooped down upon this city like eagles to their nest. Gone also is that merry gang of Russian painters who used to settle down to work only after having philandered away the assumed value of ten years' anticipated earnings.

Or is Paris really better than anything else? As for myself, I have reaped in Italy a most precious harvest. I have met of course, but few people, in fact I have met only one person, but what a person—Rossini! The press had made him into a sort of overstuffed gluttonous cretin. And what do you think I found instead? I found that very same artist's soul, so wonderful, so modest, which I have always delighted in finding in you (although he doesn't have your fire) and I now spend many an evening with him discussing everything that has even the remotest connection with music.

Then I have discovered in Rome one Abbé Santini who possesses, as if concealed deep down in the unexplored recesses of the earth, veins of pure gold and silver and whole rock-clusters of diamonds and emeralds. As far as I can gather, he has collected every single musical score that has ever been written in Italy. His set of Palestrina is complete and of course unique . . . I have had copies made of whole stacks of this music and when I travel to Russia, I will be followed by a veritable caravan . . .

Probably, when you were in Italy, you too had quite a good time. Is it possible that you should now have forgotten her altogether or else ceased to love her? No, it cannot be; it is not like you to stop loving . . . I feel that way because I know only too well that no one, who once knew you, has ever been able to forget you or cease loving you and that happens, I believe, only to those who are themselves a scintillating source of light and love (*"un foyer éclatant de lumière et d'amour"*).

To which Glinka replied:

"Your friendly and kind letter gave me so much pleasure that I forwarded it to my sister who will hardly delay showing it to our Petersburg brotherhood, which includes your dear brother Dimitri Vassilievich. . . . If the great Allah wills it, I will be back in St. Petersburg by May of next year, 1854, and will spend the following winter there. What fun it would be if you could join us there. I doubt whether you would find anywhere else a more devoted group of amateurs of classical music . . . During the winter of 1851-1852, we played the works of many a composer, but we are not very well acquainted with those old Italian gentlemen—we don't have them over there."

II

Stassov followed up this invitation and returned to St. Petersburg. Playing four hands with Glinka, he realized now that the latter was not a great pianist. Moreover Glinka disliked the "meat-mincing" style of playing so popular with many contemporary virtuosi. He had even invented a superlative for this word and spoke about "that super-meat-mincing Liszt." Above all else he valued softness of touch, smoothness, grace and neatness of performance. About Liszt, in general, he had many reservations: in Chopin's *Mazurkas,* his *Nocturnes,* his *Etudes,* in other words—in all the more dashing fashionable concert stuff—Liszt, he said, was good even though he performed them *"à la Française, avec exagérations."* He was far less good when he played Bach—whose *Clavecin bien temperé* he knew, incidentally, by heart—or Beethoven's *Pastorale* (which he himself had transcribed for the piano) and the same could be said of his interpretation of classical music in general.

Occasionally Glinka would reminisce about other great pianists of his day. "Even when improvising," he said, "Hummel played softly, neatly, as if he had thoroughly studied and memorized everything beforehand." But his great favorite was Field: "With Field," he said, "you had the impression that his fingers, instead of hitting the keys, dropped on them of their own free will, raindrop-like, scattering like so many pearls over a velvety surface."

Stassov gazed at him in rapture. Although by this time Glinka had become very stout and looked older than his 50 odd years, there was an ethereal quality, a sort of Mozartian lightness about him, about his voice, his small twinkling eyes, his whole person in fact, and the contrast between his outward ponderosity and this inner lightness was as charming as it was unexpected.

Stassov kept insisting that he write his reminiscences. But

for the time being, Glinka much preferred to talk about the past with a group of friends over a bottle of wine, than to write about it. His stories were invariably colorful, interspersed with pithy observations and full of good-natured humor and Stassov would sit for hours listening, holding his breath, avidly absorbing every word.

III

Glinka was born on March 20, 1804 on his family's estate in the Government (i.e., Province) of Smolensk. At a very early age he was turned over to the care of his grandmother, an old and ailing woman who doted on him. He was a sickly, nervous child and so she presently moved him, his nurse, and his wet-nurse into her own room which, in winter, was as hot as an oven and where the windows were opened only in an emergency. Little Misha was allowed out of doors only in summer and even then only on warm days. He was fed tea with heavy cream and was stuffed with home-made milk rolls. His grandmother spoiled him beyond all measure and had there not been within him a basically sound core, he might easily have turned into a little monster. Although these years of hothouse existence failed to warp his character, they wrecked his health permanently. All his life Glinka was to suffer from various ailments, both genuine and imaginary.

Like most musically gifted people, Glinka remembered well his first impressions of sound. As a child, he loved the tolling of bells and used to imitate them by striking copper pots and pans. On festive occasions his uncle, who lived in the neighborhood, would send over his private serf-orchestra to play *Ecossaises*, *Mazurkas* and other dance music, but little Misha didn't want to dance. Instead, he would stand quite close to the orchestra, fascinated, and sometimes he would pick up a violin or a *piccolo* and try to join in. Dinner was served to the tune of Russian folk-songs played by 2 French horns, 2 flutes, 2 clarinets and 2 oboes and it was these sad

melodies which, he claimed, predetermined the whole subsequent course of his life. "On one such occasion," he related
to his friends, "when I was ten or eleven years old, they
played Crusel's *Quatuor for Clarinet and Strings* which made
an indescribable, novel and enchanting impression on me.
All that day I was in a state of feverish excitement, I felt as
if something inexplicable and yet wonderful were happening
within me, and the next day during my drawing lesson, I
was simply unable to concentrate. The teacher scolded me for
my absent-mindedness and finally, having guessed what was
the matter with me, said he had noticed that I could think
of nothing but music. 'What can I do about it?' I replied,
'music is my soul!' "

Glinka started taking piano and violin lessons when he
was still very young. But he preferred orchestral music.
"Apart from Russian music," he said, "my favorite orchestral
works were Boieldieu's *Ma tante Aurore,* Kreutzer's *Lodoiska*
and Méhul's *Les deux aveugles.* I did not like Hirovetz, the
Czech composer, at all, partly because I found his sonatas
much too long and confusing, but especially because they
were very badly printed and on dark days I had trouble reading the score, for which I was quite often rapped on the
fingers with a pencil."

But it was difficult to punish him, for he was a gentle, meek
and dreamy little fellow.

Glinka remained in the countryside until the age of thirteen when, in a carriage padded with fur to protect him
against the cold, he was taken to St. Petersburg and there
placed in a "Gentlemen's Boarding School," one of several
pre-collegiate institutions which were just then coming into
fashion in Russia and from where, upon graduating, the
young gentlemen could join the civil service without having
to attend a university. Here Glinka was able to pursue his
musical studies under the supervision of qualified teachers.
He had particularly warm words for Karl Mayer with whom,
on graduation day, he played Hummel's *Concerto for Two*

Pianos in A Minor. His violin lessons gave him trouble, however. *"Glinka,"* his teacher complained with his heavy German accent, *"Fous ne shouerez shamais du fiolon!"*

But even school discipline and the companionship of rowdy classmates failed to toughen him. His closest nursery friends had been his younger sister and his nurse's little daughter. Having thus grown up among women, he was invariably attracted to them. All his life, in fact, the poetical friendship of a woman was as inalienable a part of him as was music itself. In most cases, this relationship was a purely sentimental one, on the borderline between friendship and love. For women fall but rarely in love with a man who blushes at the slightest provocation and who regards them, moreover, with a sort of superficial tenderness, as one would a friend with whom it is fun to chat pleasantly or to play games or to sing, but no more. Glinka spoke particularly fondly of one beautiful young girl who played the harp and for whose sake he first began to compose music. "She had a clear, genuine sorprano and she sang very naturally and pleasantly," he related. "I was deeply moved and inspired by her admirable qualities and her kindness to me. She used to call me 'my little nephew' and I called her 'my little auntie.' She loved music and when I was playing with my uncle, she would often sit for hours by the piano and sing our favorite passages in her lovely silvery voice. . . To please her, I ventured to write a set of variations to her favorite theme in C major from Wegel's opera *The Swiss Family Robinson.* Then I composed some variations for harp and piano to Mozart's *Theme in E Major* and after that I wrote a waltz in F major for the piano on a theme of my own inspiration. These were my first attempts at writing music. In those days I hadn't even the faintest notion of figured bass."

At the age of eighteen Glinka graduated as valedictorian and joined the civil service. But the sweet opiate of art was beginning to tell. He neglected his work and on more than one occasion his superiors urged him to give up his "silly pastime." His family, however, took a more lenient view and this had its good points since, thanks to them, he gained admittance to many a fashionable salon where ladies young and not so young played the harp and warbled Italian arias. He even started taking singing lessons himself with an Italian by the name of Belloli. Now and again, when one of these sweet creatures happened to strike his fancy, he composed a piece of music for her. This was something very unusual for a nobleman in those days. Finally, even his family grew worried. As one of his relatives put it: "Besides enjoying it yourself, your piano-playing may help you meet pleasant, indeed useful people. Composing, however, will bring you nothing but envy, trouble and disappointment!" "To some extent," Glinka added ruefully, "I have already experienced the truth of this warning!"

It was about that time that he met Nestor Kukolnik, the writer. Though an interesting conversationalist, Kukolnik hated arguments. If he happened to disagree with his friend, he would fill Glinka's glass and announce sententiously: "Misha! My agreement is not available! Let's have another!" In his home, Kukolnik had removed a partition between the dining room and a small dark passage and had installed an enormous Turkish divan which stretched out across the entire length. At night, when his guests had tired of playing or singing or reciting or drinking and dancing, sheets and blankets were spread out on this couch on which five or six of them could stretch out with ease. The only problem consisted of finding one's particular place at night and extricating oneself in the morning. Conversation resumed at breakfast, after which the musicians would settle down again to their playing and those who chanced to have a job or had other matters to attend to would go into town for the day, only to reappear in the evening. In later years Glinka never tired of reminiscing with a touch of nostalgia about the exhilarating times spent with Kukolnik's "brotherhood," as he called it.

In 1828 he resigned his job. His health had been giving him more and more trouble lately and this, coupled with his work and his multiple social obligations, was beginning to hamper the free development of his talent. Two years later, a further deterioration of his condition prompted him to do something he had always dreamt of doing—he went abroad, to Italy.

The purpose of this trip was twofold. On the one hand Glinka hoped to improve his health and on the other, he wished to study musical theory. Actually he succeeded in doing neither. Even in Italy his nerves gave him no rest. The pain, at times, was so great that he would roll on the floor in agony. Neither did he discover the type of music teacher he was looking for. Although he used to refer to Italians as "singing birds without taste," Italy was still the land of singers, and his own singing improved accordingly. The excellent technique he acquired there, the knowledge of the human voice and its possibilities, were to serve him later in good stead. His sojourn in this luminous, melodious and colorful land ("*O Dio!*" he kept exclaiming, "*Che tinte!*") produced upon him the same effect it had on so many other Nordic artists: it laid bare certain unsuspected facets of his innermost being. But it was only in Berlin, on his return journey, that he discovered a really good teacher, a German by the name of Siegfried Dehn.

As was often the case with Glinka, even this episode was linked to yet another sentimental entanglement. "Dehn," he related, "is now the foremost musical magician in Europe. I had met in Berlin a singing teacher called Taeschner, who had in turn introduced me to one of his pupils, whom I shall call Maria. She was only about 17 years old. She was part-Jewish, tall of stature but not yet quite formed; her face was perfectly beautiful, she looked like a Madonna. I began to teach her singing and even wrote some exercises for her; years later I re-arranged some of them and they became the Jewish song for my opera *Prince Kholmsky*. I saw Maria practically daily and I gradually realized that I was becoming more and more attracted to her—an attraction which she, apparently, reciprocated . . ." Glinka, for some reason, omitted to add that he nearly married her. "But," he resumed, "that is neither here nor there. . . It is through Taeschner that I encountered Dehn. I worked under Dehn's guidance for five months or so. He used to make me write fugues for 3 and later 4 voices; actually these were only skeletons of fugues, they had no words and were invariably based on themes by well-known composers, but they were written in accordance with all the rules that govern this type of music. Dehn compiled for my benefit a series of courses on the theory of harmony or figured bass, of melody or counterpoint and of orchestration, all of which fitted into four thin copybooks. . . I undoubtedly owe more to him than to any other of my teachers. He put some order, not only in my knowledge of music but also in my whole concept of art and it was only afterwards that I began to work consciously, instead of groping, as it were, in the dark. He never plagued me in that pedantic classroom manner. Nearly every lesson opened up some new interesting horizon. . . Of course, even five months with Dehn were insufficient to turn me into a punctilious counterpointist. But this was perhaps for the best, since the rather rigid German approach to counterpoint is apt to hamper the free play of one's fantasy." And Glinka would burst into peals of laughter as he related how his Milanese teacher Basili insisted on giving him excruciating assignments in order to *"sottilizzar l'ingegno,"* as he put it. Indeed nothing could have been more alien to someone like Glinka than to "refine his inventiveness."

His father's sudden death brought him back to Russia before he had completed his studies. He would not have stayed very long in St. Petersburg, however, had he not once again fallen in love and this time in all seriousness. Glinka never liked to talk about his marriage, for it ended in a painful separation. Unfortunately, the delightful little blonde head which swept him off his feet and which he first perceived as her maid was combing out its golden locks, was devoid of any content. Indeed his wife had so little understanding for his vocation that she would even complain about his spending too much money on sheet music. "On another occasion," Glinka related, "Beethoven's 7th Symphony was being performed in Count Vielgorsky's house. It was an exceptionally successful performance. After the *adagio,* Professor Soliva, who taught at the School of Dramatic Art and was a very good theoretician, jumped up and exclaimed: *'E una cosa che fa stupore!'* I myself was so deeply moved that when I got home my wife asked me solicitously: 'What is the matter with you, Michel?'—'It's Beethoven!' I replied—'But what has he done to you?' she said, and I had to explain to her that I had just been listening to some admirable music."

One day as he, his brother Dimitri, and Serov were resting after playing eight hands on the piano, Stassov brought up the subject of *A Life for the Czar* and while they remained seated at their pianos and the guttering candles glowed faintly in the twilight, reflected in the black lacquer of the instruments, Glinka started to describe the agonizing, wonderful days when his first opera was born.

"Though I lived at the time a rather secluded life," he began in his low even voice, "I used often to visit Vassili Andreyevich Zhukovsky, the poet, who lived at the Winter Palace (where he was tutor to the Czarevich, the future Emperor Alexander II) and where once a week a select group would assemble in his rooms: Pushkin, Prince Viazemsky, Gogol, Pletniov. . . One day I mentioned my intention of writing a Russian opera, whereupon Zhukovsky suggested that I take for my subject the story of Ivan Sussanin. He wished to write the libretto himself and on the spur of the moment he recited to us the now-famous lines: *Oh! But it is not for me that blows the desolate, stormy wind . . .* (from the *trio* with choir of the epilogue). But Zhukovsky's other occupations kept him too busy and so in the end he referred me to Baron Rosen, a prolific writer. My own imagination, however, forestalled that of my librettist. By what seemed like a stroke of magic, I suddenly saw it all quite clearly: the over-all plan of the opera, the juxtaposition of Russian and Polish melodies, the various musical themes and even the minute details of their ultimate elaboration."

—"How did the Baron work?" Dimitri Stassov asked with a twinkle in his eyes, for the friends had heard many a story about Baron Rosen.

Glinka pounced at the bait: "He had quite a bit of trouble," he explained, "for it was necessary for him to adapt his lyrics to an already existing score that often required most unusual metres. But he was really very clever at it! For instance, I would ask him to write so many lines of such and such a character with so many feet or syllables each, some of which were often quite unconventional, but he never batted an eyelid. When I came to him next day, or the day after —there they were! Zhukovsky used to tease Rosen about it and claim that his pockets were crammed with snippets of prefabricated verse and that I had only to say what I needed, for him to plunge his hand into a pocket and produce what I had asked for. . .

"I admit," Glinka added, "that the famous *trio* was inspired by the great passion I had for my fiancée at the time. I was staying in the country that summer and couldn't bear to be separated from her even for a minute. I felt deeply every word of the *Adagio* (or is it the *Andante?*) which goes: *Why do you tarry, beloved one?*

"In April of that year, 1835, I got married. Rosen presented me with an epigramme of rather doubtful quality, which he insisted that I use for my *Quartet*: 'But you don't understand,' he pleaded stubbornly in his rather heavily accented Russian, 'This poetry is really of the very best vintage!'

"I wrote to my mother that my heart had come to life and my music had resuscitated. And this was indeed so. After the

wedding we went to live in the country. I had taken with me
the libretto for two acts of my opera and I well remember
how, all of a sudden, as we were driving along in our carriage somewhere beyond Novgorod, the music of that choir
number came to me, which goes: *As the spring floods merrily,
laughingly spill over the pastures ...*" and Glinka's fingers
ran lightly over the keys as he played the tune.

"I don't recall much of our life in the country," he resumed. "I remember only that I worked very hard setting the
lyrics to the score and composing additional scenes. Every
morning I would work in the vast cheerful hall of our house
at 'Novospasskoye.' The whole family was there, I remember:
my sister, my mother, my wife. The greater the noise and the
louder they talked or laughed, the faster I progressed. The
weather was lovely and I used to leave the door into the
garden open so as to let in the wonderful balmy air of the
countryside."

Vaguely, at first, but soon more definitely, Glinka sensed
that he was blazing a trail, that he was performing a feat—
that he was creating Russian music. The idea had been with
him for a long time. Already from Italy he had written that
he was not only creating a Russian theme for an opera, but
that he wished the music itself to be strictly Russian in character: "I want my fellow countrymen to feel thoroughly at
home in my opera," he wrote, "I don't want foreigners to
regard me as an impostor, a sort of crow in peacock's plumage!" What he was looking for was a Russian plumage and
when he found it, he made it sparkle more dazzlingly even
than that of a peacock. He had long ago tired of the Italian
sentimento brilliante. "We people of the north," he used to
say, "feel differently. With us it is either frenzied gaiety or
else bitter tears. With us love is invariably coupled with
sorrow."

A Life for the Czar was accepted readily by the administration of the Imperial Theatres, but on one cruel condition:
that he relinquish his copyrights. The rehearsals began. At

one of them the Emperor himself was present. He asked Glinka: "Are you satisfied with my artists?" Glinka was a shrewd psychologist. "Especially with the conscientiousness and zeal with which they perform their duty, Sire!" he replied without flinching. The Emperor was most gratified.

When Glinka recalled the opening night of November 27, 1836 his voice shook a little with emotion. For it was a veritable triumph. Indeed it was the only unqualified success of his whole life. During rehearsals of the *Polonaise in C Major,* and of the *Choir in D Major,* where the *pizzicato* of the strings reproduces the ripples of the balalaikas, the musicians laid down their bows and applauded and this ovation meant more to him than all the enthusiastic praise of profanes among the public.

Illness prevented him from attending the dress rehearsal, but on opening night he sat in a box of the second tier. The hall sparkled with diamonds, decorations and dashing uniforms. The *Trio* in the first act was applauded but after the Polish scene, the audience remained ominously silent. The composer became worried and descended into the wings. Fortunately this silence turned out to be merely in anti-Polish demonstration, for the Polish mutiny of 1830 was still fresh in everyone's memory. Whatever doubts may still have lingered in his mind were dispelled by the *Duo* of Petrov (singing Sussanin's part) and Vorobiova, who were both remarkable artists. Glinka was in a state of complete rapture. He was summoned to the Imperial box where the Czar Nicholas congratulated him and the ladies graced him with a smile. Next day he received a present from the Emperor—a 4000-ruble diamond and topaz ring.

The opera was not only an artistic success; it was a patriotic triumph. As far as "society" was concerned, Glinka's music was *de la musique pour cochers.* The few existing newspapers did not even bother to comment on it. Only the *"Northern Bee"* published an enthusiastic review by Prince Odoyevsky and a critical reply by Bulgarin. Although with the exception of Odoyevsky, Glinka's friends—the writers of the Zhukovsky group—did not care for music, regarding it as a somewhat noisy rival of their own silent art, they rejoiced sincerely at their "dear Mikhail Ivanovich's" success and, at a dinner party given by Vsevolozhsky, the director of the Imperial Theatres, a toast in verse—the joint product of Pushkin, Count Vielgorsky, Prince Viazemsky and Zhukovsky—was sung somewhat hoarsely to Prince Odoyevsky's music.

Occasionally, when Glinka happened to be in a good mood, his young friends would beg him to sing to them. Whereupon, seating himself at the piano, throwing back his short torso and shooting a sidelong glance from below his glasses at his listeners, he would sing excerpts from his operas, oddly interspersed with a few Italian melodies and if his mood was especially good, he would stay up singing until all hours of the night. His voice ranged somewhere midway between a tenor and a baritone. Though not very good, it had so much feeling that even the great Petrov himself, they felt, could hardly have done any better.

When he sang his own *romances* (which were, incidentally, of very uneven quality) his listeners had the peculiar sensation of participating in the process of creation. For joyous or sad, these melodies seemed to reflect their own feelings of the moment. "This is better even than Schubert!" thought Stassov, for they seemed reborn each time he sang them, retaining the very flavor, the languor, the state of delicious trance which had cradled them.

IV

The success of *A Life for the Czar* gave Glinka new wings. Understanding and sympathy were to him as vital as the very air he breathed. He immediately started work on another opera on the subject of Pushkin's *Ruslan and Liudmila*. But this time progress was much slower: it took him six long years to complete it. Indirectly, success brought Glinka also material security: the Emperor appointed him Kapellmeister of the Imperial Chapel. "Glinka," said Czar Nicholas, "I have a favor to ask of you and I trust that you will not deny it. My singers are famed throughout Europe, it would therefore be worth your while to take care of them. Only I beg of you, do not turn them into Italians!" The poor composer was so overwhelmed that instead of replying, he merely bowed repeatedly.

Success had also an adverse effect, however. His new duties took up much of the time which he might otherwise have devoted to composition. He made many new friends, was invited everywhere and wherever he went he was obliged to perform and to sing. He became so popular that he often didn't get enough sleep and in his own words, "started leading the life of a post horse."

As usual, he was often in love. Princess Sherbatov, the young widow to whom Lermontov dedicated such beautiful lines, often invited him to dinner, promising him "a slice of the moon and a piece of fur" (which meant that she would light a round chandelier in the sitting room and allow him to wear her sable stole). But though she was very attractive, their relationship did not go beyond a poetical friendship. There were to be many such "slices of moon" and "pieces of fur" in his life! Another platonic involvement seems to have been of a more serious nature. In his "Reminiscences" he refers to her only by her initials "E.K.," but Stassov knew that they stood for Ekaterina Kern, the daughter of Pushkin's heroine, to whom the poet had dedicated his *I Recall a Cherished Moment* and whom he used to call the "sinner of Babylon." By no means beautiful, she had an inspiring face, with the flushed cheeks and wild staring eyes of a consumptive. Though this passion was short-lived, it hastened Glinka's separation from his wife. This was no easy matter, for at first Mrs. Glinka stubbornly refused him a divorce and maligned him continuously. Then she remarried even before

the divorce papers had come through and was nearly prose-
cuted for bigamy. All this entailed tedious court proceedings
which caused Glinka acute mental anguish.

But he overcame this crisis too. He was always happy when
working and ever since the spring of 1841, he had again felt,
in his own words, "unusually inclined to compose music."
By the following spring, 1842, his new opera *Ruslan and
Liudmila* was ready for submission to the director of the
Imperial Theatres.

"I led a very pleasant life," Glinka recalled. "In the morn-
ings, I would re-arrange the dance sequences or put the final
touches to the unfinished scenes. Around noon I would stroll
over to attend a rehearsal at the Opera House or at the School
of Dramatic Arts. I would lunch at my mother's and then
spend a few hours with my family. In the evening, I would
nearly always go to the theatre where I would stay most of
the time in the wings. When I got home my little sister Olga
would greet me with peals of laughter and when I asked her:
'Why are you laughing, Olgine?' she would reply: 'You're
back, which means that we'll have fun!' And thus life sped
by on golden wings. . ."

Ruslan was the zenith of his creative career. Like every
intelligent artist, Glinka fully appreciated the significance of
his work. He realized that *A Life for the Czar* paled in comparison with this new opera. And yet *Ruslan and Liudmila*
never really "got across" to the public. He had first been
attracted to Pushkin's fairy tale because of its lush coloring
and the diversity of its moods, which offered a vast scope to
his fantasy. Moreover, the subject enabled him to play up the
contrast between the two predominant elements, one Russian,
the other Oriental, and just like Pushkin himself, Glinka had
an amazing ability to project himself into another, alien
world. For the first time in the history of European music,
the genuine East was pictured with unprecedented force.
Unfortunately Pushkin's tale lacks dramatic interest. The

poet wanted to adapt it to Glinka's music himself, but he was killed just then in a duel and the transcription was done, therefore, by untalented amateurs who turned this graceful fairy tale into a top-heavy and endless pageant where, in the words of a witty contemporary, in every scene someone seems to fall asleep, while the audience sleeps throughout. The richness and variety in *Ruslan and Liudmila* is centered in the music, but this music was too novel and too profound to be appreciated by Glinka's contemporaries. Those who came not to listen but to watch (and they were in the majority), quite naturally found the opera tedious and their boredom was relieved to some extent only by the ballet scene, the sets and the costumes with which the administration had been most lavish.

Ruslan and Liudmila opened on the night of November 27, 1842, six years to a day after *A Life for the Czar*. "When it was all over," Glinka related, "and I was called out to take a bow, the applause was half-hearted and there were many whistles of disapproval, especially from the stage and the orchestra pit. Before going down I turned to General Dubbelt, who sat in the director's box and asked him: 'They seem to be whistling. Should I go out?'—'Sure, why not?' he replied, 'Christ suffered even greater agony!' " The Emperor and his family left before it was over and the Grand Duke Michael would joke that he would punish delinquent officers by sending them to *Ruslan* instead of to the guardhouse. Even Count Vielgorsky, a friend and a fellow musician of Glinka's, told him quite candidly: *"Mon cher, c'est mauvais!"* Again with the one exception of Prince Odoyevsky, the critics' reviews were laconic. Nevertheless, *Ruslan and Liudmila* survived through thirty-two performances that season.

The following year, the Italians arrived and Rubini, Tamburini and the admirable Pauline Viardo definitely stole the show. *Ruslan* was dropped from the repertory. This was a terrible blow for Glinka. He again sought escape from Russia and seized upon the first opportunity, in the summer of 1844, to go abroad.

V

The last 12 years of his life sped by in travel, illness and work, but although he searched for a subject and even began to compose, he wrote no more operas.

His first stop abroad was Paris which he loved and which he described as "a fine, cute little town" where life was temperate and wholesome (for in those days gambling was rare and one didn't have to go constantly to parties); here he was never bored, for as the mood dictated he could go for walks, or sit down for a drink with friends at a streetside cafe or listen to the Italian opera. He had always approved of French women, but he found their male counterpart (*le Français mâle* as he put it) cold, selfish, superficial and corrupt. Moreover, nowhere else, he claimed, did money play such an all-important part in everyday life.

He was less enthusiastic about the celebrated musicians he met during his travels abroad. "As a child," he said, "I had never liked Meyerbeer's music. Now when we met, he spoke to me with typically Jewish servility and amiability. Mendelssohn I met once in Italy. It was a fleeting encounter. Sobolevsky brought him to see me one day when I was ill and he spoke to me in a rather bantering tone, probably because he had the somewhat undeserved reputation of being a first-class pianist. I myself didn't play, but after much coaxing he agreed to perform a light *Rondo*. In Paris, a man called Souza introduced me to Hector Berlioz who happened to be contemplating a trip to Russia with the hope of reaping a harvest of something more than applause! He was very kind to me—which cannot be said of most Parisian artists who are, as a rule, terribly arrogant. I used to visit him two or three times a week and we would discuss his work very frankly. I liked his music, especially his more fantastic pieces."

Berlioz liked his Russian colleague's work too, and even wrote two long and eulogistic articles in the *Journal des Débats*. Glinka was overjoyed, for this paper had a large circulation, wielded considerable influence and could be found in all the coffee shops of St. Petersburg. These two articles, plus a very flattering review by Prosper Merimée were, in fact, the best reviews that had as yet appeared on Glinka in the press. Berlioz performed several of Glinka's works at the so-called "Festival Concerts" which he gave from time to time in a large circus on the Champs Elysées, with the participation of two orchestras and a choir of 360 singers. But the admirable *Lezginka* was not appreciated by the audience, partly, perhaps, because of its novel and daring harmony. The vocal works, moreover, were badly performed, the singer was nervous and sang off-key. After that Glinka gave a concert of his own works that cost him a lot of money and was quite successful, but this success was that of an *oiseau de passage* as the French say; it involved no commitments on the part of the native artists and could not hurt their pride, since they knew that the Russian composer was merely a visitor in Paris and his music, therefore, was unlikely to cross the frontiers of his motherland.

In Spain, which was his next destination, Glinka fell frankly in love with everything and everybody. Indeed it became a sort of second home for him. He loved the Spanish countryside and the character of the Spanish people and especially the Spanish music and dances. He had never expected such warm hospitality, such nobility of feeling. "Over here," he wrote, "no amount of money can buy you friendship or favor, but with kindness you can obtain anything in the world." Here he reaped a rich musical harvest. From an orchestral point of view, his *Jota Aragonesa* and his symphonic picture, *Recollections of a Night in Madrid,* can match the best works of Liszt and Berlioz. He was the first foreigner to delve, fully armed with the weapons of modern harmony, into the treasure house of Spanish folk songs and to transform them into symphonic music.

Stassov was greatly thrilled by this new type of music and searched in vain for an explanation why his friend's output was so meager. Could it be his poor state of health? Or his roving life? Or the congenital laziness of an aristocrat? And yet Glinka was not lazy. He knew how to work. Moreover he liked to work. As a child, he had only to busy himself with something to become, in his own words, "a fragile, untouchable mimosa." Indeed he was capable of such concentration, that not even the presence of other people in the same room would disturb him. Of course, he had inherited quite a few of the atavisms of a spoiled aristocrat, but these showed up rather in his physical appearance, his way of life, his attitude towards women.

Wherever he went, in Warsaw, in Paris, in Madrid, he surrounded himself with the type of women who, in nineteenth century Europe, were commonly known as *"grisettes."* He enjoyed their merry prattle and their carefree laughter, while to them he was an amusing little old fellow in whose company they never felt shy. And since with age, his imaginary and real ailments demanded increasing attention, whenever he happened to be away from home and far from his mother's or sister's loving care, he would look around for a "nurse," who had to be invariably young and pretty and who acted as part-time concubine and part-time attendant. Though there were many of them in his life, he remembered all their names and about all of them he spoke with his usual kindness, making them seem perfectly charming.

In Warsaw, for instance, there was "nurse Thecla" who was so kind and so helpful, and who had but one defect—a marked addiction to vodka. She was succeeded by a little Parisian girl, Nini. Lolo was a twenty-year-old Andalusian gypsy, with a tiny foot and a pleasant voice, to whom he gave singing lessons and who taught him Spanish songs. After which there was another French girl, Adeline who, though not very pretty, had a sweet expression and would sit in the first row of the stalls at his concerts and burst into tears from sheer emotion whenever he was called out to make his bow. There was only one whose name he never mentioned—a seventeen-year-old serf girl who was his sister's personal maid, a sweet and funny little thing who used to refer to *A Life for the Czar* as "our opera."

But although in everyday life he was a typical Russian aristocrat, with all the shortcomings of his set and times—in matters of art he was a severe and exacting technician. He knew that the first commandment of an artist is to be at all times an innovator, to always march forward. "I am often accused of laziness," he would say, "but when you suffer from constant nervous trouble and when you have as severe a concept of art as I have, it is not possible to write a lot. You can't imagine how difficult it is not to repeat oneself." This, surely, was not the language of an aristocratic dilettante!

VI

One day, Stassov dropped in to see Glinka at an unusually early hour. As he climbed the stairs, he heard the dulcet voice of *"Dasha"* Leonova, Glinka's favorite pupil. The piano broke off suddenly: "No, Dasha! This passage should be sung far more languorously!" and in his rather croaky voice, her teacher proceeded to show how very languorous this could be. Glinka came out to meet him, dressed in a brocade robe, and led him into a small parlor adjoining his bedroom, where Stassov sat waiting for Leonova to finish her exercises. Behind the bedroom door he could hear the merry trilling of many canaries. Presently Glinka appeared, patting his hips and obviously pleased with himself. "Forgive me, my dear friend Vladimir Vassilievich," he exclaimed, "but I had to finish Dasha's lesson. I have rearranged some of my old *Romances* for her and have set Lermontov's *Prayer* to music for two voices, choir and orchestra. My old bones get a kick out of that sort of thing. Besides, the music may be of some use to Dasha." Glinka crossed the room. The canaries fell silent. Many birds of different types and coloring were kept in open cages and as he half-opened the bedroom door, they fluttered out into the room and settled on his head and shoulders. They had apparently established a good relationship with their master. The rays of the early sun lit up the stumpy figure in the flowing robe and the sparkling coloring of the birds' plumage. "Look!" Glinka said, "I'll stir them up a little!" and he picked up a violin and started to fiddle and the room resounded with the answering twittering and whistling of the tiny creatures. "This little grey fellow over here is the leading *tenore di grazia* of my choir. He is quite tame and the more noise there is around him, the merrier he becomes. . . On my name-day, coming April 21st, I will release all the members of my little serf-orchestra, every last one of them!" Stassov couldn't help feeling that in some way Glinka was himself a singing bird, who had been born into this world to bring happiness and joy to mankind, except his release wouldn't come until his time was up.

Stassov had brought along Serov's transcription for eight hands of several excerpts from *A Life for the Czar*. Glinka leafed through the score with unrestrained enthusiasm. "I'd never have been able to do such a job," he said, "and yet it is I who wrote this rubbish. You're right, I have really given up composing nowadays. I merely keep rearranging my earlier compositions. But there's no doubt about it, Serov has a special talent for this sort of thing! Take this score here for instance. When I look at it, I say to myself: '*A Life for the Czar* is already forgotten. Sometimes they play it at the circus, and even then only because the star-singer happens to be sick and the stand-ins don't know anything else. Because *my* operas can be sung by anyone!'. . . And yet I know that it will be of some significance in the annals of our Russian art, whatever that fellow Rubinstein may or may not be writing about it abroad—and incidentally, he is a worse pianist than even Liszt! He has now undertaken to introduce our national music to the German public and has as a result merely messed everything up for us! As for my poor old woman (Glinka always referred to his first opera as his 'old woman') he claims that she's a failure, *'es ist gescheitert,'* he says! And yet she isn't at all *gescheitert*. Though, I grant you, nobody understood her significance at the time. If I'm not mistaken, only my old friend Aleksei Petrovich Melgunov realized its importance. He sent me a review he had written and I, the fool that I was, forgot all about it. I was far too absorbed by my young wife and my even younger fame!" Glinka searched around in a drawer of his desk. "I still have it," he continued, "here it is, you should read it, Vladimir Vassilievich! After all, you too are a critic of mankind."

Stassov picked up the closely written pages and when he got home and began to decipher them, he flushed with excitement, so pungent, truthful and valid were Melgunov's remarks. "The main elements in music," Melgunov wrote, "are melody and harmony; they are like contour and coloring in pictorial art. It is by the individual characteristics of these elements that one distinguishes one school of art from another. . . Glinka has undertaken a task—that of expressing in every musical form but especially through the medium of opera, the lyrical quality of the Russian character. . . In so doing, he has not confined himself to an approximate imitation of the popular folk song, no! He has studied very thoroughly the structure of Russian songs, the way in which they are performed, the outcries, the sudden transition from solemnity to cheerfulness, from loudness to quiet, the subtle interplay of light and shadow, and also the development of the musical period, in fact all that is so unpredictable about the Russian song, which allows no laws but its own. In short, he has discovered and explored a melodic and harmonic system that is specifically Russian and which derives from the very sources of Russian folk music. . ." And Melgunov predicted that a purely indigenous Russian school of music

would develop in Glinka's wake. Stassov read on and his
heart thumped with emotion. His own innermost thoughts
were reflected in these yellowing pages. Yes, indeed, one day
there *would* be a Russian school of music! Glinka would be
followed by others and it would be his, Stassov's job to find
them and encourage them until they stood firmly on their
feet!

VII

That winter Stassov made the acquaintance of two musicians who were to become the first apostles of this new musical creed.

Aleksander Sergheyevich Dargomizhsky was a small man
of about 40, with a sardonic smile, who dressed with a claim
to fastidiousness in a long brown frock coat with a large silk
bow tie. His face looked greyish, sallow and unhealthy, a few
sparse hairs curled on the top of his head, a pair of tiny
eyes twinkled—intelligently and mockingly. He spoke in a
squeaky soprano, played the piano with zest and wrote operatic music.

Glinka had known Dargomizhsky for many years and
despite the age difference between them they addressed each
other by their first names. Although he gave his young colleague every encouragement and hoped that he would, one
day, become a proficient composer, Glinka couldn't help feeling some misgivings about Dargomizhsky's unscrupulous pla-
giarizing of his own music. Once, as he was listening to the
Princess' aria from Dargomizhsky's still unfinished opera *The
Woodsprite* (in Russian: *Russalka*), he remarked: "Look here,
doesn't this rather resemble my Gorislava's aria?"—"So what,
brother?" was Dargomizhsky's bland reply, "All the foreigners are copying you, why shouldn't we Russians be
allowed to pluck out a few of your feathers for a change?"

Glinka had been among the first to appreciate his young
friend's earth-bound comic gift and he kept urging him to
write a comic opera, but Dargomizhsky took offense. In his

opinion, a comic talent was an inferior sort of talent. His feeling for Glinka was a peculiar combination of envy and enthusiastic admiration. For one thing, he resented the fact that Glinka was the idol of one Liubochka Belenitzina, with whom Dargomizhsky was himself very much in love and then he couldn't forgive Glinka for having been the first to blaze the trail and reap in Russia success, fame and devotion.

The other musician whom Stassov met that winter was Mili Balakirev, an 18-year-old pianist and composer. Balakirev had been brought to St. Petersburg from Nizni-Novgorod by one Ulybyshev, a music-loving landowner and a friend of Glinka's. Ulybyshev was an unusual man. Many people mistook him for a gentleman-dilettante. Actually, he had a great fund of musical knowledge, had written and published in French a biography of Mozart and was now writing a polemical treatise on Beethoven. His views on Beethoven provoked general indignation, but considering the times, they cannot be denied a measure of originality: for Ulybyshev claimed that with Beethoven had begun the period of decline of classical music. He had also another hobby: translating Dante.

When Ulybyshev brought Balakirev to see Glinka for the first time, the latter asked the young man to sit down at the piano and play first alone and then four hands with him. He was quite flabbergasted by Balakirev's talent. He was all the more pleased with his visitor in that he assumed the young man might feel shy in the presence of a celebrated composer. Actually, if anyone needed heartening, it was rather Glinka himself, for Balakirev's self-assurance and the intolerance with which he commented on everything and everyone were so great that they would have been disconcerting had they not been typical of a first-generation upstart intellectual. Glinka, however, he treated with respect. In fact, he seemed to know all of *Ruslan* by heart, as well as a good half of his songs. Balakirev had written a few things himself and he now played the *Allegro* from his still unfinished *Concerto in F sharp minor,* which he followed with his *Fantasy on Two Themes from 'A Life for the Czar,'* and Glinka had to concede that it was a masterpiece.

. Shortly thereafter Balakirev performed in public at a University concert under the baton of Karl Schubert. In March 1856, he gave a concert of his own works which received good reviews in the press. Among those who praised him warmly was Serov. Glinka did not hesitate to predict that this man would one day become a great musician. "He will be a second Glinka!" he told his sister Liudmila Ivanovna Shestakova and urged her to entrust the young man with the musical schooling of her little daughter Olechka when she was old enough to take music lessons. And yet, though flattering, the adulation of his disciple both irked and frightened him.

VIII

Toward the end of 1855 Glinka felt once again inclined to travel. "I thank my stars," he said, "that I am able to flee Russia, where with my character and under present conditions life has become intolerable." "Life," he added, "is a counterpoint, a symbiosis of opposites." This symbiosis of opposites, this latent ambiguity permeated also his feelings for Russia. Glinka shared this complex—this simultaneous *odi et amo,* this sensation of being at the same time attracted and yet repelled—with many of his Russian contemporaries. Abroad he felt homesick and claimed that Russian music could be created only on Russian soil. Yet whenever he returned to Russia, he realized that it was only in Paris or Berlin that he was able to "live and let live" and work in peace. What hurt him more than anything else, however, was the realization that although he had opened up to them the innermost secrets of their musical treasure house and thus also their own soul, he was neither understood nor appreciated by his countrymen, and that open wound would simply not heal.

At times Stassov wondered whether this was not the primary reason for Glinka's long silence. He kept nagging him. He reproached him for his laziness, for neglecting to make the most of the creative genius with which he had been endowed. Why didn't he write another opera? he asked. Why didn't he draft a Russian national system of harmony? A comparative study of ancient Russian church music and of the religious music of the West had convinced Stassov of the continuing importance of the ancient ecclesiastical modes, of the so-called "plagal cadences"—when the chord of the subdominant immediately precedes the tonic. He had discovered that they had been used by every composer in their moments of major creation, particularly Chopin. This had become a sort of obsession with Stassov. He expected all music of the future to proceed from these "plagal cadences." And Glinka had agreed and had asked him to supply him with the necessary documentation. But when Stassov mentioned the voluminous treatises of the musicologist Adolf Marx, Glinka begged for mercy. Rather than try to understand Marx, he said, he much preferred to go to Berlin to look up his old teacher Dehn, who would initiate him into the intricacies of German musical wisdom. The very idea of resuming the life of a student made Glinka feel like a young man again.

Meanwhile, he copied out medieval church psalms, transcribing for three male voices certain parts of the Russian Orthodox mass. He promised his friends that he would surpass even the great Bortnianski, the pundit of Russian early 19th century church music, whom he reproached for being too "honey-sweet." For his part, Stassov rejoiced at having been able to "jack up" even the great Glinka himself.

IX

Glinka had planned to leave Russia in April 1856. He had been living with his favorite sister Liudmila Ivanovna

Shestakova, as he was wont to do when he was in St. Petersburg. He had been ailing since Christmas and had hardly
ever left his room. His little niece Olechka was now his main
joy and solace. He could spend hours with her, sprawled out
on the carpet, playing with her and her pet kitten. With true
feminine intuition, Olechka realized how very kind and
gentle he was and she ordered him about unceremoniously,
only to remark afterwards: "Missia is an obedient fellow!"
He would sing children's songs to her and, one day, Stassov
found him dancing a mazurka with her fat and protesting
nanny, while Olechka watched and roared with laughter.

For the last time he and his friends got together for an all-
night revel. For the last time he played and sang without
stopping until dawn. He sang to them his latest piece, a
romance which he had written to Pavlov's words:

> "Tell me not that your heart
> Grieves over a stranger's suffering! . . ."

When he reached the cycle of songs entitled *Farewell, St.
Petersburg!* and intoned Stassov's favorite:

> "Let me sing a last song
> And then rip apart the strings of my heart . . ."

he felt a sudden lump in his throat and his listeners also
wept. How young he had been when he had written it, just
before one of his earlier departures from St. Petersburg,
how full of strength and faith he had been then, and how
tired, how spent he was now. . .

The day before his departure, on the 26th of April, Stassov
dropped in to see Mrs. Shestakova and suggested that her
brother have his picture taken. His last lithographed portrait
was outdated, having been made 14 years earlier. This time
Stassov, who loved all that was new, suggested that he be
photographed. Liudmila Ivanovna promised to persuade
Glinka to go to the photographer Levitzky, which he did,
half-heartedly, though.

His friends had arranged for him to travel free, by post-chaise, in the company of a German acquaintance of theirs, who played the bass fiddle and was also going to Berlin. They were to set out at 1 p.m. After sitting down for a short prayer, according to Russian custom, Glinka, Liudmila Ivanovna and Stassov got up, crossed themselves, took their seats in the chaise and drove out together to the gates of the city. There Glinka got out and warmly embraced first his sister and then his friend, after which he walked away a few steps, spat on the ground and exclaimed: "I hope I never see this horrid country again!"

At first, the news they received from him was good. He was working with Dehn and was happy. Meyerbeer showed him every consideration. At Glinka's request, he staged Gluck's operas at the Berlin opera house; he even performed Glinka's own works at a Court concert. On the way home from this concert, Glinka caught cold. And then his friends in Russia learned that he had died quite suddenly on the 3rd of February 1857.

A memorial service was held in the Court chapel on Koniushennaya Street, where Pushkin's burial service had been held twenty years earlier. A few mourners huddled at the front of the dimly lit church. Mrs. Shestakova knelt and as the priest intoned the mass and the choir echoed the response, silent tears streamed down her cheeks. Stassov stood with bowed head. It occurred to him that some mysterious destiny seemed to guide the lives of great people to their final goal. How often had he heard Glinka complain about his "unlucky star." And yet, all things considered, fate had not treated him so badly. The loyalty of his friends, the devoted love of his family, the tender friendship of women had constantly graced his life. His childhood had passed amidst the plenty of the Russian countryside and the wealth of Russian sounds. Fate had then taken him to Italy, without which experience the creative energy stored up within him may well never have erupted with such force. Like Goethe and Duerer before him, he had absorbed the Italian sunshine, inhaled the fragrant aroma of Italy's lemon-trees, hearkened to the music everywhere about. Next he had familiarized himself with that most severe of all musical disciplines—the German counterpoint, and yet the absorption of this discipline had not curbed his innate inventiveness. And then, by what seemed like a further stroke of magic, just when he had needed to plunge back into his native soil to seek inspiration for his first opera, he had fallen in love, however briefly, and had thus been forced to stay there. No, however unbearable the hardship and suffering may have seemed at times, Glinka had been really a favored child of Fate!

Stassov couldn't help also reflecting on the likeness of Pushkin's and Gogol's exploits. But Pushkin, at least, had had forerunners—he had been preceded by Batiushkov, Derzhavin, Zhukovsky. Glinka had had nothing but the fathomless depth of Russian folk music before him!

CHAPTER THREE

BALAKIREV

"In him there was an overwhelming magic,
An unfathomable might ..."
LERMONTOV, *The Demon*

I

A little brass tablet above the doorbell read: "Messieurs
Stassov." Actually, besides the "Messieurs," i.e., the four Stassov brothers, there were also a number of women living in
the house: Vladimir Stassov's brother's Nikolai's wife, their
three daughters, a sister—Nadiezhda, two old aunts and an
adopted niece with her governess, who was regarded as a
member of the family. Old man Stassov had left a small capital, which was managed by brother Aleksander. The latter
had been in his youth a follower of the "nihilist" Petrashev-
sky and had barely escaped arrest. He had kept up his earlier
friendships and one could, therefore, meet in the Stassov
house the elite of the liberal *intelligentsia* of the day; the
historians Kostomarov and Pypin, Arseniev, Spassovich, etc.
Brother Dimitri's friends belonged mostly to the musical
world. The great Anton Rubinstein himself would often
come and play to them. People kept dropping in at all hours,
but Sunday was the official reception day, when guests would
begin to arrive in time for lunch, staying on far beyond midnight. Theirs was indeed one of those typical intellectual
homes—hospitable and totally free of prejudice—that were
so distinctive a feature of prerevolutionary Russia.

It was an easy-going existence and yet Vladimir Stassov
could ill afford to be jobless, for he had always hated to count
pennies. A distant relative of his happened to be employed
at the St. Petersburg Public Library, which had recently been
put under the care of a new director, the energetic Baron

Korf (a former schoolmate of the poet Pushkin). Stassov remembered the library as a typical Government institution—inefficient and uncomfortable. Now, under Korf's guidance, it changed beyond recognition: everything was geared to providing better service for the public, the book funds grew by leaps and bounds, available resources were sorted out and catalogued. A better occupation for Stassov could hardly have been thought of. In 1857 he applied for and was given a job there.

Working in the Art Department, he started a catalog of "Rossica" and published several articles on the Public Library in the press. This made his name known to the director who presently invited him to help with the compilation of a series of historical studies which Czar Alexander II had requested the Baron to write. In other words, Stassov was to be a "ghost writer." He accepted and joined the Baron's personal staff. It was a secret to no one, not even the Emperor, that it was Stassov who did most of the work and as it had been agreed between him and the Baron that he would be rewarded in terms of money and promotion, but would receive no decorations and as the Baron backed him up in every way, he was made, presently, director of the Fine Arts Department with the title of "Excellency." What meant far more to him than any promotion, however, was the fact that he could now devote himself entirely to his vocation—serving the cause of Russian art—without worrying about his daily bread.

He was soon plunged in a maelstrom of activity: organizing interesting exhibitions under the Library's auspices, compiling remarkable yearly reports, engaging in research in the various fields of the history of art. Now also began his zealous and never ceasing dedication to Glinka's memory. An invisible bond of love and sorrow seemed to tie him to all those who cherished the Master's memory and above all to Glinka's foremost follower, Mili Balakirev.

II

Mili Alekseyevich Balakirev was not quite eighteen when he first met Mikhail Glinka. In terms of age, therefore, he was almost a *Wunderkind*; his whole appearance and manner, however, were already those of a genuine *Wundermensch*. Just as Athena is said by ancient legend to have sprung from the head of Zeus fully equipped, helmeted and spear in hand, so Balakirev seemed to have been born scribbling a score, a conductor's baton in his hand. He looked all of thirty; his face was framed by a full-grown beard, his features were handsome if somewhat coarsely cut and nothing, at first glance, betrayed either the refinement or the nervous temperament of an artist. Occasionally, however, a glow would appear in his eyes and a note of restrained emotion would sound in his voice.

Perhaps subconsciously, because he wished to enhance this impression of manhood and maturity, he disliked to speak about his recent adolescence and his not-so-remote childhood. Even those close to him knew little about him. They knew only that he was the son of a junior government official in Niznii-Novgorod; that his parents were both musical; that his mother, who died young, had taught him to play the piano; that when he was ten years old, he had taken a few lessons from a pupil of the famous Field and had played Hummel's *B minor concerto*—the same which Glinka had once played for its author. They knew also that he had studied mathematics at the University of Kazan but had not completed the course. His real schooling had been in the home of the wealthy landowner Ulybyshev, where all music lovers of the province liked to gather.

Ulybyshev had a fairly good library of music and every Thursday and Saturday (which were "off-days") the orchestra of the local theatre would play at his house. Sitting in Ulybyshev's small drawing room, Balakirev would talk music with his host far into the night. Soon the latter entrusted his young protégé with the preparatory training of the orchestra which numbered some twenty instruments. In the end, just before departing for St. Petersburg, Balakirev was also allowed to conduct the concert performances.

Had Stassov not known about these facts, he might have been inclined to regard Balakirev's knowledge of music as sheer sorcery. But even knowing it, he was amazed. Both in his compositions and his improvisations, Balakirev displayed a complete mastery of harmony and counterpoint. His knowledge of instrumentation was striking. His musical memory verged on the miraculous; he never forgot anything that had been played to him even only once and knew virtually all the classics by heart. He played the piano as well as Anton Rubinstein, without the latter's dazzling technique, of course, but with greater depth and penetration. Besides his knowledge of the orchestra, the powerful magnetism of his personality seemed to hold out the promise of a great conductor's career, of another Berlioz. His judgments, moreover, were all carefully weighed, solid, authoritative. And this was coupled with an idealism, a devotion to art such as Stassov had never yet encountered. By all rights, such a man was entitled to tread the road to European fame. Of him, as of Napoléon, one felt like saying: *"Il sait tout, veut tout, peut tout!"*

Although fourteen years his senior, Stassov looked up to Balakirev and the two young men soon became deeply attached to each other. Their friendship was a momentous experience. Continuing and deepening through the years, it never became commonplace as so often happens. The prose of everyday existence played but little a part in their lives and was, moreover, consciously or unconsciously excluded from the area of their association. Their friendship rested on a higher plane, where there were none of the trivialities of life, but only the more significant interests of the arts and the spirit. There was even a certain ceremoniousness about their relations: they did not address each other by their first names for instance, as is the custom among friends in Russia.

In those days Balakirev lived a secluded life, far removed from the flurry of activities and interests that involved Stassov. He was poor, gave lessons and prepared himself for action, for struggle, for glory, with the seriousness and concentration of a novice about to take the vows. It was as if poverty and continence were already an integral part of his life. Even the tiny room he rented in the apartment of one Mrs. Sofia Ediet—a Russianized German—resembled a monk's cell. Contrasting with the cold and indifferent background of the city, the warm friendship of Stassov who believed in him and valued him, meant a great deal to Balakirev.

With his fiery, well-nigh Italian temperament, Stassov was always bubbling over with feeling for something, or even for nothing at all. He liked Balakirev not so much as a man, but because of his unyielding idealism, his frank and bold truthfulness and because Balakirev was to him the live embodiment of his own dreams of a Russian school of music.

III

The early sixties in Russia were an extraordinary period. Shaken out of its inertia by the disastrous Crimean War, the Government had just embarked upon the road of reform. One change was following the other in quick succession; everything was being overhauled more rapidly even than in the days of Peter the Great. Moreover all this was done not by revolutionary forces from below, but by the authorities themselves from above: the emancipation of the serfs, the reform of the judiciary by the establishment of open trial by jury, the introduction of universal military service, the creation of rural and municipal organs of local self-government (the so-called *Zemstvas*)—there remained but the "crowning of the edifice," i.e., the promulgation of a constitution!

Meanwhile, a real wave of optimism was sweeping the

country. Among the cultured classes, in the *intelligentsia*, a spiritual movement was emerging which was to engulf Russia for half a century. Though it did not, as yet, bear the name of "Populism" (in Russian: *"narodnichestvo"*), in fact it constituted its preparatory stage. A peculiar religion in atheistic array, a social and humanitarian religion, it engulfed even the more remote areas of human endeavor—the arts, literature, music. Faith in the Russian people, the "common people" and in a higher order of truth and goodness which the latter supposedly alone possessed; the urge to serve this people, to merge with it as one, to atone for the sins committed against it (and especially the greatest sin of all—centuries of serfdom)—those were the main tenets of the populist creed.

Though he did not fully share these beliefs, Stassov stood close to them. And because of that, the Russian *intelligentsia,* for all their dislike of government officials and their distrust of artists, were prepared to forgive him both his soiled and worn uniform-jacket and his "aristocratic whims," i.e., his interest in art and music ("the peasant," they claimed, "has no call for either!"). And even those who refused to have anything to do with him and who regarded his activities with a tinge of sarcasm, never denied his "intellectual honesty," which was the highest praise they could award to one who did not quite "belong."

Balakirev was even more of a stranger to this movement. Deep-rooted emotional ties (of bourgeois or ecclesiastical origin) bound him to a remote, long-vanished Russia. There was about him an authentic "earthiness" which made him yield but reluctantly to Stassov's cosmopolitan tolerance. If, as far as Stassov was concerned, there existed literally no distinction between Jew or Gentile, in Balakirev there were unmistakable seeds of reactionary chauvinism; he held no brief for foreigners, especially Germans, Jews and Poles. Besides, like all artists, he was an individualist; he distrusted and feared the masses and these feelings, too, were just the

opposite of "Populism." And yet even he, under Stassov's influence and because of the very spirit of the times, absorbed
many an idea, many a sentiment, many a prejudice held by
the Russian *intelligentsia* of the sixties.

They frequently played music together and at the piano
Balakirev, of course, excelled. It was he who interpreted the
works they played, throwing new and unexpected light on
long-familiar passages. Stassov had a better knowledge of the
classics, of the old Italian composers and of ancient Church
music. Mili, for his part was, like all creative temperaments,
narrow-minded. While not rejecting the classics altogether,
he was relatively indifferent to them, holding that the great
gems of classical music constituted foundations upon which
one should build, but that there was no need to become
obsessed with them. The classics were something well-known,
they could be taken for granted, whereas he was interested
in exploring new paths. And he never ceased to marvel at
the magnificent mystical rhetorics of a Liszt, at the *chiaros-
curo* of a Schumann, at the dazzling coloring of a Berlioz
orchestration. He liked Chopin, but valued him less highly.
Both he and Stassov (though the latter without much conviction) despised the *petit bourgeois* Mendelssohn and neither
of them could stand "that pompous exhibitionist" Wagner.

But if in music Stassov bowed generally to his younger
friend's leadership, in all matters "intellectual" it was Stassov
who led. They loved to read aloud to one another, which
Stassov did with his usual mastery for hours on end, while
Balakirev listened, pacing the room, sitting down, jumping
up again or even stretching out on a couch. Occasionally,
absorbed by their reading, they would forget to trim the
wick of the oil-lamp and it would begin to smoke, black
soot would fill the room, penetrate their nostrils, their
throats; they would start to sneeze and to cough and the
landlady would have to be called and the windows opened.

What didn't they read! Homer and Shakespeare; Gogol and
Nekrassov; books on natural science (which were required

reading for the *intelligentsia* of their day); Belinsky, Chernyshevsky. For some mysterious reason, the latter's rather primitive *What is to be done?* made a particular impression on
Balakirev; reading it, he said, helped him to understand how
operas should be written—however, he never got around to
composing one.

Neither of the friends had an exceptionally keen intellect.
Stassov was more experienced and better educated perhaps,
but then Balakirev was cleverer by nature, more spontaneous,
more of a non-conformist. He approached the few intellectual problems (outside of music) which interested him, in his
own manner, indifferent to the accepted clichés.

One problem, however, really fascinated him, one to which
"Populism" provided such a welcome, idealistic answer. What
sort of a people were the Russians, this people who had produced a Glinka and who were now expected to work miracles
and to create a new, heretofore non-existing Russian school of
music, a people whom Nekrassov and Belinsky, each and
everyone, the newspapers and the periodicals, the lectures
and the proclamations besought one to love and whom he
himself loved so intuitively ("deep down in his guts," as he
was wont to say) without questioning, as one loves one's
family? Why *should* one love them?

The answer was: for many reasons. Because they had suffered and were still suffering; because Fate had passed them
by; because of the tremendous forces lying locked up within
them; because they loved God and made fun of the clergy;
because they worshiped ikons and at the same time despised
them; because they were the bearer of the great Message of
Truth and because they retained ideals of meekness and
resignation; because they were born rebels, ever ready to
revive the times of Pugachev; because they had remained
true to the communal way of life. In other words, because of a
thousand contradictory qualities and characteristics and because of the mysterious, luminous, flickering, iridescent con-
notation of the word "the People." And yet, like a doubting

Thomas, Balakirev wished to lay hands on the wounds in order to convince himself of the People's qualities. Therefore, together with his friend, he avidly read everything that related to the Russian people, *their* people.

Alas, when they read the Russian historians and especially the fashionable Kostomarov, they couldn't help feeling depressed. For everything in Russian history seemed rotten to the core, false, mean! St. Petersburg was the non-Russian capital of a completely Germanized empire and the St. Petersburg period of Russian history was, thus, utterly loathsome. But then the Moscow period did not fare any better! Stassov had bitter words for the ancient capital of Russia: "... that no-good, blowzy, toothless, untalented, cringing, servile old bigot!" He couldn't forgive even Glinka for having chosen as an opera subject "that apotheosis of Russian boorishness in its Muscovite version!" *"A Life for the Czar,"* he would exclaim bitterly, "is an opera with a cancer that is slowly gnawing it to death!"

But Balakirev disagreed. "Our people have indeed been defiled," he replied. "In fact, the only aspects of their national life which have remained unimpaired are those which have had no connection with the State or with politics in general, i.e., art." In this judgment he was influenced, probably, by a school of thinkers which had preceded the Populists and to whom he felt a considerable affinity, namely the Slavophiles. Except that in setting the people up against the State and in regarding them as the harbinger of a supreme Message of Truth, the Slavophiles shared with the Populists an ardent faith in the people, whereas Balakirev, for his part, believed that the State had made so many inroads, that only art had survived. Furthermore, the Slavophiles' hatred was focused on the St. Petersburg period of Russian history, whereas the two young friends followed Kostomarov's lead in contending that the ancient Free City of Novgorod alone had been endowed with every quality of intelligence, talent, foresight and progressiveness.

But there was something else, something even more fundamental that differentiated Balakirev from both Stassov and
the Populists. Even when he seethed with indignation, deep
down in his heart Stassov *believed* in the Russian people,
whereas Balakirev *did not believe* in them, which was why
he was drawn into the camp of reaction. For even the more
sincere, idealistic reactionaries had a basic contempt for the
people; they too did not believe in them. And because of
this lack of faith in the people, they craved for an autocracy,
for a paternalistic trusteeship over the people.

IV

They lived rather far from each other. Hansom cabs were
not expensive, but they crawled along at a snail's pace and
in bad weather the trip was not very enjoyable. Sometimes,
therefore, instead of meeting as was their wont in Stassov's
office, at the Public Library, or in a little pub nearby, the
two young men would communicate by letters. However, if
one of them chanced, or imagined himself to be sick (and
this happened quite often, as both of them were hypochon-
driacs), the other always came to see him. Stassov had only
to feel slightly feverish to stay awake all night, awaiting to
be told in the morning that he was down with what was, in
those days, known as "the typhus." Balakirev, for his part,
was always complaining about his doctors: "My health," he
would write, "is not improving because my doctor is a dunce
in medicine and assures me that I am in perfect health,"
and he would take to his bed, and demand to be enter-
tained by "that nicest of human beings," Stassov, without
whom he felt bored and sad. And soon the Ediets' tiny
apartment would resound with Stassov's booming bass voice,
his noisy indignation, his boisterous cheerfulness and the
political news of which he invariably was the bearer. But
presently even he would calm down and the two friends
would start to play four hands at the piano (Balakirev had

a magnificent Becker instrument, bought on credit, which he was paying off with the money he earned giving piano lessons) or else Stassov would read aloud.

Balakirev composed much during these years. Stassov's vociferous faith in him had, perhaps, something to do with it. Upon orchestrating Glinka's *The Night Parade,* Mili made a present of it to his friend who was genuinely delighted. "Whenever I happen to hear *The Night Parade,*" Stassov would say, "I await the mystery-laden beat of the opening of the grave; then, suddenly, the atmosphere becomes somehow bewitched, and Napoleon himself appears." And he would add: "I know someone else who, one day, perhaps, will conjure up similar miracles!"

And Balakirev did so under Stassov's very eyes and with his participation. For Stassov was continuously searching for themes and subjects for his friend. It was to Mili that he first suggested the saga of *Sadko* for a symphonic poem, but without success. Before that, at Stassov's insistence, Balakirev had written the incidental music to Shakespeare's *King Lear,* for which Stassov unearthed and copied out some ancient English tunes which were barely known at the time, even in England. At the same time he couldn't conceal his impatience at Balakirev's slowness. It took the latter two and a half years to produce the overture, four intermissions, the procession and a few short interludes! "I always work slowly," Mili would explain apologetically, "and in this case I have furthermore to adapt myself to Shakespeare, which makes it doubly difficult."

Stassov wanted *King Lear* to be performed at the Aleksandrinsky Theatre but the management was interested only in the overture and this Mili wouldn't hear of. When *King Lear* was finally completed, Balakirev, like Pushkin before him, missed his "silent companion of the night," but at the same time he was glad that his long labor was over. Work never came easily to him, it involved always considerable strain. "Somehow," he wrote, "my head feels weak, my brain is aflame, my legs are cold as ice, I am overcome with a sort of nervous shivering. Yesterday, for instance, while composing the procession, I thought with such concentration, that for a moment I believed I was going mad."

But all this work and effort were not wasted; *King Lear* and especially the procession and overture succeeded splendidly. Together with Mendelssohn's *A Midsummer Night's Dream,* this is probably the best incidental music that has ever been written to Shakespeare. As Stassov listened for the first time at a University concert to the brass fanfares, the muffled drums, the Shakespearean grandeur of this music, so strictly classical in form, he exulted at the thought that it was dedicated to him.

It was during these years of friendship with Stassov that Balakirev also wrote his three overtures: one each on a Russian and a Czech theme, and the third composed on the occasion of the celebration of Russia's first millennium, which he later renamed *Russ'* and which he conceived as Russia's "instrumental drama." Although the influence of Liszt and Berlioz is unmistakable, these three pieces are completely original, for Balakirev wrote them with utter dedication.

He did not actually create the themes of these overtures but, like Glinka before him, borrowed them from folk songs that had struck his fancy; he used them as a point of departure for something unquestionably his own, developing them with such fire and sparkle, that it became quite unimportant how or where they had originated. That Balakirev was also not devoid of melodic talent, however, can be seen from the charming songs he wrote at the time.

Balakirev's Piano Concerto and *Fantasy on Oriental Themes* (which he later renamed *Islamey*) also date back to this period. But in the latter work, as was only too often the case with him, the original freshness of inspiration was weakened by continuous subsequent changes, which resulted in the piece being "overdone." He also began a symphonic poem on the theme of Lermontov's *Queen Tamara,* which was to become, in time, one of his best-known works.

He felt particularly inspired by Lermontov, his favorite poet, as though there existed "a special kinship" (as he put it) between them. He realized, of course, that Pushkin was both more mature and more accomplished a poet, but Lermontov attracted him by the inherent magnetism of a strong and determined personality. "If only Lermontov had lived forty years," he used to say, "he would have become our foremost poet and one of the greatest in the world."

And yet, creative work alone was not enough. Balakirev longed for action; he longed to influence others. Friendship with the non-musician Stassov was not enough, either; what he needed were disciples, followers. Presently, such a group of disciples started to gather about him.

The most promising of these young men was a seventeen-year-old highschool boy, Apollon Gussakovsky. Balakirev and Stassov became genuinely devoted to him, because of his talent, his pleasant and cheerful disposition, his kindly laughter, his Bohemian irresponsibility. With his swarthy, yellowish complexion and bright, slanting eyes, he looked more like a Malay than a Russian. Gussakovsky was one of those gifted dilettantes, who are often seen in the company of creative artists and who, to a superficial observer, may even seem their equal, but who fail to stand up to the test of life, fall behind and may end up, more often as not pleasant but good-for-nothing Bohemians. Gussakovsky, furthermore, was handicapped by having too wide a range of interests; he studied chemistry and geology, improvised brilliantly and planned to write some incidental music to Goethe's *Faust,* as well as a symphony. All this was most promising, but it led to nothing. Lively, talkative, restless, he was always in a hurry, never finishing one thing before tackling something else. Although he often went hungry, living on poorly paid private lessons for which he didn't even always collect, he never lost heart; cheerful, noisy and tireless, he would rush into the Public Library to see Stassov, show him one of his latest compositions and then rush off again, to give a lesson, or on some mysterious "feminine tryst." Stassov had good reason to fear that in music, as in everything else, Gussakovsky, with his "mercurial instability," would remain "half-baked."

About the same time that he met Gussakovsky, Balakirev made the acquaintance of a young guards officer by the name of Modest Mussorgsky. They met in the house of "that old sorcerer Aleksander Dargomyzhsky" (as Mili called him) in whose salon "all kinds of musical people" were wont to congregate. Mussorgsky played the piano with considerable spirit and even did a bit of composing. He asked Balakirev to give him lessons in musical theory and in composition, but he turned out to be rather dull as a pupil and—what was worse—obstinate.

But then how quick to catch on, how elegant, how talented, intelligent and bright was yet another new acquaintance of theirs, Cesar Cui, an army engineer. He likewise did not devote too much time to music, but he had received some basic instruction at the hands of the Polish composer Moniuszko. Cui was of French origin with an admixture of Polish blood, through his mother. When Balakirev met him, he was working on an opera on the subject of Pushkin's *The Caucasian Captive*, and had already written several good songs. His attitude toward Balakirev was one of respect, but he had a quizzical smile and there was an ironical glint in his small bright eyes, as he peered at him through his spectacles. Though his comments were caustic and to the point, he showered Balakirev with compliments and stressed their community of ideas and aspirations.

A little later, Stassov and Balakirev made the acquaintance of a professor of chemistry by the name of Aleksander Porfirievich Borodin. Tall, good-looking, with flashing oriental eyes, Borodin suggested cheerfulness and kindness, strength and talent. His talent was highly original, but he too had little time for music.

Thus, gradually, a circle of musicians formed around Balakirev. To these young men (Cui and Borodin were actually older than he, Borodin by fully two years!) Balakirev was the *maître*. The only professional musician among amateurs, he literally overwhelmed them with his knowledge, his authority, the soundness of his judgment. His word was law. He would look over their work, arbitrarily change the tonality (he had a marked partiality for some tonalities and an aversion for others), add whole passages of his own invention and adapt everything to his own taste and fancy. He was a born despot and this despotism was further enhanced by the attitude of those around him. But his despotism was disinterested; he could in all truth say: "Not for us the glory, but to Thy Name!" He lived only for art, for music, for Russia, and demanding nothing for himself.

But soon Balakirev began to feel hemmed in in this narrow circle of admirers. He craved for wider fields of endeavor and, especially, for some way of making use of his knowledge of the orchestra and of the art of conducting. And in this he was supported by Stassov and all the others, although with the insight born of devotion, Stassov could not help feeling that Balakirev was not so much a man of action, as one who cherished dreams of action. Nevertheless, some of these dreams were now beginning to bear fruit.

V

Outwardly at least, Balakirev's life in those years was poverty-ridden and monotonous. True, from time to time this monotony was broken by trips to his birthplace, Niznii-Novgorod, or the Caucasus, or Moscow...

The sight of the Moscow Kremlin, Red Square, the cathedrals, the view across the Moskva river and all the treasured antiquities of Russia's ancient capital awakened Balakirev's sense of patriotism (which had never been more than dormant anyhow) as well as a feeling of pride in being a Russian. He was convinced that he had succeeded in instilling into his works "a particle of the Kremlin" and even, to be still more accurate, of the Kremlin towers! He felt a sudden urge to write a symphony in honor of the Kremlin.

During his several trips to Niznii-Novgorod, his old and annoying father kept nagging him to use his St. Petersburg connections in order to obtain his reintegration in the Civil Service, so that he might become eligible for a pension. His youngest sister was growing up fast, but there was no money for her education. Balakirev succeeded in obtaining for her a government scholarship to an Imperial Institute for Young Ladies. But to achieve this he was forced to plead, to pay calls on the Governor-General's wife, to play the piano in the house of the headmistress—all of which pained and disgusted him.

In the Caucasus, he took a vacation at Piatigorsk and Zheleznovodsk. The majestic beauty of the Caucasian landscape captivated him and, like Lermontov before him, he was quite overwhelmed by its towering ranges, its inhabitants —the Circassian mountaineers—their customs and even their national dress. Like Lermontov too, he purchased a Circassian costume, which he wore with childlike joy and in which he even had himself photographed (he sent a print to Stassov). As he strolled about the neighborhood of Piatigorsk, he read and re-read his favorite poet and literally "inhaled Lermontov with every breath."

The rest of the time Balakirev stayed in St. Petersburg. Occasionally Liudmila Ivanovna Shestakova, Glinka's sister, would invite him out to the country, to visit them in their summer cottage. Occasionally too he would visit the Stassovs in their country place, near Pargolovo. Most of the time, however, there was plain living, creative work, daydreams and dreams at night—ever so live and clear—about music, about musicians, about notes and tonalities. Sometimes these dreams were so vivid that he would awaken in the morning unrested, drained of all strength.

On once such an occasion, he dreamt of Schumann. He could not afterwards remember the details of the great composer's face; all he remembered was that it was a pleasant face. He asked Schumann whether the latter spoke French and Schumann answered "Yes!" with a kind nod. Whereupon Balakirev proceeded to shower him with compliments in that language, saying: *"Vous voyez devant vous un musicien russe qui est votre grand admirateur!"* Schumann replied something equally pleasant and Balakirev was about to question him about the finale of his *C major symphony,* when Schumann vanished. Then, somehow, he managed to get hold of him again and Schumann gave him his calling card, which was very crumpled. Balakirev would have liked to ask him for his autograph, but was unable to do so. Then he again remembered that he had wanted to talk to him about the finale of the *C major symphony,* but by that time Schumann had again vanished, this time for good, and Balakirev awoke.

For a long time afterward, he felt stimulated at the thought of this fancied meeting. But his joy was tempered by the annoyance at not having been able to find out why Schumann had departed from the classical form in his *finale,* why he had not stuck to a *rondo,* or a *sonata.*

Even in those early days, there was an inner weakness behind the show of strength though few people except Stassov noticed it at the time. In the presence of others, to the world at large, Stassov kept extolling his friend's amazing powers. "Balakirev soars like an eagle far ahead of them!" he would say. Balakirev's personality, he asserted, was of the quality of highly tempered steel, of a diamond of the purest water; nothing could bend or break him! And yet, Stassov knew that somewhere there was a crack in the casting, a flaw in the diamond. "Some day," he said to himself, "this man will fail and break down."

For one thing, there was about Balakirev an extreme, an

unmanly nervousness which bordered on neurasthenia. Also, he was superstitious and fainthearted to the highest degree. Even when all was well with him, he feared the worst, for surely this was merely the calm before the storm; surely some new and unexpected blow of fate lurked just around the corner. Moreover, he was becoming a misanthrope—not out of any particular disillusionment in man, but beforehand, as it were, as though he were inviting fate to strike.

He was still quite young—26 years old—when he made to Stassov a confession which would have sounded more natural on the lips of an aging Schopenhauer. "If the others are human beings," he said, "then I do not consider you and me human. I have lived in their midst, I am to some extent still compelled to do so, but I feel like a dog in a hencoop. Inwardly I had already renounced them, only to find later that society was necessary as a source of life-giving sap, and yet I cannot find my place in it. . . That is why I feel such an aversion to performing in public; my fingers become paralyzed when you ask me to play *Lear* or anything else for that matter, for our society is perfectly indifferent to it anyhow . . . It has always been terrible for me to realize that, having written something, there is no other way of hearing one's own compositions except at a concert; it's like confiding one's innermost emotions to a policeman. . . I am through with people; in fact I only go to them now sometimes, because it is necessary to eat and drink."

Stassov feigned to echo these thoughts. He even planned to write a book entitled *"Le carnage général"* (in Russian: *Razgrom*), which was to be his *magnum opus,* his "Ninth Symphony" and in which he proposed to prove that it was natural for the public, for the broad masses everywhere and always, to have bad taste and to approve and extoll only those works and only those artists that had no real or lasting value. In his heart, however, Stassov was a very different person; he loved people and far from being a misanthrope he was an extrovert, a philanthropist in the fullest meaning of those words.

He was thus both right and wrong when, writing to Balakirev on the occasion of one of the latter's periodic spells of sickness, he said: "Come back and you will be mended, not like one patches up an old toothless nag which the Tartars are about to drive to the slaughter-house, but as one mends a young, impatient, fiery, wonderful, pure-blooded Arab stallion which has temporarily injured its priceless foot by stumbling over a chance cobblestone, but which will in time gallop away again, wonderful and unrivalled with spreading tail, flying mane and flaming nostrils, leaving everybody gasping at the sight!"

But a few chance cobblestones or the fact that it was harnessed to a dray cart were not alone to blame if, all too early, the priceless thoroughbred began to stumble; it was simply too fiery, too untrained, too nervous to clear the hurdles it encountered on its course. Life, like a clumsy jockey, broke its back.

CHAPTER FOUR

BORODIN

"Devines si tu peux, et choisis,
si tu l'oses!"

CORNEILLE

I

"Alles gaben die Goetter, die unendlichen,
Ihren Lieblingen ganz.
Alle Freuden, die unendlichen,
Alle Leiden, die unendlichen, ganz!"

"The eternal gods endowed their favorites fully: with endless joys, with endless sorrows," wrote Goethe about himself.
One of these favorites of the gods, a living witness to their
generosity and greed, was born in St. Petersburg, in the barracks of the *Izmailovsky* Regiment of the Foot Guards on
October 31, 1833. His name was Aleksander Porfirievich
Borodin (with the accent on the last syllable).

He was an illegitimate child, the son of one Luka Semiono-
vich Ghedeanov, a scion of the Princes of Imeritia, an ancient
Georgian ruling family. Because of that he was given the
name of one of the Prince's bonded servants. His father was
52 years old at the time, his mother—25. Lively, intelligent,
beautiful, she had easily turned the old man's head, as she
was to turn many others in her life. She soon left Ghedeanov
and married an army doctor by the name of Kleinecke.

"Sasha" Borodin grew up as a gentle, sickly child. He was
surrounded by so many women (his first playmate was also a
girl, his cousin Marie) that he even got used to talking about
himself in the feminine gender. The Kleinecke house—a
large four-storeyed stone building with a courtyard and a
little garden in the back—contained many invaluable hiding

70

places, where Sasha's imagination could escape into a world of fantasy which even little cousin Marie was not always allowed to penetrate: "I've got a lofty palace there," he would say, "which rises all the way up to the sky."

His love of music showed up early. As a child of eight, he would be taken by "Fräulein Louise," his German maid, to listen to the military band playing in the square in front of the barracks of the *Semionovsky* Foot Guards. He soon made friends with the musicians. They allowed him to inspect their shining instruments, even to touch them, and to watch them playing, pursing his lips as they did. Later, at home, he would try to pick up on the piano the tunes he had heard. Presently, his mother invited a ferocious-looking, dashing corporal of the *Semionovsky* Guards to teach him to play the flute and the plaintive sounds of the two instruments would echo through the house. Fearful for his health, his relatives advised his mother not to let him overdo these studies. But she seemed to have an instinctive faith in his musical destiny and although she herself had been poorly educated, she decided that he should be encouraged to take up a learned career and spared no money on his education. For fear that he might catch some disease or come into contact with undesirable elements he was not allowed, however, to go to school. He wasn't even allowed out of the house alone, but only in the company of Fräulein Louise or the housekeeper, and up to the age of fourteen he would often have to be taken by the hand in crossing the street. In due time, tutors came to his home. He studied with considerable facility.

He was already quite grown-up when two other little boys, *"Mitia"* and *"Enia,"* came to live with them. Though they had different patronymic names and surnames they were, in fact, his half-brothers. Being considerably older than they, however, he took little interest in them.

At the age of nine, he experienced something like a first love. The object of his passion was a tall and buxom girl by the name of Elena. Indeed, it may have been precisely because of her size and girth that the puny little fellow fell in love with her for when they danced he could just barely embrace her knees. But when she danced with the grown-ups, he was madly jealous of her, while poor cousin Marie was jealous of him. This first love inspired him to write his first composition, a polka which he named Helene after his heroine. It was written in the minor key (perhaps because he felt unhappy) which gives it an odd, rather charming flavor. Curiously enough, it had a striking resemblance to the *duo gracioso* of Vania and Sussanin in Act III of Glinka's *A Life for the Czar.*

Presently, however, he acquired a real playmate, a boy of his own age by the name of Misha Stieglev. When they first met, they promptly and without uttering a word seized each other by the hair, threw themselves on the floor and proceeded to pummel each other with all their strength. Then, having thus expressed their joy at this encounter, they started to chatter away like old friends, discovering that they had countless interests in common: from Walter Scott to music and from Latin to sweet cakes. They soon became such bosom friends, that Misha's parents who lived out of town, in Czarskoye Selo, would allow their son to stay overnight at the Kleinecke house, which was closer to the school he was about to attend.

About this time, Sasha Borodin fell a victim to another passion which was to last him through life. He took up chemistry. Something very powerful drew him to this particular branch of science. It was as though far from discovering something entirely new, he were returning to a half-forgotten homeland, where everything, however mysterious, was nevertheless familiar, so that he had only to find his bearings and refresh his memory to know exactly where he stood. The speed with which he assimilated his new interest bordered on the miraculous. He was given a room where he set up a laboratory where all day long crucibles and retorts bubbled and hissed and from which, sometimes, there emanated the most unbearable fumes. But soon even this room became too small for him, he spread out his paraphernalia all over the house until everywhere, on the washstands and window sills, in the most unexpected places, liquids could be found cooling, solutions crystalizing, suspicious-looking fluids trickling out of one container into another, whilst elsewhere something would suddenly explode with a tinkling of shattered glass. He actually succeeded in concocting certain unknown compounds. In fact, had it not been for Misha Stieglev, who kept dragging him away to the piano whenever he could, he might easily have given up music altogether.

Both boys read music easily and together they learnt to play many a classical work by heart, such as the Haydn and Beethoven symphonies. But best of all they liked Mendelssohn. In order to familiarize themselves with the chamber repertoire, Misha learnt to play the violin and Sasha Borodin —the cello. Then they took to attending the symphonic concerts at Pavlovsk in the summer, and Karl Schubert's St. Petersburg University concerts in the winter. At the age of 13, Borodin composed his first "serious" work—a concerto for flute and piano, which he first performed, of course, with Misha Stieglev.

His years of childhood and adolescence, surrounded by all these adoring women and in the company of his friend Misha, passed quickly. He was not yet sixteen when he was received with high honors into the Academy of Medicine and Surgery as a real "grown-up" student. His way of life, however, changed but little. True, he was now no longer led across the street. But even so, whenever he went out, his mother or Fräulein Louise would inspect him carefully, for he was a very absent-minded boy and was quite capable of tucking his trouser-cuffs into his high boots (which simply was "not done" in nice circles). On one occasion, he went out without any trousers at all! He was also somewhat more free now in the choice of his friends and acquaintances, even though here again his mother kept a watchful eye. Despite her own fairly libertine life, she was a woman of firm rules and principles as far as others, and especially her children were concerned. She had grown up in the half-German town of Narva and had acquired from her daily contacts with German circles a sound respect for the latter's neatness and good manners, as contrasted with the often somewhat boorish ways of so many of her Russian friends. She therefore encouraged her son to associate with German boys.

In the evening, the young people would dance, with decorum and restraint. There were of course no drinking parties, no smoking and still less politics or discussions of those "problems" that haunted so many students of his day. And then of course there was work—in the anatomy theatre, or in the dissecting room (where he once got poisoned with corpse venom) or in the chemical laboratories. When in his third year, Borodin requested the celebrated Professor Zinin to allow him to work in the Academy laboratory. The latter was at first skeptical, but he soon became convinced that the young man was capable of working like an experienced scientist.

Chemistry! The natural sciences! What could be better, more sublime, more wonderful? This conviction was shared and propounded with all the ardor of neophytes by most Russian intellectuals of the day. For wasn't this the best and fastest way to achieve paradise on earth? Wouldn't the scientific approach solve all harrassing problems? Science and science alone! That was the answer! Music was on a different, a lower plane—that of entertainment, of pleasure, of "having fun," of "aristocratic leisure" that it ill-behoved to indulge in at a time when the peasant, the poor *muzhik* craved for knowledge and when there were so many more serious things to think about!

And yet music was by now an integral part of Borodin's life, he couldn't get rid of it. He and Misha Stieglev had recently become acquainted with the two Vassiliev brothers

of whom one had an admirable bass voice, while the other
played the violin. They now performed trios—Vassiliev playing the first violin, Stieglev the second and Borodin the cello.
It was somewhat more difficult to organize a quartet, for the
viola had to be hired, but they had only to be told that somewhere chamber music was being played, in order to plod
there on foot (they had not enough money to pay for their
cab-fare), whatever the distance, whatever the weather. Most
often they played at the house of a government official by the
name of Gavrushevich, himself a fair cellist. So many musicians used to gather there, that they could play even the
double quartets of Spohr and Gade, the quintets of Boccherini
and, more rarely, the quartets of Mendelssohn and Beethoven.

Sometimes Serov would put in an appearance at these
gatherings. He would drop a few comments and then sit down
to play the cello. He was passing through a nationalist phase
at the time, extolling Glinka and arguing angrily with the
German guest musicians. Sasha Borodin sympathized with
him, for he too liked Glinka.

One day he mentioned to his host that he had written a
few songs. "Why don't you try your hand at chamber music?"
Gavrushevich queried; "why not write a quintet with two
cellos for instance?"—"No, no!" Borodin replied, "It's too
difficult." He didn't mention that he had already been trying
stubbornly for a long time to write not only a trio for flute,
piano and violin, but also quartets, quintets and even sextets,
though he had never finished them or showed them to anyone. At times a veritable passion to compose would seize him,
like the urge which overcomes an alcoholic or an inveterate
gambler, and he would lose all count of time. At such moments he would stay glued to the piano for days on end
searching, improvising, staring out into space with dull, unseeing eyes. Sometimes this "musical madness" would become
collective. On one such occasion, having sat down with three
of his companions to play at 7 p.m., they stayed up all night
and all of the following day, recovering their senses only at

dusk, after playing for 24 hours at a stretch without even realizing it. From time to time someone would bring them tea and sandwiches or else Borodin's mother would tiptoe up to the door and peer into the smoke-filled room, only to retire again without daring to interrupt them.

Oddly enough, his studies did not suffer from these spells of music mania. He was first in his class in every subject. Nevertheless, Professor Zinin advised him to concentrate on chemistry and not to "chase two hares," as he put it. Borodin was quite indignant at this flippant comparison. He preferred to compare his two hobbies to two muses in classical mythology, or rather to two beloved women: one fashionable, up-to-date, emancipated, intelligent, with whom it was possible to live a lifetime of reason, of usefulness and to whom everyone around him—his mother, Zinin, his relatives—were hopefully expecting him to propose; the other strange, half-crazy, wild, with whom you could not join in life, to whom you could only devote rare moments of passionate inspiration, about whom you could only dream.

II

In the spring of 1856, when he was not yet 21 years of age, Borodin graduated from the Academy of Medicine and Surgery with the title of Military Doctor and was appointed interne at the St. Petersburg Army Hospital. It is here, in a hospital, that he met for the first time someone, with whom his name was to remain associated in the memory of man.

It happened on a cold but clear day late in September. The garden of the hospital was densely carpeted with yellowing leaves which rustled underfoot. Occasionally, a patient's robe or the uniform of an attendant would flicker for a minute white against that golden background. Borodin was on duty that day, but there were few patients in his section so that he was rarely disturbed. And so presently he struck up a conversation with the officer on duty, a very young subaltern of the *Preobrazhensky* Foot Guards by the name of Modest Petrovich Mussorgsky who soon confided to him that he was only 17. He had a typically Russian face, snub-nosed, like that of a country yokel or small-town merchant. Upon observing him more attentively, however, Borodin noted that there was about his features something both sensitive and fine. His manners were distinguished, aristocratic even. And he had also that artless candor, that easy-going outspokenness typical of a young boy of good family. Borodin himself was also artless after a fashion, but his manner was more restrained. Within a quarter of an hour it was as if they had known each other all their lives.

The disastrous Crimean war had just ended. A new Emperor had ascended the throne and his accession had been accompanied by a sort of vague and therefore all the more wonderful feeling of expectation—of reforms, of changes, of something new and fair. Such a feeling of expectation can be experienced by entire nations or by individuals, especially when the latter are very young. Occasionally they are shared both by the nation and the individual. Such was the case with these two young men in uniform.

They spoke of the war; of the coming emancipation of the serfs and they rejoiced. How could they not rejoice? Weren't they, after all—however aristocratic their origin—related to the Russian peasantry? Take the Mussorgskys: although they had lost their princely title, they descended from Rurik, the first ruler of Russia, and yet one of Modest's grandmothers was a serf-girl and his cousins were at that very moment, possibly, tilling the fields barefoot. With his usual frank simplicity, Borodin agreed with him. He too, although the son of a Georgian prince, had been registered at birth as of serf origin, and it was only upon entering the Academy that he had been promoted to the class of "merchant of the 3rd (i.e., lowest) guild." Borodin told Mussorgsky how he had seen some domestic servants being made to run the gauntlet for killing their master, and how—weakling that he was—he had fainted at the sight.

That same evening they met again at the house of Dr. Popov, the head physician of the hospital. His daughter was of marriageable age and parties were given for her, to which the officers and doctors were invited. Mussorgsky made a somewhat different impression on Borodin than he had in the morning. He flirted with the daughter of the house and her friends and spoke with a nasal twang, mixing Russian with some French expressions that were not always accurate. His spotless dark-green Guardsman's uniform, his wasp-like waist, his patent-leather boots, his carefully manicured hands and well-oiled hair made him look every inch the professional Guards' officer. Moreover, he was obviously doing well with the ladies and this made him appear a bit foppish. But he was at the same time courteous, his manners were perfect and everything about him was so genuine, that Borodin gladly forgave him this foppishness. Besides, he himself, with his tall, slender figure, his huge and admirable Georgian eyes and flushed cheeks, involuntarily attracted the ladies' attention. After dinner Mussorgsky was asked to play, whereupon he sat down at the piano and tossing his little hands somewhat coquettishly, proceeded to perform excerpts from *Il Trovatore, La Traviata* and various other favorites from the fashionable drawing-room repertoire of the day. He played extremely well, with considerable brio and the ladies were delighted.

They continued to meet there, occasionally, until Dr. Popov stopped giving parties and Borodin left the hospital. They did not see each other again until three years later, when they met once more at the house of one of Borodin's teachers. By that time Mussorgsky had resigned his commission and wore a well-cut grey coat. A pair of mauve-colored gloves lay, together with his hat, on a chair. He had changed considerably, had grown stouter and looked much older than his twenty years. His manner too, had changed; gone now were his earlier foppishness and Guardsman's mannerisms.

They immediately struck up a conversation. Borodin had now virtually given up music, being busy preparing himself for his doctor's degree which he was to take with honors shortly thereafter. The rest of his time he spent at the laboratory, where he was engaged in independent chemical research. In contrast to Mussorgsky, he had hardly changed in the past three years. Even the stormy period of early youth had not left much of a mark. Prompted perhaps by a definite purpose, his mother had engaged a pretty young chambermaid by the name of Annushka, and Borodin right away had fallen in love with her. In his spiritual life, the struggles, the conflicts, and indecisions that are a prerogative of youth seemed nonexisting. Even the indecision of choosing between music and science, which had so long plagued him, had now been satisfactorily resolved in favor of science.

As though he wished to reproach him for this development, Mussorgsky began to relate how he himself had given up his regiment to devote himself entirely to music. At first, Borodin took this to be just a bit of innocent bragging. "He must have experienced some unpleasantness in the service," he said to himself. But Mussorgsky was quite bubbling over with enthusiasm; he started to tell Borodin about the various people he had met since they last saw each other. "Stassov," he said, "is a veritable well of wisdom. Cui, the young artillery officer, writes charming music. But Balakirev is the greatest of all. He is really unbeatable—a luminous personality!"

Their hosts begged Mussorgsky and Borodin to play four hands Mendelssohn's *A minor (Scotch) symphony*. Modest frowned a little and said that he would be glad to, "Only please do not ask me to play the *andante,* which is not symphonic at all, but merely another 'song without words' put to orchestra. . ." Whereupon they played the first part and the *scherzo* after which, without getting up from the piano, Mussorgsky started to speak about Schumann and his symphonies. "How fine, how profound this is," he murmured as he strummed fragments from the *E flat (Rhenish) symphony*. Suddenly, he stopped "because what follows is nothing but musical mathematics." These excerpts from Schumann and especially his comments pleased Borodin; he became suddenly interested. "Of course they're not his own ideas," he said to himself, recalling the 17-year-old little Guardsman and his brave performance of *Il Trovatore* three years ago. "He probably borrowed them from those men about whom he keeps speaking. But he does play well, and that Schumann fellow is good too." And out of politeness Borodin asked Mussorgsky to play one of his own compositions, whereupon the latter began to strum his *Scherzo in B flat*. The more he played, the more fascinated Borodin became. At first, he didn't like the *scherzo,* he felt confused by its novelty. But gradually he came to like it. If Mussorgsky was able to compose so well, his words about having given up his military career to devote himself to music might not be idle bragging after all. Upon reaching the *trio,* Mussorgsky muttered with set teeth: "and here now begins something oriental. . ." All this, Borodin felt, was new, unexpected, interesting.

Soon, that very autumn in fact, Borodin departed for a trip abroad, to Heidelberg, on a scholarship from his former academy.

III

For some time already, voyagers between St. Petersburg and Moscow travelled by rail. Those who went abroad, however, still had to take the post chaise, just like their forebears. Although it was now late in October, Borodin booked an outside seat, next to the coachman, for being warmly dressed, he did not fear the cold. Besides, an outside seat provided a far better view and this made the trip less tedious. There was still another advantage: you could stretch your legs, which was quite impossible inside. The seat, however, was

very narrow and on the other side of the small partition the
coachman kept blowing his horn, unfortunately, out of tune.
The chaise left St. Petersburg late in the evening. Before
its departure everybody had, according to the old Russian
tradition, sat down in silence, for a minute, to pray for a
successful trip. The horses travelled at a brisk trot and by 11
p.m. they had already reached the first relay station, Kipen',
where the passengers got out for a cup of tea, after which,
having lowered the leather curtain with its tiny oval window,
those on the outside seats settled down for the night. Borodin's neighbor, a Hamburg merchant, fell asleep immediately,
but Borodin himself couldn't sleep. Through the window he
could see the barren fields, the sparse, puny fir and birch trees
lit up by the dim glow of the moon, the rare hamlets. He
hearkened to the whooping of the coachman, the trot of the
horses, the wheezy snoring of his sleeping companion. As
sometimes happens when travelling, hundreds of unrelated
thoughts came to his mind: his childhood, Fräulein Louise,
the corporal who had taught him to play the flute, little
cousin Marie . . . Marie, who had wanted to marry him
when he was a child, had married one of his friends instead
and had died, three years ago, in childbirth. This had been
his first experience of death. . . But he did not dwell long on
his cousin's passing and on the thought of death: he lived
for the future and thoughts about his work, about chemical
formulae and musical themes, jostled one another in his
head. He hardly slept at all that first night and next morning
he smiled when the Hamburg merchant, having awakened,
complained of insomnia and promptly fell asleep again.

The road ran first due west through Yamburg, Luga, picturesque medieval Narva and then south-westward, along
the shores of Lake Peipus. It wasn't possible to read and so he
watched the desolate landscape and chewed pretzels and pep-
permints. Only the following night did he fall, out of sheer
fatigue, into a fitful sleep. And so through Riga, Mitava,
Shavli and on to Koenigsberg. . . By the time they reached

that city (where he was to take a train to Berlin) he had got to know most of his travelling companions, whom he found all very nice. Like brothers they shared their provisions at the relay stations, drank *Kümmel* together, told one another their respective life stories or sang sentimental German songs. In the train as he neared Berlin, Borodin made up his accounts: the whole trip including post chaise and train fare had cost only 80 silver rubles (i.e., 40 U.S. dollars)!

IV

Russian travellers arriving for the first time in Germany in the sixties of the last century were as a rule at first pleasantly impressed. Everything struck them as so clean there, so neat, so cozy, so comfortable, from the huge eiderdowns and spotless white sheets, the crisp rolls served with the rather watery morning coffee and the little circlets of fresh butter, to the cozy *Kneipen,* the low prices and the rather idyllic way of life of that still provincial and patriarchal country. Sasha Borodin was amazed to notice, for instance, that on Saturdays, German women washed not only the sidewalks, but even the streets. His room was always spotless, too, and over his washbasin, on his towels and even in the most improbable places, there were embroidered moralizing exhortations, such as: *Morgenstunde hat Gold in Munde,* while his wastepaper basket was adorned with the words: *Werft hinein das Papier, denn dazu steh ich hier.*

Heidelberg had all the charm of a small university town that can be found the world over, in Oxford and Cambridge, Bologna and Coimbre, Iena and Tübingen. These towns live *for* their universities and *by* them, as though they were devoted to the cult of something special, something sublime. The crowds of young people milling about their streets give them an air of festive unconcern. And even the toothless street-sweepers, or the old rather grim landladies have a kindly smile when speaking of "those young people." The

whole town seems to live for the sole purpose of providing
food, drink, clothes and entertainment for the students,
participating thus in a way, in their peculiar, carefree life.
Even the milkman takes pride in having celebrated scientists
for his clients as if, because of this service, he were himself
a party to their discoveries.

In Heidelberg, Borodin worked with the famous chemist
Erlenmaier. He lived that first winter at No. 11 Friedrich-
strasse, in a room with blue wallpaper, which a hanging drape
cut in two and for which he paid only eleven *gulden* (plus
one *gulden* for a perfectly adequate meal). He got up early,
at 5 a.m. and immediately went to work at the laboratory.
Besides his university courses, he also took English, Italian
and riding lessons. Occasionally, he would break the monotony by going to a concert, or visiting friends. He did not
see many Germans, however, for they disgusted him by their
pettiness and narrowmindedness. He preferred the company of Englishmen and of his own compatriots—the celebrated chemist Mendeleyev and the equally well-known
physiologist Sechonov. He liked the former for his self-con-
fidence and dedication. But he liked Sechonov even better.
The latter was a follower of the radical Herzen and was
violently critical of the Czarist Government.

But all these kind friends could not provide him with what
he missed most—the coziness of a home. The latter he
found in the house of a Russian lady, a Mrs. Bruger, who
lived in Heidelberg with her children. She was wealthy,
beautiful and unhappy, being separated from her husband
who refused to grant her a divorce. Borodin began to spend
all his free time in her company. He would come to her to
tea, stay for dinner, read the Russian papers and magazines
which she received regularly or play four hands with her on
the piano, while she mended his gloves, helped him choose
a new hat or suit, tied his ties for him. She claimed that she
had maternal feelings for him. Was it only maternal? Who
knows? She was afflicted by consumption. In the spring she

left Heidelberg for Italy for a cure, returned early in the summer, only to die there shortly thereafter.

Throughout winter, the Russians in Heidelberg would study or work; come summer, they would start out in a merry group led by Borodin and Mendeleyev, with a considerable stock of energy and much smaller reserves of money, to explore neighboring Switzerland or even Italy—some of them by train, but most of them on foot, with rucksacks on their backs. In the fall they would return to their studies with a store of wonderful memories: the honey-sweet smell of Swiss Alpine pastures, the transparent blue of mountain lakes, the trickle and crash of waterfalls and the tinkling bells of grazing herds. And also the blue sky, sultry air and hallowed beauty of Italy.

To the great joy of his mother, Borodin's studies proceeded successfully. Articles began to appear over his signature in the scientific press. This was particularly welcome news since her own circumstances were steadily deteriorating, largely due to the dishonesty of her agent and to her own reluctance to replace any of her staff. She found it ever more difficult to send her beloved Sasha his monthly allowance. Because of that, also, her younger sons were given a far less thorough education than their elder brother had enjoyed.

V

Spring came, that delightful Heidelberg spring. Borodin now lived at No. 2 Karpfengasse, where he had also installed his laboratory. He took his meals in a boardinghouse, run by the wife of a retired Russian professor, a Mrs. Hoffman, and which was frequented by other Russians. It is here, one day in May, that he made the acquaintance of his future wife, Ekaterina Sergheyevna Protopopova, who had just arrived from Russia to study music. The daughter of a Moscow doctor, she was a proficient pianist, and a great admirer of Schumann. She had been sent abroad by the doctors, for she suffered from asthma and they feared that she might become consumptive. The money for the trip had been provided by the proceeds of a concert which she gave at some friends' advice on the eve of her departure. Although it was not generally regarded as a health resort, the doctors had recommended Heidelberg because of the well-known mildness of its climate.

Upon learning that Mrs. Hoffman's newest guest was a talented pianist, her Russian boarders decided to dispatch a "deputation" to beg her to play for them. Borodin was one of this group. She accepted gladly and on the very first day of her arrival, after dinner, the "concert" took place.

Borodin took an immediate liking to the young girl. Like many of her contemporaries of the Moscow *intelligentsia,* her manners were somewhat awkward and her aloofness seemed to discourage any familiarity. But this first impression was immediately made void by her obvious gentleness, the sweetness of her face, the soft expression of her beautiful dark eyes, the kindness in her voice.

She began with Chopin's *Fantasy in F flat* and Schumann's *Schlummerlied.* Borodin stood by the piano; he had already found time to inform her that he was an "ardent Mendelssohnian." He did so perhaps, by way of a challenge, for he knew that Mendelssohn was not very fashionable in progressive musical circles. Though Chopin and Schumann were a real discovery for him, he felt little kinship for Chopin, finding him a bit too fragile, like a hot-house-bred flower. But Schumann, Schumann! . . . Here was a genuinely free-soaring spirit! Mendelssohn seemed in comparison, all of a sudden, vapid and insipid, like the colorless transparent water of a pond. From the look on his face, the young lady could see that he indeed "worshiped" music, as he had said. He kept begging her, insistently, almost ordering her to play more. She had had mixed feelings about Borodin when she first saw him, for one of her Moscow friends had met him during a steamer trip on the Rhine and had described him as a quite exceptional, "luminous" young man in every way; talented, handsome and brilliant. Obviously her friend had fallen in love with him; she even had a photograph of him. But Ekaterina was not impressed. She didn't care for handsome, effete-looking men. Nevertheless she had been curious to see him and upon meeting him at the Hoffman's she had been forced to admit that he was even handsomer in real life than in the picture; moreover he seemed, also, both intelligent and witty.

Thereafter, every morning, when most of its guests had left for their respective courses and labs, Mrs. Hoffman's boardinghouse would echo to the sound of Ekaterina's scales and exercises. The rest of the time she spent stretched out on a sofa, reading and smoking (although this was bad for her). In the evening she would again play and—at Borodin's insistence—mostly Schumann. Presently, they discovered in Heidelberg several other amateurs of music and before long they were able to perform a few chamber pieces. Schumann's *Quintet* drove him quite wild with enthusiasm. Borodin and young Ekaterina Protopopova soon became good friends. In the afternoon, at five, having finished his work in the laboratory he would drop by at the Hoffman's to pick her up and they would roam about the countryside together. The neighborhood of Heidelberg is most picturesque, with the silvery Neckar winding its way swiftly between high, steep, green banks, with its cheerful farmhouses and charming country *Kneipen* where they serve the celebrated Heidelberg beer in high earthenware *Schoppen*. At first Ekaterina refused to allow him even to take her by the arm, insisting that she could manage even the steepest paths without help. But then, when he remarked one day all of a sudden: "Do you realize that I spend sleepless nights because of your Schumann?" and added with a disarming smile: "By the way, when will you finally let me hold your arm?" she gave in. On one occasion, she came to fetch him at his home, and he was so flustered by this unexpected visit that he sprang up and started, for no particular reason, to show her his clothes closet. By eight o'clock, they were usually back in town for a hasty dinner, after which the music sessions in the small sitting room of the *Pension Hoffman* would resume until, and sometimes beyond, midnight. And so day after day.

Occasionally their excursions would take them farther afield, down the Rhine for instance, to Coblenz, past the many castles ruined, past the vineyards, past the Lorelei. And everything they saw appeared to them in a miraculous light, far more miraculous than anything the legendary Lorelei herself could have devised. Even the names of the towns they travelled past on their journey—Bingerbrücke, Rüdesheim, etc.—remained forever associated in their minds with this sensation of magic. Occasionally, on Saturdays, they would go to Mannheim, to listen to a fashionable young German composer by the name of Richard Wagner. Once or twice they travelled to elegant Baden-Baden, where symphonic concerts were given in the gardens of the *Kursaal*. There, Ekaterina one day exclaimed: "Wasn't that passage from one tonality to the other beautiful?" Borodin stared at her incredulously: "Do you mean to say that you have absolute pitch?" he cried out, "Why, that is so rare!" And he became suddenly pensive, absent-minded, remote. For a long time he remained seated, gazing into space with happy, unseeing eyes. She couldn't quite understand his surprise, for there seemed to be nothing particularly unusual about it. But Borodin, who was so reluctant to acknowledge his own exceptional musical talents, was quite overwhelmed by what he regarded as a token of intellectual superiority. Here, obviously, was someone very special, here was a chalice filled with a rare essence. Suddenly he realized that he loved her.

VI

Hereafter, Borodin could never again quite forget about music. In the past, he had often been able to sacrifice his artistic inclinations to other, temporarily more important interests. Now, Ekaterina, his "sweet little woman" (as he liked to call her) was to become the very symbol of music, a live link with the world of arts.

For a long time, her health did not improve. Indeed, if anything, their long walks and the atmosphere of constant exhilaration in which they lived, contributed to its deterioration. Until the end of summer she still breathed freely. But with the advent of autumn, she began to cough, to spit blood. For a while, she succeeded in concealing her condition from Borodin and he for his part, what with his work and his happiness, noticed nothing. When he did notice it, however, he insisted that she go and see a specialist. The latter, with typical German rudeness, barked: "Unless you leave Heidelberg immediately for a warmer climate, you won't survive a month! Why don't you go to Pisa?" She was at first quite desperate. But Borodin was soon able to impart to her a little of his own gay vitality and inborn optimism. He accompanied her to Italy, planning to stay with her until she was installed before returning to Heidelberg. The dread day of parting came. Borodin had packed his bags and had gone to call on two Italian professors of chemistry of his acquaintance and Ekaterina was lying prostrate and sobbing on the bed when she heard him bounding up the staircase and he suddenly burst into the room. "Katria!" he exclaimed, "Imagine what has happened. . ." It appeared that his Italian colleagues had suggested that he stay and work with them in Pisa.

Now, thanks to the warm Pisan sun and his own loving presence, she soon made rapid progress. He, for his part, resumed work on his music; he started to play the cello with the local opera orchestra, made many friends among the local musicians and even began to compose a *quintet* "in Glinka's spirit" (as he put it) and a *scherzo* for piano *à la* Mendelssohn. They returned to Russia only in the autumn, when Borodin was offered the prized post of associate professor of chemistry at the St. Petersburg Academy of Medicine and Surgery. The following spring, 1863, they were married.

CHAPTER FIVE

THE YOUNG MUSSORGSKY

"How would I have liked to be Manfred!"
MUSSORGSKY

I

Shortly after his return to St. Petersburg, Borodin made the acquaintance of Mili Balakirev. They met at Botkin's, one of his Heidelberg friends and Borodin immediately realized that this was the man of whom young Modest Mussorgsky had spoken in such enthusiastic terms.

Though only 24 years old at the time, Balakirev was by now already fairly well known in the capital. Commended for having founded the Free School of Music, an undoubtedly progressive institution, he was blamed for performing at the school's concerts amateurish works of young men whose only merit seemed to be that they professed his own absurd theories. What these theories were exactly, nobody quite knew and though they all kept showering praise on one another and regarded each other as "geniuses," in fact they were, likely as not, just a bunch of ignorant youngsters who had taken it into their heads that it was not necessary to study music in order to become a musician!

Upon meeting him, however, Borodin found Balakirev so pleasant and interesting to talk to, that he gladly accepted the latter's invitation to drop in to see him, quite informally, the following Wednesday.

The first person he saw upon entering Balakirev's study was Mussorgsky. A tall, heavily built gentleman was seated at the tea table. The host introduced him as Vladimir Vassilievich Stassov.

After tea, Balakirev announced: "And now I would like

to acquaint you with the work of one of our absent friends, an 18-year-old naval cadet by the name of Rimsky-Korsakov, who is for the time being at sea. You will see for yourselves how much freedom, how much maturity there is in this work!" Whereupon he and Mussorgsky sat down at the piano and performed the *finale* from Rimsky-Korsakov's first symphony.

Borodin was quite overwhelmed by the beauty of the piece and by the intelligence and vigor of the performance. He couldn't quite make up his mind which of the two played better. Balakirev had a delightfully soft, almost feminine touch, but Mussorgsky's playing had more brio and power. Then Mussorgsky sang in a small but excellent baritone voice a few of Glinka's and Balakirev's songs, after which they all begged Borodin to play one of his own compositions. But the latter refused point-blank: "I'm no musician!" he protested, "I'm a chemist!" It was a most pleasant evening all around. Borodin noted, however, that although Mussorgsky seemed thoroughly at home in the company of these older men, there was something about Balakirev's attitude toward him that made Borodin suspect that young Modest was a bit of a Cinderella, and that he knew it and resented it.

II

Modest Petrovich Mussorgsky was born in 1839. Up to the age of ten, he lived with his parents on their country estate in the Government of Pskov. Here young Modest got to know something of "Holy Russia": the green fields sown with flax and dotted with birch coppices, the pine forests, the countless little lakes with their low, flat shores—the sort of countryside Pushkin loved to roam about. Like Pushkin also, he had a real *Nyanya,* an old peasant nurse who would tell him the sort of fairytales Pushkin's nurse loved to tell. His first playmates were the boys of the neighboring villages, who helped him gain an early insight into the more seamy aspects of Russian peasant life. He loved it all.

His aptitude for music showed at an early age; he was barely six when, without ever having taken a lesson, he was able to pick up on the piano anything he happened to hear. His mother became his first teacher and a year later he could already play some of Liszt's easier pieces. Aged nine, he performed at home before a large audience Field's piano *concerto* and at twelve he participated very successfully in a charity concert.

By then his family had moved to St. Petersburg, where young Modest attended the German school of St. Peter-and-St. Paul and where he studied music with the well-known Professor Anton Herke, who was so satisfied with his performance at the charity concert that he made him a present of an ornately bound Beethoven *sonata*. He did not interrupt his music studies even after joining the School of Guards' Ensigns (which the poet Lermontov had also attended in his day) and at the age of 13, he wrote his first composition, a polka, which his father proudly published at his own expense. Unfortunately, even before he left school, he acquired a taste for drinking. The director disliked boys who read too much. "What sort of an officer will you make, *mon cher?*" he would ask frigidly. On the other hand, boys who returned from furlough drunk, went unpunished as long as they got drunk on champagne and drove back to school in a carriage drawn by their own trotters, rather than in a hired hansom cab. In the *Preobrazhensky* Foot Guards, to which he was posted upon graduating from school, he found among the officers several amateurs of music; but most of them were more interested in carousing—something to which he himself was not entirely indifferent.

His father died when he was still quite a young man. He left his affairs in a state of confusion, having bequeathed the family estate to both sons in joint ownership. Modest would have been well advised to regard this as a first warning on the part of Fate, but he was too young to heed it. After all, he still had his mother and everything seemed to go on much as before. Life was not yet frightening. Life was interesting and, above all, fun.

III

Mussorgsky was seventeen years old—this happened a few months after he had made Borodin's acquaintance at the hospital—when one of his fellow officers introduced him to Dargomyzhsky's "*salon.*" Not all the seeds that are sown germinate, not all grafts take, and likewise not all meetings between persons produce the same effect: Some are productive of consequences, others—the majority, in fact—go virtually without leaving a trace. Such, for a long time, was Mussorgsky's acquaintance with Borodin. His meeting with Dargomyzhsky, on the other hand, immediately played an important part in Modest's life, for it was in Dargomyzhsky's salon that this rather primitive young Guards officer received a first insight into genuine musical culture. It was here, also, that he met some of the people who were to play an even more important part in his life and where in due course his friendship with Borodin matured.

Dargomyzhsky's salon wasn't really much to write home about. His women pupils were mostly distinguished by their gossip and the passionate adoration they professed for the "master." In return, the latter was wont to pay more attention to their looks than to their voices; thus, if somebody happened to point out to him that Mademoiselle Shilovskaya was singing pretty much off-key, he would merely exclaim: "But then she is such a darling!" One of them, a young German girl who went by the name of *Liubochka* was actually living with him maritally. The others feigned to be jealous of her. Aside from society dilettantes, the *habitués* of his salon were mostly failures; music teachers with nobody to teach, orchestra musicians without a contract, military bandsmen on half-pay. The host himself was, actually, also somewhat of a failure. He had only recently experienced yet another disappointment: Having placed vast hopes in his *Russalka,* he had finally found a good libretto and had felt his talent growing and maturing. But *Russalka* (though not a complete failure like his earlier *Triumph of Bacchus* and *Esmeralda*) was received coldly by the public. Aggrieved, mortified, he had thereupon withdrawn into the "desert"— a somewhat noisy and crowded desert!—of his salon. Here he reigned supreme; here, amidst the heady atmosphere of respect and worship that prevailed, he could at last breathe freely. Soon he was dividing St. Petersburg into two groups: those who attended his gatherings and those who didn't.

"Welcome to my house!" Dargomyzhsky exclaimed as he shook Mussorgsky's hand. "Here you will find all the devotees of real art, all those who are not bound by their jobs, their careers, official favor or official views, in other words— all the independent musicians of St. Petersburg! We are not very numerous (and Dargomyzhsky glanced about the room as if to count) but there is equality here and friendliness, in short—a genuine republic of the arts!"

After which he introduced Mussorgsky to some of the old-timers. But nobody seemed to have anything to say to the shy young man and so, presently, Modest walked up to the group that had formed around his host. The latter was talking in his high-pitched voice but with considerable authority: "I cannot argue about Glinka's idealism," he was saying, "but there is yet another aspect to music and that is truth and there —and I say so without mock-humility—I am one better than Glinka! Glinka was a great man, but he was still completely under Italian influence. He had a weakness for the rounded-off, conventional form. His recitatives are sometimes quite expressive, but I for my part want the music to follow the speech, I want it to serve the word . . ." Dargomyzhsky had a Jesuitic way of using words of praise in order to condemn. He would, for instance, talk about Glinka in the most enthusiastic terms, and claim that he himself was not worthy even "to unloose the Master's shoe-laces" and yet presently it would appear that Glinka's *A Life for the Czar* was a pretty poor opera. About *Ruslan* he expressed himself more cautiously. Mussorgsky was reminded of those underground sapping operations about which he had read at school in the course on fortifications.

Then the musical part of the evening began. "Here we like to play Russian music simply, sensibly, without any fanciful effects," Dargomyzhsky explained by way of an introduction. "In other words, just as our late friend Mikhail Ivanovich Glinka liked to hear it played." But although this was indeed what he taught his pupils to do, most of them failed to live up to his standards. Moreover, they seemed to have purposely chosen Glinka's poorest songs. Then Dargomyzhsky sang in a high-pitched tenor voice some of his own songs, as well as excerpts from *Russalka*. He sang beautifully. When he had finished, he suddenly remembered his new young guest and insisted that he play something, too. Mussorgsky's performance was warmly applauded and when the party broke up, he went out into the cold night in a mood of pleasant elation.

After that, he made a point of visiting Dargomyzhsky's hospitable salon practically every week. It was here that he first began to live the real life of a musician. His host, who appreciated frequent visitors, was friendliness itself. Occasionally he would invite Mussorgsky to take a seat at his side, on a small couch, and putting his arm through his, would talk to him, quite intimately about himself, about his views on music and on art: "He who writes for the sake of wealth or glory is not an artist, he is merely peddling his talent," he would say. "Although the articles that appear about me in the foreign press give me an occasion to make fun of all those in St. Petersburg, who keep belittling me in the drawing-rooms and in the press, I do not seek fame in Russia. I am not fooling myself! My standing here as an artist is hardly

an enviable one! Most of our music experts and reviewers
find me uninspired and uninspiring. They are so wedded to
routine that all they can think about are easy, ear-tickling
melodies in which I have no interest. I do not propose, just
to please them, to degrade music until it becomes merely a
source of entertainment. I am searching for the truth!"

Soon, however, and despite his own lack of experience,
Mussorgsky came to realize that it was only with a great
effort of imagination that one could claim that what he saw
at Dargomyzhsky's gatherings represented the "salt" of St.
Petersburg's musical earth. There was something stifling and
acrid about the whole atmosphere, as that which one finds in
a room that has long remained unaired.

And yet, every now and then, a few really interesting people would put in a fleeting appearance. Thus, Mussorgsky
met there the young music critic Serov who waved his chubby
hands and talked much and very intelligently about many
things that were quite unknown to Mussorgsky, while the
other guests listened with mute respect. Modest couldn't help
marvelling at the way Serov seemed to have caught on to his
host's way of thinking and at their manner of hissing in
unison at all and sundry. Another time, he was introduced
to a composer with the French name of Cui. They took an
instant liking to one another and had a long cozy chat. Cui
had just completed a comic opera entitled *The Mandarin's
Son*. Presently he admitted that he was engaged to be married to one of Dargomyzhsky's pupils, Mademoiselle Bam-
berg, and introduced Modest to her. He seemed very much
in love. He also spoke with a feeling much akin to love about
one of his friends, Mili Balakirev. "His is a luminous, outstanding personality!" Cui exclaimed. This was all the more
impressive because he did not look as if he were easily carried
away. Mussorgsky just couldn't wait to meet Balakirev. But
when the latter finally appeared, toward the very end of
one of Dargomyzhsky's weekly reunions, he impressed Mussorgsky as glum, pompous and stiff. He sat down at the piano,

played one of his own compositions and then said that he
was tired and drove away. But Cui had had time to introduce
Mussorgsky, and Balakirev very kindly invited Modest to
come and see him, together with Cui, on one of the following
evenings.

IV

Mussorgsky felt a little shy and a bit nervous as they walked
up the rather unattractive staircase that led to Balakirev's
humble lodgings. But he took an immediate liking to all that
he saw there: the shining black lacquer of the magnificent
Becker grand piano that took up almost half the room; the
score sheets strewn about everywhere—on the bookshelves,
the chairs, the floor and windowsills, and lastly their host
himself, who was quite different from what he had seemed at
Dargomyzhsky's. For he was now informal and gay. And then,
contrary to Dargomyzhsky, his every word, his every gesture,
however harsh, implied noble sincerity and when he spoke of
something about which he felt particularly strongly, the
very tone of his voice (for Mussorgsky did not always understand the meaning of his words) sounded convincing. Naturally enough, the conversation turned to Dargomyzhsky.
Balakirev did not deny the merits of Dargomyzhsky's operas
and acknowledged that he was continuing the Glinka tradition, though in a diluted, weakened form. "He is following
the right path, but he lacks talent," was Cui's summary.
Mussorgsky felt like asking them about that musical "truth"
by virtue of which Dargomyzhsky had claimed himself to be
superior to Glinka, but he didn't dare contradict Balakirev.
At Cui's request the latter then sat down at the piano and
began to interpret one of Schumann's symphonies commenting upon individual passages. After which he began to im-
provise, gaily and brilliantly. Everything he played sounded
new and attractive to Mussorgsky's ears. "If this is what he
calls improvising," Modest said to himself, "I wonder what

his compositions are like!" Cui also sat down and played and sang a few of his own charming songs, following which they both requested the young man to play something too. Modest felt ashamed of the poverty of his repertoire, both qualitatively and quantitatively. But Balakirev seemed impressed. Modest decided then and there to ask Balakirev to give him some lessons. He saw in this a double advantage: on the one hand, he would be able to perfect his musical education at the hands of a first-rate teacher; on the other hand he would be able to see more of this extraordinary man, to get to know him better, perhaps, and talk to him simply, as a friend, as Cui did. But he didn't dare mention it yet.

That summer Balakirev fell seriously ill and at his bedside Mussorgsky made the acquaintance of the Stassov brothers. Upon recovering, Balakirev left St. Petersburg and it was not until the autumn that Modest was able to mention, very shyly, his request. Balakirev agreed gladly.

The lessons consisted of playing four hands the works of Bach, Handel, Haydn, Mozart, Beethoven as well as those of the more recent composers—Schumann, Berlioz and Liszt. By that time, Mussorgsky was already sufficiently well acquainted with the works of Glinka and Dargomyzhsky so they left these aside. This list in itself shows that the charge that Balakirev "cultivated ignoramuses" and was "contemptuous of the classics" was unfair. However much he himself might appreciate in music all that which was new, unexplored, forward-looking, he regarded classical music essentially as a cornerstone to build upon and insisted that his young friends be "broken in" on the classics.

As they played, Mili would explain to Mussorgsky the significance of the various selections, their specific place and meaning in the history of music. Cleverly avoiding musical theory (which was never his forte) he would dwell on that which he knew best. He would talk to Modest about what he called "musical form." Although he never wrote anything but letters, Balakirev possessed beyond doubt the gifts of an outstanding music critic. He had an intuitive understanding of the inner logic of musical structure and was quick to note the slightest departure from these iron-cast rules. And in so doing, he would split up every musical composition into its component parts and analyze virtually each bar separately. He was a capricious and impatient teacher. Because he himself was quick to grasp the meaning of things, he expected others to do likewise and any delay in doing so exasperated him. He took absolutely no account of the varying degrees of knowledge of his pupils, never tried to make the meaning of his words unequivocally clear to them and hated repeating what he had already said. But all this was offset by a fiery and genuine love of art which was a source of inspiration for all those who associated with him. So, in spite of his shortcomings as a teacher, he fathered more than one musician of genius in his modest rooms. None of the great conservatories of music of the world could match this "nursery."

But Mussorgsky exasperated him. Not that the young man didn't have talent or a real gift for music but there was so much he seemed unable to understand or, worse still, which he insisted on understanding in his own peculiar way and expressing accordingly, i.e., clumsily, flamboyantly. Moreover, he was stubborn; at times he seemed actually dumb. But he was a good fellow and he seemed genuinely devoted to him, and so Mili continued to work with him. He refused to take any money for these lessons because they were friends, or perhaps because he made such poor progress. Mussorgsky was soon spending every free evening at Balakirev's— drinking glass after glass of tea, playing four hands and talking about music.

Mili introduced Mussorgsky to Apollon Gussakovsky in the hope that this would awaken in the two young men a spirit of healthy competition and they soon became good friends. Gussakovsky was already a brilliant student who composed and improvised, whereas Modest had (besides the polka he had written in his childhood) only one little composition to his credit. This small piece, entitled *Souvenirs d'Enfance* did not meet with Mili's approval. But seeing Mussorgsky's eagerness, Balakirev suggested boldly that despite his lack of theoretical knowledge, he go ahead and write an *allegro* to a prospective *Symphony in C Major*. He seemed to think that the best way to learn how to swim was to jump into the water! And to their mutual surprise, the *allegro* turned out better than they had expected after which, encouraged by this first "success," Mussorgsky began to toy with even more ambitious plans. He had recently read a Russian translation of *Oedipus Rex* and he now decided to write some incidental music to it, not only for the intermissions (as Balakirev himself had done for *King Lear*) but something along the lines of an *Oratorium for Choir and Orchestra*. How he did this is a mystery, for Mili had taught him hardly any musical theory. And yet even this *Oratorium* turned out all right.

In his turn, Modest introduced Balakirev to his mother and to his brother Filaret and Mili began to visit the Mussorgskys' home. Sometimes Mrs. Mussorgsky would take an upper tier box and they would all go to the theatre, Modest in his dashing Guardsman's uniform, his mother in a black lace or mauve widow's dress, Mili and Filaret in grey trousers with a ribbon down the seam and black dress coats, trimmed with black silk. Mili invariably wore bright red gloves.

Summer was approaching. Mussorgsky found that music was taking up more and more of his time; occasionally he would stay up all night at the piano, quietly, so as not to wake his mother and brother—improvising, playing, rewriting . . . Thus, at Mili's request, he wrote a piano transcription of Glinka's *Persian Choir* from *Ruslan*. In June, when the capital was at its best, when it had not yet become covered by dust and—though its old stones were already warming and brightening up under the sun—it was not yet sweltering under a wave of heat and stuffiness, when the Islands were radiant under their veil of young foliage

and the west wind carried with it the salty fragrance of the
distant ocean, Mussorgsky remained glued to his piano stool
(he couldn't yet, for lack of routine, compose in any other
way), working on a sonata, writing, searching, re-writing. It
turned out to be like any other sonata in the world; nevertheless, he was terribly proud of it. And yet he surmised,
correctly, that Mili would not this time "rub his tummy with
butter" (as he put it) for it. His *Oedipus Rex* was progressing
somewhat better. Mili helped him orchestrate what he had
written. Carried away by all these novel and fascinating
occupations, he took a fateful step—he resigned his commission. He felt that he shouldn't waste any more time on drill
and guard duty, on uninteresting companions, on anything
that had no relation to music. His mother and brother were
distressed. His brother knew that Modest's finances were in
poor shape and that soon the income off their estate would
not suffice to support them. Even Mili remonstrated with him
and pointed to Cui's example whose duties with the Army
Corps of Engineers were no hindrance to his work as a
composer. Actually, Balakirev feared that Mussorgsky was
simply not sufficiently talented to sacrifice his career for the
sake of music. Stassov too advised against it. He had, from
the very first day of their acquaintance, shown Modest friendship and kindness. Now, he pointed to the example of the
poet Lermontov. But Modest was adamant. "That may have
been good enough for Lermontov, but I am not Lermontov—
I am Mussorgsky!" he insisted. In July his resignation became effective and he left for the country, to stay with friends
in the Government of Novgorod.

V

There he attempted, at first, to settle down to the usual
routine—composing, improvising, transcribing, writing songs
(which were still mostly of very poor quality) and translating
Lavater's *Aussichten in die Ewigkeit,* which fascinated him.

But presently he had to give all this up; he felt tired out and his morale, too, was low. He himself attributed his condition to that mystical strain which Balakirev had noted in him. In that sense, Lavater's treatise on the fate of man's soul after death supplied an answer to his quest for the mysterious. Strangely enough, he combined at this point a genuine faith in God with a rather cynical approach to religion and the most coarse language when talking of the Almighty, until this became a veritable mania. And yet, at the same time, being a typical Russian intellectual of his day, his mind rejected God and religion as so many "prejudices." Not much is known about this period, for he himself was most reticent about it. He was beset by the perennial "accursed questions" (as he described them): what does life stand for? Does immortality exist? How is it possible to reconcile the existence of God with that of suffering and death? He sought to avoid being obsessed by them in the hope that "by developing his mind correctly," he would find comfort, just as he had found comfort, relaxation and peace in Swedish gymnastics and cold showers. By making use of mineral waters in the neighborhood, however, his health eventually improved so much that he was able to return to St. Petersburg.

He came home during the first part of August. Mili was not yet back. He had left for Niznii-Novgorod to visit his father only to learn on his arrival, that his old friend and protector Ulybyshev had died, bequeathing to him his entire collection of sheet music, as well as 1.000 rubles. Ulybyshev's sons were willing to part with the music, but they wished to pay the money off in installments. Balakirev was, as usual, hard up and so he decided to stay on and bargain with them for better terms. Without his "precious," "admirable" Mili (as he used to address him in his letters), St. Petersburg seemed to Modest a deserted city.

Nevertheless, he settled down to work. He wished to be worthy of his friend and to work hard, without wasting any time, especially since his resignation from the army had removed the last excuse for idleness. Time and again he would go back to his translation of Lavater. A sort of heady feeling drew him instinctively toward the world of beyond; he would feel a chill in the back as he read that "the soul of the departed can communicate with a man capable of clairvoyance," and that this proved the soul's survival after death. He even wrote about this to Mili. For wasn't Mili himself a clairvoyant? Didn't he too radiate a magical power?

But Mili disapproved of this mystical strain in Mussorgsky. "Modest's mind is crammed with rubbish!" he wrote, "now he keeps talking in one breath of the immortality of the soul and of infusoria!" (For Mussorgsky had also informed him that he was avidly studying the natural sciences as an antidote to his philosophical soul-searching.)

But most of his time he devoted to music. He was about to finish his *Sonata in E flat major,* which he had started before going to the country and for which he had found additional ideas at a village fete. At the same time he was also working on another sonata, "a simple little piece," as he put it. But more important still, he was full of plans for his *Oedipus Rex.*

That autumn Cesar Cui got married. Stassov was as usual indignant. To marry at the age of 23 was in his opinion just criminal. "One should get married only after having worked a bit, lived a bit, gotten tired a bit, just as one shouldn't lie down to sleep unless one has done a good day's work. Otherwise sleep is no sleep and marriage is no marriage. Actually, I don't see why I should waste my breath. Cui won't listen to me anyhow; as for you and me," he concluded his letter to Mussorgsky, "I doubt whether we will ever marry."

Mussorgsky wrote a song for the occasion, which he dedicated to the bride under the title *Meines Herzens Sehnsucht.* He was one of the ushers at the ceremony.

Shortly thereafter, Mili returned to St. Petersburg. He arrived without Ulybyshev's 1.000 rubles. Nevertheless, he seemed rested and cheerful. Another winter went by.

In many ways it resembled past winters, except that Mussorgsky had now no permanent occupation. Again he and Mili would meet, partly to study together, partly to talk and argue. Again Mrs. Mussorgsky would take them all to the theatre. That winter Modest heard *Ruslan and Liudmila* for the first time in extenso. Once or twice he even performed himself on the stage, for the Cuis liked to organize amateur theatricals. These included Cui's comic opera, *The Mandarin's Son,* from which Mussorgsky had already sung excerpts at Dargomyzhsky's.

Modest had himself now begun to dream of writing an opera. As a schoolboy he had been fascinated by Victor Hugo's *Han d' Islande.* Now he turned to his beloved Gogol for a theme. Having gone to visit Mili together with his brother on Christmas day and finding there a whole group of other visitors, he suddenly announced, between toasts, that he proposed to compose an opera on the subject of Gogol's *Night Before Christmas.* One of the guests suggested that this project would be put down in a protocol which all those present would then sign. But like so many other of his projects, this one too evaporated in alcoholic fumes.

Besides "their group" (as his composer-friends referred to themselves), he now also associated with people whom the latter regarded as not "theirs" at all, or at least "not *quite* theirs." Thus he spent much time with the Shilovsky family. Stepan Stepanovich Shilovsky had little to distinguish him apart from his fortune, but his wife, Maria Vassilievna, or *"Masha"*—as she was known even to strangers—was a perfectly delightful woman—beautiful, gay, coquettish. She had quite a good voice and would often sing—with considerable success—at her own and at friends' parties. Though she took singing lessons with Dargomyzhsky, her style was somewhat gypsy-like—both in her choice of repertoire and her technique. She had even composed a few *romances* of her own, though these, like her singing generally, seemed to serve her largely as an additional medium for flirtation. She was in

her late twenties, i.e., ten years older than Mussorgsky when
they first met. He was nevertheless very much taken by her
and she, in turn, does not seem to have been indifferent
to his attentions.

His friendship with Nadiezhda Petrovna Opochinina
was to take an even more serious turn. Tall, very good-
looking, with dark blue eyes and a deep voice, she was close
to forty when they met and in those days a woman of forty
was considered already middle-aged. She was the only sister
of four highly cultured and very attractive brothers, one of
whom—an admiral—Mussorgsky had met at Dargomyzhsky's.
No one quite knew why she had never married, though there
was a mysterious rumor linking her to a tragic amorous
experience in her youth. She had first met Mussorgsky's
mother and the two women soon became close friends. Afterwards Modest himself was introduced to her and before very
long he was calling her his "conscience" and talking to her,
for hours, about his work and his plans which, as she was
careful to stress in the beginning, was the only reason for
which "an old woman like myself" could take an interest
in him. We know very little about their relationship, except
that Mussorgsky dedicated more *romances* to her than to any
other woman; that it was to her that he also dedicated his
Impromptu Passionné (which he had been inspired to write
after reading Herzen's famous novel *Who is to Blame?*) as
well as most of those of his compositions which concern love,
such as his *Night* and *We Parted Full of Pride,* and that the
dedication to the song *Desire* reads: "In memory of her
judgment over me. St. Petersburg, 2:30 a.m." They wrote
to one another often, but none of their letters have survived
so that it is only from scattered hints, excerpts from his
inscriptions, chance remarks, etc. that one can guess his real
feelings. It was as if they were ashamed to admit their love
for one another, as if he wished to repeat with the poet:

I speak not, I trace not, I breathe not thy name . . .

It was while staying at the apartment she shared with one of her brothers in the Mikhailovsky Palace, that he was to write the greater part of his masterpiece, *Boris Godunov*. She was nearing fifty when he wrote the following letter to Stassov, which has actually little to do with love but in which he obviously had her in mind: "I am reading Darwin and I am in a state of bliss . . . When a strong, burning and loving woman clasps her beloved in her arms, he is conscious of violence, yet he has no wish to free himself from her embrace, because this violence sends him 'beyond the borderline of bliss,' because from this violence 'youthful blood roars.' I am not ashamed of this comparison: however we may twist around or flirt with the truth, he who has experienced love in all its freedom and power, has lived and will remember how very wonderfully he has lived and will permit no shadow to fall on the bliss he has known."

It is among the Shilovsky family that Mussorgsky lived the first years of his adolescence. It was an uneventful period of his life. In the spring of 1859, they invited him to stay with them at their country estate, situated in the neighborhood of one of Russia's most celebrated monasteries, *Novyi Yerusalim*. The house stood on a hill, surrounded by an English-style park and a large model farm. The Shilovskys lived in grand style, they even had their private choir which was conducted by one Depuis, from Count Sheremetev's celebrated choral ensemble. The latter performed quite adequately the church music of Bortniansky and was now studying excerpts from Glinka's *A Life for the Czar*. Besides Modest, the other guests included Dargomyzhsky and Liadov, who were in charge of the opera performances. Mussorgsky occasionally participated in the rehearsals. Most of the time, however, he spent living the leisurely life of a country gentleman.

On his way back from the Shilovskys, he at last visited Moscow The ancient capital of the Czars made an even stronger impression on him than it had upon Balakirev. Now, for the first time, there awakened within him that "feeling for history" which was later to grow so strong. Writing to Mili, he remarked: "Moscow transported me into another world—an ancient world." And he went on: "That wonderful Kremlin! I approached it with a spontaneous feeling of awe. Red Square, the scene of so much remarkable bedlam, loses somewhat of its impressiveness when seen from the left —from the side of the *Gostinnyi Dvor*—but Vassili-the-Blessed and the Kremlin wall . . . why, that is sheer sacred antiquity. The Cathedral of St. Vassili-the-Blessed gave me a sensation that was both strange and pleasant, as though any moment an ancient *boyar* would walk by, complete with long robes and high fur hat. . . You know I used to be a cosmopolite, but now I feel a sort of inner regeneration; everything Russian seems suddenly closer to me and I would be somehow upset if people took no account of Russia; I believe I'm really beginning to love her."

Thus, at first almost unnoticed, there appeared in him the first signs of "Populism." And yet for the time being, his music remained entirely "cosmopolitan"—despite Mili, despite Stassov. It was as though their words and Dargomyzhsky's "I am seeking the truth in art" needed still to lie fallow in his mind, like late wheat under its blanket of snow. As yet he was neither a nationalist, nor a realist. Even his titles were borrowed from the classical vocabulary. And yet his latest (and best) piece was beneath the surface already quite Russian in character. He confided to Stassov that this *Intermezzo in Modo Classico* had been inspired by something he had seen, that winter, in the country: On a sunny, festive day, a group of *muzhiks* were making their way across the snow-bound fields. "It was at once beautiful, picturesque, serious and amusing. And then there appeared in the distance a group of young peasant women, singing and laughing as they advanced along an even path. This scene impressed itself upon my mind in its musical form. All of a sudden, the first melody, rising and falling *à la Bach* took shape. I envisaged the merry laughter of the women as a melody from which I afterward took the middle part or *trio*. But all this was written *in modo classico,* in line with my musical studies at that time."

On January 11, 1860 there occurred in his life an event most important in the experience of any musician: for the first time, one of his compositions, his *Scherzo in E flat* was performed in public, at a concert of the Imperial Musical Society conducted by Anton Rubinstein.

Although he tried not to show it, he was of course terribly excited. And he was pained to note the contrast—quite natural—between his own emotion and the routine, matter-of-fact manner in which this event took place. The hall was not very full, for the St. Petersburg public had still to learn to appreciate symphonic music. It was cold. The candles flickered dimly overhead. Moreover, he didn't like the performance: he had not visualized the execution in quite this manner and the *tempi* were all wrong. At the end, the applause was merely perfunctory; the author was not called out. He noted with surprise that he was actually measuring the volume of applause. Could this be all? During intermission, some one had congratulated him. Mili had claimed that everything had gone perfectly well. He couldn't understand how it was that everyone seemed concerned not with him, but with their own petty affairs. Going up to Rubinstein who stood surrounded by women, he started to thank him effusively. But Rubinstein merely shook his artist's mane with an absent-minded air. After the performance there was not even the traditional celebration in a neighborhood tavern; it was too cold, his friends told him, and so he had to go home early with his mother, as though this were just another day.

And yet the event had a salutary effect on him. He began to feel that he was treading the right path, after all; he began to work with greater calm and concentration. It may have been a happy coincidence, but even his seizures ceased temporarily after this concert. By the end of the summer he felt completely well again. "You will rejoice," he wrote Balakirev, "at the change that has taken place within me and which has, no doubt, greatly affected my music . . . My brain has become stronger and has turned toward reality; the fires of youth have cooled, everything has settled and of mysticism there is now not a sign . . . I have recovered, Mili, thank God, completely!" In an earlier letter, he had sought to clarify their personal relationship: "As regards my attitude toward you," he had written, "I must explain my behavior toward you from the very start of our acquaintance. In the first place, I recognized your superiority; when arguing with you, I perceived in you a great clarity of thought and firmness. Mad as I was at myself and at you, I had to acknowledge the truth. Hence the need to stick to my guns both in my arguments with you and in my attitude toward you. Further: you are aware of my extreme softness of character which has caused me harm in my relations with unworthy people. Once I felt that my self-esteem was in jeopardy, all my pride welled up within me . . . And yet meanwhile I never forgave myself the slightest slip as regards kindness and truth. I owe you much, Mili; you did wonderfully well in jolting me out of my torpor . . . Later I understood you completely and became genuinely attached to you, finding that you, among other things, not only reflected my own thoughts but sometimes even provoked them into existence.—Our latest relations, moreover, have brought your personality so close to mine, that I have now complete faith in you: the role of a pasha *à la* Dargomyzhsky is too petty and insignificant to be ascribed to you; it wouldn't fit you anyway." And in another letter, he added: "Do you remember, my dear, how two years ago we were walking down Sadovaya Street? It was summertime, we were on our way home. We had just been reading *Manfred* and I became so electrified by the sufferings of this lofty human spirit that I exclaimed impulsively: 'How would I have liked to be Manfred!' (I was then still quite a child.)

Fate, apparently, willed it that my wish be fulfilled—I became similar to Manfred; the soul conquered the flesh."

Mili greatly enjoyed these letters, and yet somehow he
didn't quite trust Mussorgsky. This was not the first time, he
recalled, that Modest had claimed to have recovered his
health only to lapse again into despair shortly thereafter. It
seemed to be in his nature to switch from one extreme to
another. All his letters were full of unsolicited confessions,
obscure phrases, signs of megalomania. He seemed sincerely
to believe that he *was* a Manfred, a Faust. If all that he wrote
was true, he might well end up insane. And if it were
not true, if this were all exaggeration, what was the reason
for it? Why this pouring out of confessions, why this constant
soul-searching? The very tone in which Mussorgsky described
his work irritated Balakirev. "He has written an *allegro,* and
already he thinks that he has done much for art generally,
and for Russian art in particular," Mili confided to a friend.
"Can anyone that sensitive be regarded as healthy?" And he
found himself replying to Mussorgsky with unnecessary
sharpness. He even wrote to Modest's brother, Filaret, to
warn him about the dangers allegedly threatening the young
man. Modest took offense and as result, their relations
deteriorated.

About this time, Mussorgsky made the acquaintance of a
group of radical young men and when he could not be with
Masha Shilovskaya, he would go with them to a pub, to eat
crawfish and drink beer and "give hell (as he put it) to history, to the administration, to chemistry and to art." When
he learnt of this, Mili wrote him another letter, in which
he commented upon Modest's tendency to associate with
"limited personalities." Modest's reaction was swift and violent: "This calls for only one answer: 'Tell me whom you
love and I will tell you who you are.' And so, logically, I
must be limited."—"Not limited," Mili reflected bitterly,
"simply an idiot."

CHAPTER SIX

THE DELIGHTFUL CHILD
(The Young Rimsky-Korsakov)

*"On ne peut ici bas contenter
qu'un seul maître."*

BAUDELAIRE

I

At a time when Mussorgsky's genius was still shrouded in impenetrable veils, pierced only by occasional outbursts of passion for Balakirev, this "unrequited love" began to be further overshadowed by the appearance in their midst of a "green tenderfoot," a naval cadet by the name of Nikolai (or *"Kolia"*) Rimsky-Korsakov. The Benjamin of the group, he soon gained their general sympathy and Balakirev's personal devotion.

There was something just a little naive, a little clumsy about this seventeen-year-old youth; he seemed to radiate the breath of the sea, an air of purity and ingenuity. Indeed the only abnormal thing about him was his extraordinary gift for music. Everything else was simple, typical, conventional. There were literally thousands of such youths in pre-revolutionary Russia. All these groups were in a way products of the same class, a small stratum which gave Russia, apart from the army officers and government officials, also a few dozen major talents in every field of art. Nowhere else—with the exception, perhaps, of ancient Athens—was there such a blooming of talent within so short a period of time. Literature, music, the fine arts lit up the grey, cheerless skies of Russia like so many fireworks.

Rimsky-Korsakov's childhood was that of any other average child of his set. True, he did not spend it in the country, but in the small provincial town of Tikhvin. But the house—wooden, with gabled attics, columns and jug-like balustrades—lay on the riverbank at the very edge of the town and differed little from a typical Russian country mansion. He was a child of elderly parents (his father was 61 and his mother 43 at his birth, March 6, 1844). His elder brother Voin was twenty years older than he, so that he grew up among adults. Old Mr. Rimsky-Korsakov had served under Czar Alexander I as Governor of a province. But he was too gentle a man to survive under the reign of Alexander's successor, Czar Nicholas I; having shown "excessive kindness" to some Poles exiled after the 1830 mutiny, he was dismissed. Being a freemason and a stoic, he took this blow philosophically: "It's bad for my vanity but good for my morality," reads an entry in his diary on the day of his dismissal. He spent his remaining years in reading and bringing up his children.

Young Kolia had an excellent memory and studying came rather easily to him. His interest in music appeared early. As a child he would delight in listening to the chimes of the carillon in the neighboring monastery; all his life he was to remember their mournful tolling, following the death of one of the monks. Tikhvin was in those days a popular lieu of pilgrimage and the sight of these pilgrims, some colorful, others ragged, disease-ridden, blind; their monotonous chanting; the tinkling of the coins in their wooden begging-bowls as they made their way from church to church; the churches themselves, with their endless services, their festive processions, their dark-faced ikons, the sumptuous robes of the clergy, the dazzling splendor of the church plate—all that impressed itself early in his memory and was later enshrined in his work.

At the age of six, he began to take piano lessons, for which he showed little disposition. He started to compose also early though in the beginning he looked upon this more as a game, like building toy castles with wooden bricks. Thoughts about the sea, about travel to distant places, about ships took up much more of his time. The Rimsky-Korsakovs were an old Russian naval family; even now, his elder brother Voin was making a brilliant career at sea. From his recent round-the-world trip, he had kept writing home long descriptive letters which were read aloud to the whole family. And as he listened to them, Kolia himself fell victim to the spell which the sea and everything relating to the sea seem to cast over most young boys, so that when the time came for him to enroll as a Cadet in the Imperial Naval Academy, he did so gladly.

In those days, discipline at the Academy was strict; neither did it relax as far as Kolia was concerned when his brother Voin, by now already a rear admiral, was appointed director. Indeed, the latter was perhaps even more strict with him than with the other boys. However, he encouraged Kolia to resume his piano lessons and in the summer, when the cadets went off on training cruises in the Gulf of Finland, he even rented for him in Kronstadt (their summer base) a room complete with piano (due to the percussion of the firing guns, no pianos could be carried aboard ship). In reply to their father's charge of "extravagance," Voin wrote: "This is the best time in his life for him to acquire an art which will in due course be a source, not only of pleasant, but also of morally useful entertainment... I cannot say how great his inclination for music is, but I feel that his gifts are such that to neglect to develop them further would be tantamount to sinning before God, to burying the talent with which He has endowed him."

Gradually, music came to play an ever growing part in the boy's life. When he was thirteen, he was taken for the first time by his brother to the opera, to hear Flotow's *Indra*. He was thrilled—not so much by the music, as by the whole spectacle, even by the way the conductor swung his baton. Eventually, he learnt not only to watch, but also to listen; then he began to count the number of instruments in the orchestra and to hearken to their individual playing. At home, he would try to pick up on the piano the arias he had heard or, if he had been unable to find the score, would play them back from memory. On one occasion, having been put under arrest, he gave all his savings to the warden so that the latter might go and buy him the piano transcription of Glinka's *A Life for the Czar*. Writing home to his parents, he would describe in great detail all the operas he had heard; occasionally even, he would include scraps of sheet music with his own arrangements of his favorite arias. "I am learning to play by heart," he wrote, "the sextet and the madwoman's aria from *Lucia di Lammermoor*—I do wish Papa would learn to play them, too. It's really very easy; only in the sextet, the left hand needs to be more agile than Papa's is, it shouldn't follow the right hand. You wouldn't believe how much I love to decipher opera music and how, on the contrary, I dislike to play piano music. The latter seems so boring, so dry, whereas when you are playing an opera, you have the impression that you are sitting in the theatre, that you are listening or are even yourself playing or singing; you visualize the sets, the costumes—in other words, it is terribly jolly." Eventually (though again in a somewhat immature, childish way) he began to prefer some operas to others. "Italian music," he wrote, "is more graceful, whereas Russian music is more pleasant, it reminds you of the little Russian *muzhiks*, and also of the ancient times of the Slavs." As for *Ruslan*, "they say that it is a wonderful piece, that it can easily match Meyerbeer's *Robert le Diable* and the other classical operas."

At the age of fifteen, he heard for the first time a symphony concert and this event and even the programme remained forever enshrined in his memory. It consisted of Beethoven's *Pastorale*, Mendelssohn's *A Midsummer Night's Dream*, Glinka's *Jota Arragonesa*, the Interlude from *Lohengrin* and Liszt's *Prometheus*. He understood neither Liszt, nor Wagner but was enraptured by Beethoven's *Pastorale*. But he wasn't yet thinking of the career of a musician. "I should go to the country and play the piano a little," he wrote, "my fingers are, I imagine, quite wooden. But what can you do? Being an officer, I may well have to go several years without playing, the service is more useful, even though it may be less pleasant."

He displayed at this time considerable agility at climbing the masts and shrouds and once even almost drowned after falling into the sea from the height of a seven-storied structure. His musical progress, however, was slowing down. "After studying his playing," his brother Voin wrote to their parents, "I find that he seems to have no difficulty in mastering the mechanics of the piano, but he lacks taste and feeling, even when playing the things he likes most. It may be too early to expect anything better from a boy of his age; nevertheless, I deem it my duty to keep on nagging him and to make him repeat again and again the things he is playing, standing behind his back and beating time with my voice, my hands and my feet."

And yet his talent kept growing and evolving, despite the lack of expert guidance (which even his brother's substituting as a metronome could hardly replace). Voin realized this only too well and in the autumn of 1859, he engaged the celebrated Canille to give young Kolia lessons. This was the boy's first contact with a professional musician. Canille made him play Chopin, Bach, Beethoven. Together they marvelled over Glinka's operas, "the best in the world." He would also be made to harmonize chorales (without the help of a piano) or to re-arrange a piece of Church music or to write variations on a theme borrowed from a Russian folk song. Once, he was even made to write a sonata. He soon became so carried away by his musical work that he began to neglect his nautical studies, until his brother took alarm and threatened to stop paying for his music lessons unless he showed greater application. Canille was willing to go on teaching him without pay, but Kolia dared not disobey the admiral. In the autumn

of 1861, Canille spoke about his young pupil to Balakirev
and the latter invited him to bring the young boy to see him.

II

Balakirev took an immediate liking to young Rimsky-Korsakov and suggested that he visit him informally whenever
he had a free day. These visits soon became a real treat.
Temporarily to part with the austere atmosphere of the
Naval Academy, with the loving but stern discipline of his
brother and to be transported as if by magic from a young
boy's world into one where art reigned supreme, where he
could associate with the most intelligent men in Russia and
where these treated you, moreover, as an equal—why, this
was well-nigh a fairy tale!

Of these men, the most remarkable was of course his host,
Mili Balakirev himself. To young Rimsky-Korsakov, his talent seemed to "surpass the range of possibility" while his
knowledge was just inexhaustible. It was quite impossible,
however, to argue with him. His very presence was intimidat-
ing. Soon, the boy was echoing Mili's every word. Like him,
Kolia would now claim that of Beethoven's symphonies, only
the ninth was actually any good, and of his other compositions, only the *Missa Solemnis* and his last quartets; that
"Mendel" (as they kept calling Mendelssohn) had written
in all his life only two to three decent bars, and that for all
his talent, Chopin resembled at times a nervous young lady
with a marked inclination for fainting fits. Very soon he had
learnt to use all the correct musical terms which, though not
always comprehensible, were nevertheless full of charm.

With his habitual perspicacity, Balakirev realized immediately that this modest-looking youth was enormously talented. Like the other pupils before him, Rimsky-Korsakov
was now subjected to the traditional Balakirev method of
teaching ("part-talks, part-lessons"). Like them, he was given
extremely difficult assignments; like them, he was presently

advised to write a symphony. What did it matter if he knew
nothing of counterpoint or harmony and had only the vaguest
notion of that notorious ban on parallel quints and octaves!
In Balakirev's view, this knowledge could be acquired by
studying the major composers and by trial and error. Then,
having suggested a certain tonality and a number of key
themes (also with their respective tonalities) and having
advised him to consult Schumann's *Manfred* and *Symphony
No. 3,* Glinka's *Jota Arragonesa* and *Prince Kholmsky* and
lastly his own *King Lear,* Balakirev left him to his own
devices.

Being both capable and observant, Rimsky-Korsakov had
soon "put his symphony to simmer." Each excerpt was played
over in Mili's presence; he would approve some, but replace
most of them with his own suggestions. Then, again jointly,
these ready excerpts would be orchestrated. Rimsky-Korsakov
was somewhat more proficient at instrumentation than at
anything else, for Balakirev had given him excerpts to read
from Berlioz's *Traité de l'instrumentation.* But even then
there were abysmal gaps in his knowledge. He knew nothing,
for instance, about strings and insisted in writing endless
legati which no violin could ever have performed. Be it as it
may, by May 1862 the first movement, the *scherzo* and the
finale of his symphony were ready. It had immediately (especially the *finale*) great success with the members of the group.
Stassov "ooph-ed!" and "ah-ed!" and slapped him on the
back, Mussorgsky embraced him, even Balakirev glowed with
satisfaction. Only the *adagio* was now missing, it seemed to
elude him—which was relatively unimportant considering his
friends' professed prejudice against anything melodic.

Balakirev had never yet been known to devote himself to
someone with such concentration and passion. Rimsky-Korsakov was clearly his favorite pupil, it was in him that he
placed his greatest hopes. For Balakirev was as rarely mistaken in others as he was about himself. Let Stassov proclaim
him a genius, let all these young men hearken to his every

word with rapt attention, *he* knew his own limitations, he
knew how short-lived his moments of inspiration were, how
easily he got out of breath. If he lived on in the memory
of man, it would be not on the strength of his own compositions—of that he was now sure—but because of those he had
discovered, inspired and fostered to do still greater things.
He felt a real physical need to be the "spiritual forebear"
of a new generation of Russian musicians to an even greater
extent than Glinka had been. And yet until now, none of
his pupils had given him any real satisfaction: young Apollon
Gussagovsky was clearly "rotting away" (as he put it), Modest
was behaving more and more foolishly, Cui's talent was too
impersonal, too inhuman; alone *"Korsinka"* was enormously
gifted, alone he was soft and malleable like wax, a wax which
only Balakirev could shape and mould to the image of his
dreams. There was perhaps also another reason; what Mili
needed above all at this point may have been simply plain
human love and tenderness. But though Korsinka kept gazing
up at him rapturously, deep down in his heart Balakirev
sensed that this too was merely a mirage, that he would once
again be cheated of the fulfillment of his dreams, that (in his
own words) Rimsky-Korsakov was for the time being still "a
delightful child," but that when his gift reached full bloom
he, Mili, would be already an old man, he would no longer
be needed. And he felt himself torn between the wish to
enjoy to the hilt the satisfaction of the moment and the
anguish of anticipation at the thought of what must inevitably follow.

By now Rimsky-Korsakov had completed his course at
the Naval Academy. There remained the traditional three-
year training cruise which would mark the beginning of his
career as a naval officer. The very thought of having to part
with Balakirev and his friends, however, of having to interrupt for several years his musical studies filled him with horror. For by now he knew that his destiny was that of a
composer, not of a sailor. He had recently lost his father and

though nominally he now passed under his mother's control, in fact it was his brother Voin, the admiral, who would hereafter have the decisive voice in the shaping of his career. "Surely he doesn't think of becoming an artist!" his father had exclaimed shortly before his death. And yet that was precisely what the boy intended to do. He knew that his symphony was good, that he was on the right path. "By remaining in Russia," he wrote, "I might not be happy, but at least I would be following the career for which I was destined at birth." For his part, aside from the personal sorrow he felt at the thought of parting with his favorite pupil, Balakirev feared that such a prolonged absence might "demagnetize" the boy (as he put it), that he would be lost to art. During the heated discussions between the members of the group as to whether Korsinka should agree to sail or not, he argued that no effort should be spared to prevent his departure. He even tried to mobilize his connections in the Navy Department, but there he was told that the boy's only other alternative was to resign. Cui and Mussorgsky took it all far more calmly. "Yes," Mili retorted, "but then you are already a mature artist, whereas Korsinka is still a green tenderfoot. Neither in character, nor in talent has he yet matured!" To which Cesar replied: "That's just it: the voyage will develop both the one and the other. Let him live independently for a while, let him see the world, meet people." And Modest thought likewise, even though he himself had acted differently. And in the end, Rimsky-Korsakov gave in.

His mother and brother had all along been strongly in favor of the trip, though from very different motives. Though entirely dependent on her elder son's support, the mother had never really gotten on with him, while he treated her with courteous aloofness. With Kolia it was quite different: he was very close to her. But then, all of a sudden, she noticed that since he had met that wizard Balakirev, he too had begun to elude her. Who knows, perhaps the trip would bring him back to her? The admiral, on the other hand, regarded the whole thing essentially as a sort of "trial by sea water." For all one knew, Kolia's interest in music might be just another passion—like botanics, or numismatics. "Any passion," he wrote, "has perforce to be strong, which does not mean that it cannot be overcome. Take for instance love for a woman—and such a love is of course far stronger than, say, love of art. Why, even that love can be overcome through an effort of will-power, whereby the latter emerges strengthened, and without will-power there can be no success in anything, even in music. On the other hand, if this passion persists, well then it will have proven that it is indeed real. In Kolia's case, he will come back with a hardened character, having developed his mind through reading and travel, and he will then be able to devote himself fully to music. And if his musical urge vanishes, why then there will be no need for regrets, since its very transience will have shown that it was not really serious in the first place."

On October 20, 1862, the clipper *Almaz* weighed anchor with the 18-year-old Nikolai Rimsky-Korsakov aboard. He left with a heavy heart, as though he were going into exile.

III

The members of the Balakirev Gang did not forget their absent friend. Mili wrote to him continually, Cui more rarely. Contrary to his brother's hopes, Kolia did not take to this phase of the service, though he bore it stoically, as one bears a rough sea, or the heat in the tropics. He realized that he would never become a good sailor. Of course he enjoyed the sensation of travelling, of seeing new countries, but he described life on board, in the cadets' wardroom in pretty gloomy colors: "Each one does exactly as he chooses, without regard for the others: one reads, the other keeps yelling at the top of his voice, a third stays awake all night and sleeps all day, a fourth gets up during a meal and re-

lieves himself in front of everyone. . ." In the beginning he
tried to compose. He finished the *andante* to his first symphony and wrote and orchestrated a trio for the *scherzo*. This
in itself amazed him. "I can't understand," he wrote, "everything around me is unattractive, completely unmusical,
coarse, ugly, nasty, and yet I find it possible to compose even
in this rut." But this soon changed. "I don't seem to be
able to compose anything, or concentrate on anything. Only
random bits and snippets come to my mind and the devil
alone knows how good they are."

His spirits revived somewhat upon learning that the
andante which he had twice sent to St. Petersburg had finally
arrived there and had been performed by his friends and
that they had liked it. "Balakirev's news cheered me no end,"
he wrote to his mother, "he is always so encouraging . . . At
present I am glad, happy, satisfied. I will now write a new
symphony, *Symphonie en C-Minor No. 2 par N. Rimsky-Korsakov*. Ah! If only it turns out to be good! Mother, though
every passion is a vice, nevertheless do cross your fingers,
perhaps all will be well!" But this second symphony went
off to a poor start and he wrote to her again, this time in
despair: "In Russia, music is just making its first steps and
yet the Russian musicians are not just ambling along, they
are flying forward. Why is that? The frightening thing about
it is that I myself feel somehow apathetic toward music, I
have become indifferent to it. Voin will rejoice, he will claim
that he always knew this would happen, that he always told
me that my ravings about music were perhaps just idle talk
and that when I grew up to be more responsible, I would
forget all about it. Well, I may truly forget all about it. But
the trouble is that, while I will have stopped running with
the fox, I will not have learnt to bay with the hounds. And
so what? And so we will just have to drudge and toil and
tow the line and become a mediocre person!" And he goes
on in the same spirit: "Musically I am becoming ever more
obtuse and stupid. Not one of these months of enforced

idleness will be forgiven me, not one but that will claim its
toll one day. After three short years, I will have acquired
a will of iron, my character too will have hardened, my
nerves and music will have become of steel and I will have
grown incapable of producing anything decent."

Of course, this fear of acquiring "nerves of steel" was
merely a neurotic outburst and his brother was able to
counter, quite rightly, that one did not necessarily have to
have over-sensitive nerves in order to create. At his age, moreover, there was little danger of his fingers stiffening beyond
repair, while musical technique could always be acquired
later. Balakirev wrote to him much in the same spirit, with
the difference that while the admiral had little faith in
Kolia's ability to stand up to this challenge, Mili never
doubted it. And he begged his young friend not to waste
time in moping, but to read all he could. In answer to which
Rimsky-Korsakov dutifully plodded through the Iliad, the
Odyssey and the other ancient classics, as well as the works
of Bielinsky and Schlösser.

His friends did their best to avoid being too sentimental
in their letters (after all, this was the age of "thinking realism" and even nihilism, when Turgenev's hero Bazarov would
beg his friend Arkadi "not to talk so prettily" and would
proclaim that "nature is not a sanctuary but a workshop"!)
but they did not always succeed. Thus, while Kolia signed
his letters to Mili: "devotedly yours Rimsky-Korsakov," the
latter assured him that "I am ever so bored without you
even though I am very busy and should thus have no time
for boredom. I am all the more bored, because with the sole
exception of Cui, I do not expect anything from anyone any-
more . . . Of you I expect much; indeed I place all my hopes
in you. . ." Rimsky-Korsakov had asked Balakirev to criticize
his work without restraint or pity. To this Mili replied:
"You will in your lifetime have many an opportunity, no
doubt, to talk about music in your letters to friends and I
would advise you once and for all not to obey blindly any

self-styled 'authority.' Trust yourself more than anyone else. You may have faith in my critical ability, for instance, in my understanding of music, but even my views should not be binding upon you, for otherwise this will turn us into just another conservatory of music."

Rimsky-Korsakov hastened to follow this advice. Thus he refused to alter his *andante* as Balakirev had advised him to do. "You don't like it, I believe you when you say that it is poor, but I also believe that were I to change parts of it, I would thereby be changing the whole *andante*. It may well sound harsh, as you say, but I like that harshness. . ." Neither did he accept Mili's offer to score the symphony in his absence.

It was, of course, easy for the teacher to be liberal-minded and for the pupil to make a show of independence as long as they were separated by thousands of miles of ocean and as long as their "spiritual communion" was in writing. As soon as they met again, Balakirev's despotic disposition was bound to impose itself with renewed vigor.

CHAPTER SEVEN

THE BALAKIREV GANG

> *"Despite his great talent, he did a lot of harm. He origi-nated the bizarre theories of this strange group."*
>
> TCHAIKOVSKY

I

Gradually it became apparent to musical circles in the Russian capital that for all his cantankerous disposition, Balakirev was the gravitational center for a somewhat un-usual group of young men in army or navy uniform who composed strange music and propounded an odd musical philosophy. The very fact that they wore uniforms, of course, was regarded as conclusive proof of their dilettantism.

The *"Balakirevtzi"* or "Balakirev Gang" (as their foes called them) were probably the last to be aware of the stir they were creating. They had started off simply as good friends, exchanging occasional visits, swapping musical gossip or showing one another their latest compositions. But pres-ently, when their music began to be performed in public and first Stassov and later Cui gave them unqualified praise, while rejecting all those who did not belong to their "clan," the other critics took alarm. Many of them were composers in their own right; they felt personally singled out by these attacks, they replied in kind and it was thus, in the heat of newspaper polemics, that the "Balakirev Gang" received its baptism of fire.

In those days, the influential musical circles of St. Peters-burg centered around the Imperial Musical Society. The I.M.S. (as it was called) had been founded, among others, by Dimitri Stassov and Anton Rubinstein. It was headed by a board of five directors under the "august auspices" and chairmanship of the Grand Duchess Elena Pavlovna, an aunt of Czar Alexander II. Rubinstein, however, was the most powerful member of the board. He also conducted the I.M.S. concerts which were started during the winter of 1859-1860 and were the first regular series of symphonic concerts to be given in Russia.

Although, under the terms of the I.M.S.'s charter, there existed a Program Committee, the latter concerned itself solely with new, hitherto unperformed works. The selection of classical music and of those contemporary works that had already been "accepted" was Rubinstein's monopoly as conductor, and he had a marked partiality for the compositions of third rate Germans.

But it was neither his errors of taste, nor his preference for the classical pundits of music which alienated Balakirev and his group. What they could not forgive was Rubinstein's treatment of their idol, Glinka. Besides, they disliked his own compositions, finding them banal and of unequal quality. They even denied his talent as a pianist. To them, he was merely a brilliant virtuoso who excelled at so-called "drawing-room knick-knacks" or music *"con brio."* They refused to acknowledge his great human qualities and his innate distinction of manner. They mistook his vanity for ambition and his brutal frankness of speech for insolence. "To tell the truth," Balakirev remarked, "I don't find it very flattering to be compared as a pianist to either of the two Antons—Anton Rubinstein or Anton Kontsky"—a remark that was all the more malicious considering the different qualifications of the two Antons in question. Among themselves, Balakirev's friends invariably distorted Rubinstein's name, turning it into "Dufferstein" or "Bullystein." In public, however, relations remained correct.

A revealing incident occurred, one day, shortly after a rather successful performance of Mussorgsky's *scherzo* at an I.M.S. concert. Two of the directors who were well disposed towards Balakirev—Kologrivov and Dimitri Stassov—persuaded the Program Committee to ask Mussorgsky for another composition. He offered them excerpts from his *Oedipus Rex*. The committee members seemed soon to have repented their "rashness," but feeling themselves morally committed, they resorted to what they regarded, no doubt, as a tactful and clever escape ruse: Having selected a choir piece "shorter than a hen's beak" (as Mussorgsky himself put it) they made an unheard-of suggestion concerning its performance: the composer was invited to attend a rehearsal after which he himself would decide whether his music was worthy of being performed in public. "Feeling acutely the need to protect my integrity," said Mussorgsky, he flared up and demanded that his composition be returned. "That motley gang," he complained to Balakirev, "has the nerve to want to teach me a lesson!"

II

During the winter of 1860, Anton Rubinstein set about the realization of an important and difficult plan—the establishment of the first Russian conservatory of music. His first step was to set aside the profits from the I.M.S. concerts in a special fund for this purpose. Then he wrote an article which appeared in *The Century* and in which he expounded his views on the subject. "The conservatory," he said, "will provide us with Russian music teachers, Russian musicians and Russian singers, who will work as only those can, who visualize art as a means of existence, entitling them to public recognition, respect and fame. . ." What he meant to say, actually, was simply that music in Russia was to be henceforth the business, not of dilettantes, but of professionals.

At first Rubinstein's aims were completely misunderstood. His article aroused a storm of indignation. He was practically accused of inviting musicians to work not for art's

sake, but for money or for the satisfaction of their personal
ambition. The disciples of the great dilettante Glinka felt
personally attacked. They took up the challenge. Yes, they
retorted, they *were* dilettantes; moreover they were proud of
it! In the *Northern Bee* Stassov rebuffed Rubinstein in ruth-
less terms. He denied any analogy between a university and
a conservatory (this similarity was Rubinstein's main argument). A university, he wrote, "only conveys knowledge."
A conservatory, however, "is not satisfied to do merely that—
it insists on interfering in a most noxious manner with the
creative work of the student-artists . . . It attempts to cut them
all down to the same academic level . . . Besides," he added
rudely, "Rubinstein has nothing in common with either our
country or our art!" As for Rubinstein's complaints about
"dilettantism," what was frightening, Stassov said, was not
the compositions of "dilettantes" but the works of those
"untalented composers" who had acquired fame through a
different type of music, namely one that appealed essentially
to the masses. This, obviously, was an aspersion against
Rubinstein's own compositions. Other members of the
Balakirev group spoke in still more violent terms, though not
in public. "Unconditional surrender to Mendelssohn," exclaimed Mussorgsky, "that's Dufferstein's motto!" Balakirev
himself saw in this project nothing but "an attempt to set
up in Russia a Department of Music to educate musical
officials, who would then subject Russian music to the com-
mand of Baltic generals!" Even their perennial opponent,
Serov, agreed with them. "The education of our youth," he
exclaimed angrily, "is being entrusted to an illiterate, untalented pianist who, moreover, is an ignoramus in the field of
musical education!"

All this was of course greatly exaggerated. The very idea
of a conservatory implied, it is true, a spirit of academicism
which could easily turn it into a stronghold of routine, but
then the same could be said of conservatories all over the
world. Actually the Conservatory *did* raise the level of musi-

cal culture in Russia. The unconventional way chosen by
Balakirev and his friends was not necessarily the right one for
everybody else. If an original and powerful talent does not
require the strict rule of school discipline (indeed such a discipline could even harm it) for the average musician—the future music teachers and orchestra players—a conservatory was
indispensable. Unfortunately, there were at first several
mediocre teachers on the staff. Rubinstein himself was no
pedagogue. During his classes, when playing Beethoven's
sonatas, he would glance around at his pupils from time to
time to ask: "Do you understand?" Naturally, what they
understood was only that the music and the interpretation
were equally "divine" and that the maestro's head reminded
them of Beethoven's. There was something very powerful,
indeed leonine and yet at the same time childishly candid
about Rubinstein's features, his voice, his manner, in fact
his whole personality. Those who knew him never forgot
the admirable image of this inspired artist. Which was,
maybe, more important than the theoretical analysis of a
Beethoven sonata.

III

The tide of the times was favorable to Balakirev's "skiff."
He had always had faith in his vocation as a conductor and
his hopes soared with the inauguration of the Free School of
Music which offered him at last the opportunity to engage in
this new type of activity.

The School had been conceived as a counterweight to the
I.M.S. and the Conservatory. Though it was likewise supposed to satisfy the growing need in Russia for musical training and good symphonic music, it was to do so in a very
different way. Indeed, the spirit and character of the two
establishments were in sharp contrast to one another.

The Conservatory was a regular State-institution of
higher education, specializing in the field of music. Its

diploma awarded graduates the honorable title of "free artist" which assured them a number of privileges. Jewish graduates, for instance, were allowed to reside outside the Jewish Pale.

The founders of the Free School, however, were not content to be "free artists" in name only. They proposed to dispense with many hallowed features such as examinations, diplomas, patronage and state control. Admission was not to be restricted to a limited number of prospective professional musicians. True to the democratic-populist spirit of the times, the School was expected to bring musical culture to "The Masses." Tuition was to be free and the classes were to be held in the evenings or on Sundays so that the worker, the shop clerk, the seamstress or the chambermaid might find there an opportunity to make use of their leisure. The primary accent was to be laid on lessons in singing for which "the masses" had supposedly a greater aptitude. These were to be the responsibility of one Gavriil Yakimovich Lomakin, an experienced choir master who was, with Balakirev, the co-founder of the School. Glinka had rated him highly. Later he had taught singing at Stassov's school. He was now in charge of Count Sheremetev's private choir, which he had brought to a high point of perfection. Balakirev reserved for himself the instrument classes.

Of course, although the teachers worked without pay, the very principle of free tuition implied the existence of funds which had somehow to be obtained. Balakirev and Lomakin therefore organized two benefit concerts, the first of which was held in March 1862 and the second a week later. The Sheremetev choir participated and Karl Schubert conducted. The Free School concerts soon became a regular feature of the St. Petersburg musical season, alongside those of the I.M.S. Balakirev conducted the orchestra and planned the programs.

Although they had fewer connections than Rubinstein, Balakirev and Lomakin were able to recruit a number of prominent trustees and, despite the progressive spirit of the School, these included even the heir apparent, Grand Duke Nikolai Aleksandrovich, who contributed 500 rubles.

Balakirev's programs were, as a rule, far more selective than Rubinstein's. Mili was not one to curry favor with the public by catering to pseudo-democratic tastes. Rather than lower himself to his audience's level, he sought to raise its standards of musical appreciation to his own exacting heights. It was some time, however, before he was able to master completely the difficult art of conducting. His only previous experience had been with Ulybyshev's little orchestra many years earlier. Whatever he may have learnt then had by now been forgotten. Besides, the magnetic quality of his personality—so compelling in a restricted circle of congenial friends —was apt to dispel itself in a concert hall and did not impress either the orchestra or the audience. His followers, of course, studiously ignored this and in the press both Stassov and Cui praised Balakirev inordinately (although in private Cui was a little more conservative in his comments) while the hostile critics, headed by Serov, went to opposite extremes.

IV

Meanwhile, to Stassov's surprise and dismay, his "favorite foe" Serov had suddenly become a celebrated operatic composer in his own right. Stassov had long regarded Serov as a superficial windbag or as he would put it, "a barren figtree." In his eyes, Serov had been guilty of a number of crimes: he had scorned Glinka and Russian music generally; he had dared to predict that *Ruslan and Liudmila* would soon be dropped from the operatic repertoire and forgotten (and— which was worse—he had been right!); he had become a ludicrous *Zukunftist,* a standard bearer of "that Teuton" Wagner! And now, through sheer stubbornness rather than by virtue of his talent, he had succeeded in getting his opera *Judith* accepted at the Mariinsky Theatre.

Stassov did not even bother to attend a rehearsal until, one day, he received a letter from a Greek lady friend of Serov's in which she announced that "In three days' time this 200-gun vessel will be launched and at the sight of majestic Judith all will be confounded—Glinka, Wagner, Meyerbeer. . ." She added that Serov had been grieved to note his friend's indifference. At first, Stassov was inclined to shrug all this off as the ravings of a love-sick woman, but then, overcome by curiosity, he attended the dress rehearsal and noted with some consternation that the "Greek odalisque's" raptures (as he called her) were shared by the public. Although the house was almost full, there reigned as he entered such a hallowed silence that for a second he thought that he was alone. And when the curtain fell, the roar of applause was such as he had never heard before, even at the ballet. During the intermission, he visited Serov in his box. The acclaimed composer was beaming with joy and his tiny body was twitching all over with emotion. He welcomed his old friend effusively, but Stassov remained aloof and instead of commenting on the music, spoke at great length about the sets and costumes, whereupon Serov's face immediately fell and Stassov beat a hasty retreat.

The final curtain fell amidst a new storm of applause. As he roamed the corridors and listened to the enthusiastic comments of his acquaintances, Stassov recalled something he had often deplored before, namely that a crowd, as if prompted by a sort of collective, warped instinct, is invariably attracted by cheap effects and false values. Although he would never have admitted it even to himself, apart from the disgust he felt over this triumph of poor art, he had also a feeling of personal injury, because the success had been scored by Serov, of all people.

As ill luck would have it, his friends were all out of town. Balakirev was in the Caucasus. Cui, forgetful of his duties as a critic, had left for the country. Only Mussorgsky was there, but then what good was he? True, Modest had also criticized

Serov's opera, but how listlessly, how colorlessly! Stassov poured out all his resentment in a letter to Balakirev: "Mussorgsky seems to have become a complete idiot!" he wrote. "I could have whipped him yesterday. I think that if he were left to his own devices or if he were lifted out of the environment into which you dragged him against his will and given a chance to indulge without restraint in his natural inclinations, he would soon sprout moss and weeds like everybody else. Where are you, where are you? Why aren't you here, right now?"

Balakirev's reply was a cool and level-headed appraisal of Serov and his opera: "I can find no spark of genius in it," he wrote. "But then where should it come from? . . . The over-all result is weak, the fantasy poor. The Serov we all know shows in every note—spineless, sour, open to every chance influence. And yet it is obvious that he has a head on his shoulders and that he is a musician. . . There is a lot of Verdi in him . . . It's all served with the most fashionable sauce, but then this sauce was brewed not by Serov, but by Berlioz, Wagner and the others. As for the public, all that one can say is that if it has indeed been taken in by this masterpiece of petty-bourgeois operatic art, this proves merely that it has at least risen above the level of Varlamov and Guriliov . . . Which is of course lamentable! As you know, for all its uncouthness, I prefer the Orthodox Church to the civilized petit-bourgeois Protestant creed, just as I prefer Czar Nicholas I to that sweet constitutional dreamer Katkov."

Mussorgsky was equally objective (and this is precisely what Stassov mistook for "idiocy"). He too wrote Balakirev a letter in which he gave a very sound analysis of *Judith*'s merits. It contained, he said, many interesting ideas which, if not overtly expressed, were at least, as he put it, "implied." It had of course many Meyerbeerian features. Obviously, the *Wagnerkindchen* had not quite made the grade. But the opera showed talent even if, like all cosmopolitan music in Russia, it had no future and led nowhere.

V

Young Kolia Rimsky-Korsakov returned from his cruise on the clipper *"Almaz"* in October 1865. Some time, however, elapsed before he was able to find his bearings, on land and in the world of music. At first he lived in Kronstadt, coming into St. Petersburg only occasionally. When he finally moved into town, he noted with some bitterness that there was no place for him in his brother's large apartment, the Admiral's young wife objecting, apparently, to their living all together under the same roof. He therefore took only his meals there, living in a small furnished room, which he rented for 11 rubles a month from a typesetter, on Vassilievsky Island.

His official duties did not take up much of his time and he gradually lost interest in naval matters. Although he had corresponded with his musician-friends and they had extended a warm welcome to him on his return, he felt at first like a stranger in their midst. During his absence they had acquired new interests which he was unable to share; they were concerned with countless minor problems which meant nothing to him; they had even picked up expressions or coined words which were new to him. He was most anxious, therefore, to catch up on all the latest news and gossip.

Although they all disliked him heartily, the concerts which Richard Wagner had given in St. Petersburg the year before had somehow alarmed Balakirev and his friends and "stirred them up." They continued to maintain that Serov was insane to claim that Wagner "had discovered new horizons" in music. There was no doubt, however, that Wagner was a remarkable conductor. Furthermore, he had introduced an unheard-of innovation: he stood facing the orchestra with his back to the public! But his music was repulsive; it was affected, insincere and lacked simplicity. The orchestration was of course brilliant but there was something about it that was profoundly alien to the Russian character. "Wagner," barked Stassov, "is not an operatic but a symphonic composer. He is at his best in his musical pictures, even though he but scratches the surface, whether it be the gallop of horses, or the flight of a bird, or fire, or water, or a storm, or a crowd, or a celebration, or a bacchanalia, or just noise or conversation. Take these pictures away from him and nothing remains of Wagner!" Cui was even more violent: "He's a good conductor," he wrote, "but he plays uninteresting things: Beethoven's *Third* and *Fifth Symphonies* and his own compositions. He has absolutely no talent. His melodies are even cheaper than Verdi's and more bitter-sweet than Mendelssohn's at his worst. All of it is coated with a thick layer of decay. His orchestra is decorative but uncouth." He granted, however, that Wagner's visit had done the local conductors some good: Even Karl Schubert ventured now to turn his back to the audience, Liadov Sr. had begun to swing his baton with a little more zest and Balakirev himself, ever since Wagner's visit, was conducting with greater vigor.

Balakirev was fully aware of Rimsky-Korsakov's predicament. He realized that his young friend suffered from being neither fish nor fowl, neither sailor nor musician. He decided that it might be a good thing to have Kolia's *Symphony No. 1* performed in public and he urged him to complete it. In general, throughout this difficult period, Balakirev was to his younger friend both a father and a brother and Rimsky-Korsakov found himself enmeshed in a web of devotion and consideration from which it would have been difficult to extricate himself, even if he had tried. But he did not try. On the contrary, he submitted to it and, as a result, he was gradually "led back to musical health."

Dragging half-heartedly his symphony out of a trunk, he added the missing *trio* and *scherzo*. But he composed these without faith or enthusiasm, mainly to please his older friend. Then he orchestrated and re-orchestrated the whole thing under Balakirev's direction and finally re-wrote it hastily, leaving many mistakes in the script.

Rimsky-Korsakov's *Symphony No. 1 in E flat minor* was

performed in public for the first time at a concert of the Free
School on October 19, 1865. This occasion was probably as
memorable for Mili as it was for the composer himself. The
School's modest budget had allowed, as usual, for only two
rehearsals. But Balakirev conducted with fire and enthusiasm
and after the *andante* and *finale,* the public called for the
composer who appeared in his naval uniform, bowing
clumsily and obviously ill at ease. The whole audience stood
up like one man and applauded long and loud "as a token
of appreciation for youth, talent and art," as Cui put it. For
once, Cui's review was enthusiastic and unqualified. "At last,"
he said, "we have a real Russian symphony." After the concert the composer was invited to a banquet given by the
School, where again he was toasted and welcomed as the first
Russian composer of symphonic music.

But although Rimsky-Korsakov was in a state of perfect
bliss, this triumph did not go to his head. He continued
to believe that he was indeed the poorly educated, uninteresting little naval officer such as he appeared to others. He
went on to look up, not only to Balakirev because he regarded conducting as a mysterious and awe-inspiring craft,
but also to Cui because a critic performed a function no less
important—that of sitting in judgment and handing down
verdicts. For Rimsky-Korsakov was one of those people in
whom genuine modesty is sometimes combined with an
almost insane subconscious vanity. A single word could
scathe him, even if he would never admit it, and his friends
did not spare him. For one thing, they considered him a poor
pianist. But then on that score Borodin too was the target
of many a good-natured taunt. And *he* was already a mature
composer. Even when Borodin played his own *First Symphony* four hands with Balakirev, the latter would jump up
suddenly and say: "No, I'd better play it with Modest!" and
as he took his place, Mussorgsky would point at Borodin's
clumsy white hands and remark jokingly: "It's not your
fault . . . How can you help it with those paws?" and Borodin

would join in the laughter. But although he too laughed at
their taunts, Korsakov felt miserable and in Balakirev's
presence he would play, of course, worse than ever.

At home, therefore, he practiced diligently and eventually
he made good progress. The worst of it was that his own
family and his fellow naval officers regarded him as a great
pianist, the ladies' darling. It all seemed so silly and unworthy. He was too sincere a man at heart to endure for long
this double life: of a talented composer who was at the same
time a poor pianist. In later years he would say: "Oh what sad
times those were for Russian music!" And yet these were
years of hope and expectation; he himself had just scored his
first success; other masterpieces were beginning to stir his
fantasy, *Sadko* was on his way; Borodin was finishing his *First
Symphony* and Balakirev was performing his *Islamey* and
Tamar!

Although he dared not as yet admit it openly, he was
beginning to find fault with his mentor. For one thing, in
contrast to Balakirev, he considered that a good piano technique was necessary, even indispensable for composing. And
then he was growing increasingly conscious of the fact that
his work lacked a solid technical foundation and though he
was the first to revere Balakirev's omniscience, he could not
help noting that the latter seemed intentionally to avoid ex-
plaining certain fundamental problems of musical theory.
Finally, there was something clearly very odd about Balakirev's methods of criticism.

Upon being shown a new musical composition, Balakirev
would immediately pounce upon every trifling shortcoming
and lampoon it on the piano to the point of ridicule. Then
he would suggest improved variations. He was apt to dissect
almost every bar. He would say, for instance: "The first four
bars are good, the following eight are weak, the melody which
follows is no good at all, but the transition to the next musical phrase is admirable. . ." And all his friends seemed now
to have adopted this method. Sometimes, new compositions

were not even played through to the end, or else they were begun in the middle and then played by bits and snippets, selected at random. Mili insisted, furthermore, on seeing even the earliest drafts of a given composition. As a result, the composer would lose all his spontaneity and after thinking up a few chords, would stop in his tracks in a dither of fear and ask himself anxiously whether by chance two or three notes had not crept into his work which later would cause him embarrassment?

On one occasion, Rimsky-Korsakov suggested timidly that creative work was something intimate and personal and that it was perhaps better for a composition to be imperfect so long as it was original and reflected accurately the author's intentions. To that Balakirev replied that the best method of composition, on the contrary, consisted in submitting the entire process of one's creative effort to the continuous criticism of those endowed with critical qualifications. For their part, the critics should correct mercilessly every detail, until the piece was absolutely perfect. To prove his point, he quoted the example of the Jesuits, whose every action was subject to discussion by all the brethren. Which was, to say the least, an unexpected comparison from the lips of a Russian ninteenth-century intellectual!

VI

Borodin was now also taking a course at Balakirev's "school for geniuses." He too sat "at the master's feet," or rather at his side, playing the piano four hands as best he could. He was of course older and more mature than both Mussorgsky or Rimsky-Korsakov, and he had already heard and seen much. But even to him Balakirev would explain the various musical forms, and demand corrections and changes in tonality. There was, however, a note of deference in his voice when Mili spoke to Borodin which was conspicuously lacking when he addressed the other members of the group. Borodin was graced by nature with an unusual air of distinction and a great solemnity of manner. He was in every way a *grand seigneur*; he even spoke with a sort of aristocratic drawl. His very presence made Balakirev's Saturday gatherings more festive, added a sparkle of wit and friendliness.

This friendship with Balakirev played an important part in Borodin's life. Until they met, he had regarded himself as a dilettante and had paid but scant attention to his work as a composer. Among his fellow professors his musical hobby was the subject of many a good-natured taunt. But Balakirev, with his usual insight, had understood immediately that here was a man of enormous talent whose real vocation was music. When he said so, however, Borodin merely stared at him incredulously or roared with laughter.

Borodin's apartment in the building of the Academy of Medicine and Surgery on the far side of the Neva River, was quite far from where most of his musician friends lived. So that his guests should not have to cross the rather ramshackle Neva bridges after dark, therefore, he used to invite them out early or put them up for the night. They had all taken an immediate liking to his wife, Ekaterina Sergheyevna. She suffered from asthma, however, and spent most of the winter months with her mother's family in Moscow where the climate was drier.

Balakirev's rare visits were quite a special event. They were usually preceded by endless correspondence, coaxing and persuading. When at long last the great day was set, Mili who, true to his bachelor or rather old-maidish habits, disliked spending the night away from home, would arrive early. Mrs. Borodin was not a very good housekeeper and so the meals were not very exciting, but she never failed to buy him a tin of his beloved pressed caviar. After lunch, while his host puttered around in his laboratory or gave lectures, Balakirev would lie down and take a nap. The flat was roomy but as a rule chilly, for the Academy took poor care of its tenants. But none of this mattered once the evening set in, the lamps were lit, the conversation became "concert-like" and they were able to abandon themselves to that state of intellectual effervescence which is one of the great joys of life. The hostess was usually silent, she just sat and listened, but she was such a charming and intelligent woman that her very presence was an additional delight. Sooner or later they would sit down at the piano. Borodin had taken out a subscription with a music-lending library, but their choice of selections was limited and he would always beg Balakirev to bring some music with him—one of Beethoven's quartets, or a Berlioz piece, or one of his own compositions with which Borodin was as yet unfamiliar.

Deep down in his heart, of course, Borodin knew that Balakirev was right, that music was indeed his real vocation. But it was at present too late to seek to alter his course. Nevertheless, he now made a point of playing the piano more often and, like all Balakirev's "eaglets," started work on his own symphony, which was to become the celebrated *Symphony No. 1 in E Flat.*

He composed slowly, much more slowly than his friends. Almost every bar was discussed with Balakirev and when a given passage had been approved by the Master, it was played four hands at a plenary meeting of the group when everyone was once again invited to express an opinion or proffer advice.

There is a theory among experts that folk songs, sagas and popular fairy tales are the product of an anonymous, collective effort dating back to the dawn of time. This is probably just another myth. Our folk songs and epic poems were more likely as not created by gifted individuals and then adapted subsequently by those who performed them. The first masterpieces of the "Balakirev Gang," however, seem indeed to have been the product of a collective effort. Though only one of them actually composed, the others all gave advice, suggesting a change here, an addition or a deletion there. For all one knows, these modest gatherings around an oilcloth-covered tea table loaded with cold cuts, different sorts of cheese and pressed caviar may one day rank alongside Plato's legendary symposia!

In this congenial atmosphere, Borodin the composer little by little gained in stature. His growth could be compared to that of the mythical *bogatyri*—the hero giants of the ancient Russian sagas who, incidentally, were to inspire a number of his works. For years he had remained an amateur, an imitator; of a sudden he found himself a mature and original artist, somewhat tinged by Mendelssohnian influence, but with that additional touch of the Orient which is so inherent in the Russian character.

And yet he seemed in no hurry to perform the feats of valor for which he was so well equipped. As a rule, creative work requires unremittent effort and it is only through continuous practice that a talent can retain its fertility. Like the flow of water in a pipe, it requires continuous pressure. With Borodin, however, it was different. For years on end, he would busy himself with his chemical work or his civic duties and all the while the musician in him would remain dormant. Yet, as soon as he returned to art, everything he wrote was so powerful and so original that it was as if he had never stopped. When he was "in the mood" he could remain glued to the piano for ten hours at a stretch without eating, without sleeping, without even being aware of the passage of time. Even after he had torn himself away from his composing, he would answer his wife's questions absent mindedly; he would beg her not even to look at him at such moments: "What fun is there in looking at the face of a cretin?"

Besides their weekly gatherings in Mili's apartment, the "Balakirev Gang" used also to meet at the Cui's and sometimes at Stassov's. The Cui's were famous for their culinary prowesses and one day Borodin ate so much of a stuffed goose that for several days he was too ill to go out. He didn't really mind because, like Balakirev and Stassov, he too, enjoyed being sick. For it was only through the experience of physical

anguish that he could forget his students, his chemistry, his
board meetings and reach out for a sheet of music-copy. Even
on sleepless nights, when continuous pain kept him awake, he
found consolation in the thought that sooner or later the pain
would vanish and that he would then be able to resume
composing. As for the "sundry petty swine" (as he called his
real or imaginary ailments, the rashes, the boils, the colds and
bouts of bronchitis which plagued him from time to time)
they seemed to him a veritable gift from heaven! It was
during one of these periods of convalescence, that he wrote
"out of sheer boredom" the *finale* to his First Symphony.
He wrote it straight for the orchestra, which was something
new to him and passionately interesting.

He met his friends also at the concerts of the I.M.S. and
of the Free School, which he attended regularly. Sometimes
he would even drop in at the dress rehearsals. The I.M.S.
concerts were usually well attended and on those days when
the Grand Duchess was present with her Court, the hall was
filled with chamberlains, Guards officers and students from
the exclusive "Corps des Pages" and Imperial School of Jurisprudence. The concerts of the Free School played, as a rule,
to a less numerous audience, less glamorous perhaps, but
which listened with rapt attention. Here the friends felt
at home. During the intermission, they would visit Balakirev
in his dressing room and occasionally, after the performance,
they would go on to a pub in order to celebrate a first performance, or because Mili had been especially applauded
that night or simply because they wished to get together over
a bottle of wine. But Borodin rarely participated. He had to
get home before the wooden bridges over the Neva were
closed for the night.

VII

There comes a point in the life of every revolutionary
when he has to stand up to the supreme test—the test of
power. Balakirev was now nearing this point.

It all happened with seeming suddenness, and yet there had been many signs in the sky. For one thing, his fame had grown steadily with every concert of the Free School and it had been further consolidated by the publication of a splendid anthology of Russian folk songs which he had collated and put to music with masterful skill. Besides, the number of his friends within the I.M.S. had grown. Besides two of the directors, Kilogrivov and Dimitri Stassov, they included now Dargomizhsky, who had been recently elected vice-president of the St. Petersburg branch of the society.

In the I.M.S. itself, the situation was growing increasingly tense. Anton Rubinstein did not see eye to eye with the members of the Program Committee and he was, furthermore, incensed against the administration of the Conservatory which, in his opinion, distributed diplomas all too generously. During this conflict, all the directors with the exception of Koligrivov, resigned. Finally Rubinstein himself submitted his resignation, whereupon Koligrivov recommended that Balakirev be appointed to conduct the concerts of the Society in his stead. It was rumored that during his final audience with the Grand Duchess, Rubinstein himself supported the nomination. Whether true or not, this would have been consistent with his capricious but generous nature. Be that as it may, the Grand Duchess confirmed the nomination; she granted Balakirev an audience and as he kissed her hand, the old lady's face was wreathed in smiles and merry wrinkles. In secret, she probably dreamed of taming this "wild revolutionary" and turning him into a "polished European."

In his dual capacity as conductor of both St. Petersburg symphonic orchestras, Balakirev became a sort of *arbiter elegantiarum* in musical matters. Even such famed visiting *virtuosi* as Leschetitzky and Auer had to address themselves to him personally in order to secure his participation in their concerts. He had now both the time and the opportunity to reorganize the programs, which he did with his customary energy. His foes claimed that his marked preference for composite, "international" programs was due to his vanity and his desire to see his own name posted alongside those of such great musicians of the past as Beethoven, Schumann and Bach. But this was unfair. What thrilled Balakirev was not so much—if at all—the possibility of posting his name alongside Beethoven's, but the opportunity of including in the programs of every concert a work by Glinka or by one of his other Russian friends. Thus, at one of the first I.M.S. concerts under his baton, he performed Rimsky-Korsakov's latest work, the tone poem *Sadko*.

Stassov was even more excited about this concert than Balakirev or even Rimsky-Korsakov himself. For he had a sort of paternal feeling about *Sadko*. It was he who, in the days of his close friendship with Balakirev, had discovered the symphonic potentialities of this ancient saga about the traveller from Novgorod and his visit to the realm of the King of the Seas. When Mili refused it, he had offered it to Mussorgsky. He had even given him a detailed outline on the subject. But Mussorgsky was not inspired. Beyond an occasional trip to the *Strelka*—the promontory at the westernmost point of St. Petersburg jutting out into the Gulf of Finland—Mussorgsky, like most citizens of the capital, knew nothing of the sea and cared even less. Rimsky-Korsakov, however, had pounced on the subject. His years of sailing the oceans had predestined him to become the Russian musical bard of the sea.

Although one could discern a number of influences in *Sadko* which, with his usual high sense of integrity, the composer himself readily acknowledged, the piece taken as a whole was as original as it was colorful. Perhaps because he realized that this was the product, not only of his pupil but also of a unique musical personality, Balakirev, even while praising it, seemed no longer able to find the words of enthusiasm which had come so readily to his lips when welcoming Rimsky-Korsakov's first compositions.

There is nothing as successful as success. Now that the new Russian school of music had discovered a powerful salesman in Balakirev, wider European horizons suddenly opened up before it. Balakirev received an invitation to conduct a series of concerts of Glinka's works in Prague.

Prague was not a "world capital." Indeed, it was a quiet, slightly provincial city. Nevertheless, this invitation represented an unprecedented tribute to a Russian musician and a great and promising triumph for Russian national art, generally.

CHAPTER EIGHT

BALAKIREV IN PRAGUE

> *"I pity the man who can travel from Dan to Beersheba and cry: 'tis all barren!"*
>
> STERNE

I

Ten years after Glinka's death, the Czech National Opera decided to stage both *A Life for the Czar* and *Ruslan and Liudmila*. In order to give an eloquent demonstration of Slavonic unity and also because of the technical difficulties involved, it was decided to engage a Russian conductor. The Czechs turned for advice to Liudmila Ivanovna Shestakova, Glinka's sister, and she recommended Balakirev, as Glinka's best known pupil and disciple.

In the spring of 1866, Balakirev left for Prague for preliminary talks. In Vienna, however, he learnt that hostilities between Prussia and Austria had just broken out and that the Prussian troops were fast advancing toward the Austrian capital. He had perforce to get out of the country as best he could. Later that autumn, Liudmila Ivanovna herself went to Prague (no time, no effort was too much for her when her brother's music was at stake). She was received by one of the outstanding leaders of the Czech patriots, the *Namiestnik* or Governor of Prague, Rieger; the latter was extremely kind to her, promised every assistance, including even a subsidy. It was now decided that *A Life for the Czar* would be staged by the Czechs themselves, before Balakirev's arrival; he would have merely to conduct its performances; but *Ruslan* would be staged by him. In addition, he would be invited to give, with the participation of the Czech National Opera orchestra and choir, two benefit concerts of Glinka's works. The finan-

cial terms of this contract were rather unsatisfactory, but then
money never played a very important part in his life.

Balakirev left St. Petersburg in January 1867. Prague produced on him a mixed impression. He liked all that was old,
historic: the Hradŝin, which reminded him of the Moscow
Kremlin; the old churches, houses and cemeteries; even the
Jewish synagogue. But modern Prague appeared to him dirty,
humid and dark. He had little money and so at first he took
a room at the Inn of the *Black Horse,* from where he moved
to a small, inexpensive apartment. His new quarters were
crammed and cold, the stoves smoked profusely but provided little heat. He soon discovered that there were also
bedbugs on the walls, behind the picture frames, though he
couldn't be too sure that these were not of Russian origin,
brought with him from home. He searched far and wide for
a piano to rent and finally found one; hardly had he played
a few chords, however, than he was told that he couldn't have
it for love or money: he played too loud, he might damage
the keys! The Czechs reminded him of some of the Russianized Germans he knew in St. Petersburg, and he had always
despised those. Neither did he like their language, but then
Slavs often regard other Slavonic languages as a caricature
of their own!

On the first night of his stay in Prague, he went to listen to
A Life for the Czar and was aghast. The conductor Smetana
(a well-known Czech composer in his own right) had done
goodness knows what to Glinka's opera! The *tempi* were all
wrong, the performers quite unsuited to their parts; the
Russian peasants wore overcoats with white buttons and
peaked caps on their heads; Antonida was dressed in a
Western-style jacket and Polish cap; Czar Mikhail, in the
Coronation scene, was attired somewhat like the King of
Sicily in Meyerbeer's *Robert le Diable.* The *boyars* resembled
Venetian state councillors or Medieval troubadours and the
Patriarch—a rabbi. It was as though Smetana was trying on
purpose to turn the whole piece into a farce. At Mili's in-

sistence, the Patriarch was dropped from the Coronation procession; he also tried to have some of the singers switched to other parts, but without success. With *Ruslan* however, he realized, he wouldn't have to worry, there *he* would be Czar!

Thereafter, he made it a point of attending every performance, so as to study the singers. Then rehearsals started, first with the singers alone, and later with the orchestra and choir. The latter at first sang badly though most of them tried hard, for they loved the music. The orchestra was quite good, even though its members were so poorly paid, that most of them had to perform also elsewhere, in hotels, restaurants and beergardens. Balakirev did not suspect for instance, that a shabbily dressed baritone by the name of Anton Dvorak who now gazed at him with huge, attentive, severe and slightly crazy eyes, had himself already written quite a lot of music and was about to perform in his own country a feat much resembling Glinka's.

Most of his troubles were with Smetana and the opera administration. He suspected that they were influenced by pro-Polish elements and were being purposely obstructive. For the Polish-language press was claiming that the whole venture was a "Czarist intrigue" for which the St. Petersburg government had paid 50.000 rubles—which made Mili particularly bitter when he looked around his humble lodgings and recalled that he couldn't even afford to dine in a decent restaurant.

His struggle was rendered even more difficult by the fact that he couldn't speak Czech and his German was rather poor. The "revolting pygmy-conductors" (as he called Smetana and his friends) raised obstacles all down the line: first the orchestra and choir seemed to be constantly busy, rehearsing something else; then the piano transcription of *Ruslan* suddenly vanished, only to reappear again just as suddenly, as soon as it was clear that he could conduct the opera from memory; besides, the Czechs refused to pay for the transcription of the orchestral music parts, and as Mili couldn't afford to pay for this himself, the two benefit concerts had to be abandoned. In the end, he was not on speaking terms with Smetana. Time and again he had to appeal to Governor Rieger himself. At times he felt so despondent that he was tempted to drop everything and return to St. Petersburg, but he couldn't afford to do even that. In the end, he was fortunate enough to come upon a pro-Russian Czech merchant who put his financial means at Balakirev's disposal so that the latter was able to threaten that he would resign. His threat had an immediate effect: the Czechs became frightened and, in Mili's own words, "silk-like." But even then he had time and again to resort to what is known in Biblical terms as "snake-like wisdom." Thus, upon being urged to make cuts in *Ruslan*, he at first agreed and even struck out a few bars with his pencil, only to carefully rub out his own markings with an eraser shortly thereafter, when nobody was looking.

The guiding light in this struggle was his ardent, unrestricted admiration for Glinka and his work. "Usually, when you are studying one particular piece," he wrote, "you end up by becoming dulled and impassive. Whereas here, it is just the opposite. I am falling more and more madly in love with this music . . . Tell Cesar [Cui] that *Ruslan* is superior to the *Ninth Symphony* which, with the exception of the first *allegro*—and even this is thinned out *à la* Schubert—and a few bits of the *finale*, contains nothing remarkable. The *Lezginka* alone is worth all of the *Ninth Symphony*. *In extenso*, Glinka's *Ruslan* sounds marvellously majestic. The last *Quartet in C* impresses the artists with its faultless, virgin-like beauty. My nerves are quite on edge, both because of the music and because of all this unpleasantness."

. It is hard to say, nowadays, whether Balakirev's suspicions were fully justified or whether they were partly due to his own high-strung disposition. It is also possible that those of his Czech friends who belonged to the pro-Moscow party intentionally fanned his feelings against Smetana. Be it as it may, his letters home were full of complaints, irony and indignation. He wondered, for instance, why the Czechs, who had so courageously upheld the integrity of their language against the inroads of the Germans, had fallen for all that was German in every other respect. Students of the Prague Conservatory of Music would drop in to visit him and would voice enthusiasm for his *Anthology of Russian Folk Songs,* only to hear from their teachers, when they returned to school, that everything about the anthology—the melodies as well as the harmonies—were *ganz falsch,* so that they were in a dilemma. "Ignore the self-styled experts!" Mili enjoined them, "Think for yourselves!" At first they merely stared at him, in a dumb way, then they got frightened and stopped seeing him. He kept criticizing the Czechs' lack of a sense of humor and made fun of the names of the various "pygmy-conductors," the Smetanas, the Prohaskas, the Seboras.

On the other hand, his Russian friends made fun of him and of his mission. For his part, Mussorgsky, while joining in their jokes, seized upon this opportunity in order to state, in powerful and harsh language his own faith in an exclusively national art which, alas he, like so many others, identified with hatred of all things foreign, non-Russian, European, Jewish, German.

II

On the opening night of *Ruslan,* Balakirev arrived at the opera house early and in a state of considerable excitement. As soon as he entered the hall, however, he realized from the reception given him by both the orchestra and the audience, that he had little to fear—*Ruslan* would not let him down. That night he conducted as he had never yet conducted in his life. He felt as though he were walking on clouds, in a state of blissful trance. In their turn, the musicians outdid themselves and the singers sang with much feeling. At the end, he was quite deafened by the roar of applause. While Balakirev and all the members of the company celebrated the event at the club *Besseda,* many of the audience and especially the younger generation refused to go home and groups of them roamed the usually quiet streets of the town until the early hours of the morning, singing *Bayan's Aria* or *Ratmir's Cavatina,* to the surprise and indignation of the inhabitants and policemen. This turn of events was all the more unexpected when one recalled that the citizens of Prague usually made a point of getting home early so as not to have to pay 20 *hellers* to the nightwatchman.

Some of this success was strictly political. Threatened in their national existence by the Germans, the Czechs looked for salvation toward the Russians who, for all their sins, had nonetheless built up a mighty Empire. Behind each swing of the Russian conductor's baton, they seemed to perceive the heartwarming vision of row upon row of Czarist troops, marching to their rescue. It was as if they were addressing a challenge to the Germans: "We Czechs aren't alone!" they seemed to say, "We have an elder brother! Just try and do anything to us now!"

At first, it had been planned to conclude the festivities with the solemn unveiling of a portrait-bust of Glinka in the National Museum. But the Germans became alarmed; the Austrian *Landrat* forbade the procession and in the end, the bust was transported to the Museum informally, without any ceremony, and installed there for some reason, not with the composers, but beside that of Shakespeare.

Next morning, Balakirev awoke with a somewhat heady sensation. He turned on the light and started to glance through the papers. He now knew enough Czech to be able to understand the gist of the reviews, all of which were favorable. *Narodni Listi* stressed quite correctly that Glinka had been the first to seek to express the Slavonic spirit in musical terms and expressed the opinion that the Slavonic peoples were destined one day to take the lead in the field of music.

Balakirev got up, opened the window wide and breathed deeply. He felt that he could be justly proud of what he had achieved. Within two weeks, he had rehearsed and staged an opera with a choir and orchestra he had never worked with before, with artists who were in some cases not suited to their roles, or unable to speak the Czech language. He felt that he had actually matured, grown in these past two weeks. He was now at last "a real conductor." For *Ruslan* was after all, a somewhat tougher nut to crack than, say, Liszt's *Mephisto Walzer*! If only he could stage *Ruslan* at home, in Russia, without any cuts! True, he had been forced in Prague to agree to certain cuts; thus he had dropped all the dances from Act III. But then these were not among the best parts of the opera, anyway. On the other hand, he had been able to retain parts he had never succeeded in performing in St. Petersburg, i.e. the *Introduction* and *finale* from Act V, and also the entire first scene of that same act, with Ratmir's *romance*, the *Recitative in A Minor* and the *Oriental Choir*. And he had played the extraordinary *Lezginka* in its original form, not as Liadov played it in St. Petersburg.

There were two other performances of *Ruslan*. The last one, a benefit performance which was to take the place of the two cancelled benefit concerts, yielded very poor box-office returns, so that Mili had to borrow from his Czech merchant-friend 100 *guldens* to pay for his return fare. Nevertheless, he left Prague content and happy. A foundation had been laid; however brief, this was the first attempt (since Glinka's own rather unsuccessful concerts in Paris) to make Russian music known to western audiences. Eventually, it was to conquer the world.

CHAPTER NINE

MUSSORGSKY'S CREDO

> *"All realities will sing, nothing else will."*
>
> COVENTRY PATMORE

> *"To depict the finest traits of human nature and of the masses of mankind, to delve insistently, tirelessly into these unknown lands and to conquer them—that is the genuine vocation of the artist. Forward, toward uncharted shores!"*
>
> MUSSORGSKY

> *"Teach me, only teach, Love As I ought I will speak thy speech, Love Think thy thought."*
>
> R. BROWNING

I

In the spring of 1861, Czar Alexander II proclaimed the long-awaited emancipation of the serfs. For the smaller landowners, like the Mussorgsky's, this measure—however morally commendable—was to spell gradual ruin and their eventual extinction as a class, for only very few of them had enough capital to effect successfully the switch from free part-time serf-labor to tenant farming or paid manpower.

This ruin came slowly, and it was not for the ever unpractical Modest to arrest its steady progress, however much he might try, on occasion, to take his brother Filaret's place during the latter's periodic absences, to go on business trips and venture into business deals. According to his brother "Modest, both in childhood and adolescence, and also later, when he was grown up, regarded all that had to do with the people and especially the peasants with a real feeling of love. He looked upon the Russian *muzhik* as a trustworthy human being." And Filaret added with a note of bitterness: "In this he was greatly mistaken; it caused him to suffer considerable hardship and privation; because of this love for the *paysan,* he was obliged to look for a job." Thus, Mussorgsky may have gone too far to meet his farmers' interests and shown them exaggerated trust.

Be that as it may, he now found himself compelled to tighten his belt. Then his mother gave up her house in town and retired to their country estate in the Government of Pskov. He saw her only the following year, when he himself had to travel to the provincial town of Toropetz "because of some ill-doings on the part of the agent," as he put it. It was to be their last meeting.

In Toropetz, of all places, he came upon some verses of Goethe. These were the traveller's *An die Türen will ich schleichen* from *Wilhelm Meister* which Mussorgsky re-christened *The Beggar's Song* and put to music. He himself was to become a beggar, the beggar's bard, singing the woes of the crushed and underprivileged . . . The time had come to sacrifice, once again, that freedom for the sake of which he had left the service and to put on another uniform. In December 1863, his friends, the Opochinins, helped him obtain a job with the Main Department of Engineering of the Ministry of Communications. He was then 24 years old. For the rest of his life he was to devote part of his time to his official duties.

Presently, his brother Filaret also left St. Petersburg and Mussorgsky settled down in an apartment which he shared with five other young men who all worked in various government departments. Each had his own room, but in the evening they would usually get together over a bottle of wine and read to one another aloud, or just talk, or play some music. They called this arrangement jokingly their "Commune" (Chernyshevsky's revolutionary novel *What is to be Done?* was just then the rage in Russia). As usual, Mussorgsky read a great deal and also worked on a paid translation of Gayot de Pitaval's *Les Causes Célèbres.*

II

In 1864, Mussorgsky wrote a small vocal piece which he himself regarded as his "first attempt at writing something funny." Its real significance, however, lay elsewhere for this was his first attempt to integrate the Russian peasant, the *muzhik,* in his art. Not that he could ever have been reproached for not knowing his own people. He had known and loved them since childhood. But artistically he remained long aloof of them. A month earlier, he had written a *romance* to the words of Pushkin's *Night*—a quite beautiful piece, full of daring harmonic discoveries. But there was nothing specifically Russian about it.

Suddenly, on May 22, he saw in his mind's eye a clear-cut vision: *Kalistrat,* that ragged, cheerful, sly little *muzhik,* whom the great poet Nekrassov had immortalized in his verse. Actually, this ne'er-do-well, who spends his time getting drunk, cracking jokes and making fun even of his own wife, while she kills herself laundering the rags of their innumerable offspring, is not much of a hero. And yet his appearance on Mussorgsky's roster of characters was to point the way to many other similar individuals, all of them truthfully and vividly etched, who were later to claim a place in music and literature.

And yet for a while longer, they were again dropped in favor of various Lybians and Carthaginians. But a first indent had been made.—Another year went by. Another spring came, a tragic spring. For that spring his mother, Yulia Ivanovna died. She died quite suddenly, yet fully conscious of the fact that the strange, extraordinary boy whom she loved so dearly and whose genius she alone, perhaps, understood in those early days, was now being left to fend for himself in a hostile, intolerant world.

His few compositions of that spring and of the following autumn were devoted to her memory. The first two (for the piano) were titled: *Childhood Memories.* One was subtitled *Nanny and I,* the other *The First Punishment (I am locked in a dark room).* They were pretty poor. He realized this and never published them. And yet he would hardly have dedicated them to his mother had he not attributed some importance to them. He regarded them, no doubt, as the beginning of something new, as an attempt to write, not "pure" but pictorial piano music, as a first experiment in musical realism.

That autumn he also wrote his *Cradle Song* to words taken from Ostrovsky's *Voyevoda,* in which an old grandmother sings her grandchild to sleep in terms that give a shattering impression of the Russian peasant's tragic lot. This song, one of Mussorgsky's most powerful compositions, was also dedicated to his mother's memory.

Whether because of his personal grief or because he had many an occasion while living in his "Commune" to share his friends' joys and sorrows—all of which were duly drowned in liquor—he now took to drinking immoderately, as a result of this he had another seizure, which was either a recurrence of his earlier sickness or else simply a bout of delirium tremens (he was only 25 at the time!). Be it as it may, his brother Filaret understood that unless something were done, Modest would be lost. Presently, he and his wife succeeded in persuading him to give up the "Commune" and live with them. He stayed with them several years, leaving St. Petersburg only occasionally—to accompany them to their farm of *Minkino,* or to their country villa, just outside the capital.

III

In the fall of 1866, while staying in Pavlovsk, he felt a new upsurge of creative power and within a period of a few days wrote some of his most remarkable songs. One of them, his

Gopak, was written to the words of the poet Shevchenko. The wild, fast-changing rhythm of this Cossack dance seems to impart all the warm, sultry air of a Ukrainian summer night. A few days later, he recalled in song yet another childhood image: On a warm summer night in the country, an ugly young village idiot is declaring his love to a beautiful young girl. Insistently and without restraint he keeps calling her by endearing names, begging her to love him in return. He craves for her love, and yet at the same time he doubts that anyone will ever love him, so that his nagging sounds a little like the invocations of some pagan witch doctor. There is something astonishingly daring in the very simplicity of the scene where the music, while picturing the young wooer's monotonous chanting, remains nevertheless unobtrusive, so that without the words (which he himself invented) it would mean very little, while without the music the words would mean even less. And yet blended together, the impression is quite overwhelming.

When he returned to St. Petersburg and performed before his friends his *Lovely Savishna* (as he called this song) for the first time, he found that nothing he had as yet written, not even his *Cradle Song,* had produced such an impression on them. Even Cui, who was apt to become impatient when made to listen to something he himself had not written, beseeched him to sing it over and over again. This moved Mussorgsky so much that he promptly dedicated it to him. Even Balakirev inclined his head with an air of conde-scension. As for Stassov, he now became a sort of *im-presario* to Modest, dragging him to see all his friends to sing his *Lovely Savishna* before them. It was he who introduced Mussorgsky to Liudmila Ivanovna Shestakova, Glinka's sister, in whose house Modest was soon an *habitué,* and where he met Professor Nikolsky (who taught Russian literature at St. Petersburg University) and the celebrated bass Petrov—a tall, swarthy old man (he was of gypsy origin) whom every-body called "grandfather." Petrov combined a fabulous voice with a remarkable talent as an actor. Despite their great difference in age, and although Modest treated him with ostentatious deference, they soon became close friends.

IV

For Dargomyzhsky, this evolution in Mussorgsky's creative talent was a veritable personal triumph. For he realized that he now had a disciple. He had never quite severed his relations with Modest, even though the latter, after first listening to him with wide-eyed admiration, had begun to frequent his *salon* more rarely and had finally gone over to the "Balakirev Gang" altogether. Actually, Dargomyzhsky himself spoke nowadays of the latter with more good-natured self-satisfaction than anger, somewhat like you would speak of your pet bulldog: "Isn't he fierce? And yet he obeys me completely!" For the Balakirev "bulldogs" were indeed beginning to be friendly to him; they realized that this sardonic and choleric old man was after all a "soul-mate," a "fellow-heretic," that he was one of them. Moreover, his talent had not waned with the years, especially his sense of humor—an essential quality of every real artist, without which it is hardly possible to survive, or to face the bitter truth of life. Indeed he seemed to be devoting himself more and more to the exploration of this comparatively inaccessible area of musical humor, seeking out new, wonderful images for his already extraordinarily rich and diverse picture gallery. Though suffering already from the incurable heart disease which was to take him to his grave, he had recently undertaken something even more daring—he had started to write an opera on the subject of Pushkin's *The Stone Guest*, where he not only retained every word of the original text, but emphatically declined to make use of the traditional operatic form.

What Mussorgsky was now doing, therefore, was bound to be eminently agreeable to the old composer. Let him invoke Mili Balakirev's name, so long as his real mentor was Aleksander Dargomyzhsky! Indeed it looked as if the pupil would soon outdo the master, as far as "musical truthfulness" was concerned. Presently, Dargomyzhsky came to look upon his periodic meetings with young Mussorgsky when they would sing and play their latest compositions to each other, as an indispensable part of his life.

On his side, Modest greatly appreciated this attitude of Dargomyzhsky's and even dedicated to him his *Song of Yerio-mushka* which he had written to the words of Shevchenko's poem, *Gaidamaki*. Though beautiful, this song turned out to be a little too romantic, perhaps, for a Mussorgsky piece, as though he—the Northern Russian—were out of place as soon as he tried to capture the Ukrainian romanticism of the Southern poet.

He was to dedicate yet another piece to Dargomyzhsky, something quite unexpected this time. Modest had always loved children, he would spend hours observing them, playing with them. With them he did not have to take on a pose, to talk belligerently in self-defense, as he now felt more and more the need to do when addressing grown-up people. And yet even when talking to them he would use a somewhat pompous language, such as: "Your good health, milady!" or "Allow me to kiss your fingertips, milady!" (the "miladies" in question being respectively, the twelve- and thirteen-year-old daughters of Dimitri Stassov). And the children, in turn, loved him. It is, therefore, perhaps no wonder that the idea should have come to him to transcribe into musical terms their children's world, not as their parents and the elder generation generally visualized it, but as they themselves saw it. And hardly had he embarked upon this project, than he realized that he had struck an unsuspected gold-mine.

He entitled the first piece *With Nanny*. This was a minia-ture but full-fledged drama from the life of a child, with its capricious alternation of joy and sorrow, when the fantastic visions conjured up in its mind by the nurse's fairy-tales are brutally interrupted by the crude reality of life as epitomized

by her sudden outcry: "Go stand in the corner!" This was
no longer music—this was real life! Every feeling vibrated
as in real life, every changing modulation of a child's prattle
was noted with marvellous accuracy, so that even if it may
not have been music, it was something most unusual and wonderful anyway. Dargomyzhsky never tired of listening to it.
The dedication read: "To the great teacher of truth in
music."

V

The question that now arises is: What was this "truth in
music" which first Dargomyzhsky and after him Mussorgsky kept groping for so persistently? What was this *credo,*
this dogma of "musical realism" which turned Mussorgsky
into a sort of knight-errant blazing new trails toward his often
proclaimed "uncharted shores" and inspired him to such
great deeds? And, conversely, what is the meaning and role
of any "truth" in art?

In the first place this "musical realism" was not a personal
whim, a chance caprice of Dargomyzhsky's. However intan-
gible the connotations of this oft-used and even more oft-
misused expression, it squared with certain fundamental features of the Russian character, of the "Russian soul." Much
has been said in Europe about the mystical quality in this
Russian soul, about its inherent romanticism. And yet Russian literature of the nineteenth century was born and was
to evolve essentially under the banner, not of romanticism
but of realism. True, Zhukovsky chose to imitate the German
romanticists and Pushkin and Lermontov both professed to
admire Byron. And yet it was those two who were the
creators of modern Russian prose, in its most simple and
sober form; it was they who created the Russian realistic
narrative. Indeed the main current of Russian literature, its
most significant trends have always been basically realistic.
Even its greatest magician and fantast—Gogol—was at the
same time its greatest realist. And the same can be said of

Tolstoy, of Dostoyevsky, of Turgenev, of Goncharov and of Chekhov. The drabness and greyness of the Russian landscape, the harshness of Russia's past helped produce people who were fundamentally alien to, who simply could not abide by the rhetorical pathos of French romanticism, or share the obsession with the *Übermensch* in man of its English counterpart, or cherish the vagueness and obscurity of the German romantic school. Russians are by nature cautious, distrustful, reserved and ironical. Indeed, if there ever were to be a Russian romanticism, it would have necessarily to be synonymous with truth and truthfulness, that specifically Russian brand of truth and truthfulness which, incidentally, should be handled at times—as experience has shown—with considerable caution! Russian prose is, in its essence, modest, sober, reserved. Dostoyevsky is in this regard perhaps the only exception. Those Russian authors who wished to sound more flamboyant, to sparkle and glitter—the Bestuzhev-Marlinskys, the Leonid Andreyevs, the Balmonts—produced something that rang false, like a counterfeit coin.

But if this generally realistic trend in Russian literature was thus conditioned by certain inherent features in the Russian character, starting with the second half of the nineteenth century, this trend became still more powerful, but also more complex, as a result of the growing role that the new classless *intelligentsia* began to play in the spiritual life of Russia. The *intelligentsia* infused Russian literature with its own peculiar habits, views, standards and feelings. These focused on social and ethical problems. While this *intelligentsia* professed to worship science, and especially the natural sciences, it did so largely because it regarded science as a means of resolving existing social problems. It was basically indifferent to art. As for literature, its attitude toward it was dictated by two considerations: On the one hand, like any religious creed, the dogma it professed needed perforce to embrace every aspect of man's life—both material and spiritual; it could not, therefore, ignore literature. On the other hand, because of the existing Czarist censorship, it was not always possible to discuss everything openly; ideological propaganda could therefore often best be smuggled through to the public by means of critical articles or reviews on literary subjects. Many a leader of the *intelligentsia* found himself thus literally *forced* into the position of a literary critic.

All of them—the Chernyshevskys, the Dobroliubovs, the Pissariovs, the Zaitzevs—were now unanimous in propounding the cause of realism, even though they were sometimes inclined to amend or restrict this concept. Chernyshevsky even wrote an entire treatise on the subject of esthetics. Though few people ever read it, its very publication was symptomatic of the spirit of the times. The realism of the *intelligentsia* was supposed to be somewhat different, more militant than its predecessor, to extend into every field, including that of art. Truth, truthfulness was thus to become the guiding principal *of* art, *in* art. Not only truth, but also realism in the sense that things, people, thoughts, feelings, values were to be depicted as they really were, not as it was hoped for, or thought they could be, or should be—Mikhailovsky—one of the leaders of the Populist movement—even wrote a lengthy commentary upon the peculiar beauty of the Russian word "truth." In other languages, he pointed out, there was a distinct word for truth in the sense of "veracity" and another for truth in the sense of "justice." Only in Russian were the two concepts synonymous. And what the Russian *intelligentsia* demanded of contemporary art was that it serve the dual concept of veracity *cum* justice, little realizing that in so doing, it was setting itself a romantic ideal often more remote from reality, more abstract in fact, than romanticism had ever been at its peak. The concept of "art for art's sake" was passionately condemned. Art was to stand at the service of the people, it was to be the *ancilla populi*, the votary of a new two-headed God: the God of Truth (*about* the people) and the God of Justice (*for* the people). It was then that the Russian countryside, the Russian *muzhik*, his sad fate, his needs, his strivings came really into their own in Russian literature. This was followed by yet another school, that of the so-called "civic" or "thematic" poets. And finally there came the turn of the painters, the so-called "Itinerants," who proceeded to put the *muzhik* on canvas.

For a long time the musicians remained indifferent to what was becoming a veritable epidemic, but one day there appeared in their midst, too, men who had been contaminated by popular realism or one of its affiliated beliefs. Nowadays, they would have been christened "fellow travellers." And yet, although literature and the fine arts had by now been virtually won over to the new ideas, it was necessary to possess quite a considerable dose of daring (and perhaps also blindness) to think that the same could happen to music. This was exactly Mussorgsky's conclusion. In following it up, he was not only sharing Dargomyzhsky's ideas; he was also going along with the times. But he took to this belief with the narrow-minded bigotry and passion of a fanatic and was prepared for any battle, for any sacrifice to promote its triumph. And for all its fallacy, this exiguous and controversial faith was to prove a blessing for him: It enabled him to move mountains.

At this point, it might be worthwhile to ask oneself: How was it possible that this concept of realism should have won over even those who served the most abstract, the most formalistic of all the arts? How *can* music depict and speak for truth? What sort of truth can it depict or speak for? Truth as man sees it? Starting with Beethoven, countless musicians had tried to do so. Berlioz made of this thematic, pictorial music something genuinely original, a new form of art. Liszt went even further, he gave it a deeper, indeed a spiritual context. But can one speak of thematic music as being realistic? After all, its strictly descriptive, pictorial means are limited. What it can do is merely to imply, to suggest the reality of the world as man sees it. It has access to only one of the elements that are found in this world—that of rhythm (if we except that of sound itself). Music can claim mastery in interpreting only one aspect of life, its emotive aspect, the realm of feeling and here it exercises a power unknown to the other arts. But then this power in itself depends on the existence of form. Without form, there can be no music.

There exists only one type of music, in conjunction with which it is possible to speak of realism, and that is vocal music and specifically the opera. In this field, there has long been a great tradition of "truth"—starting with Monteverdi through Gluck to Wagner. True, some would-be reformers of the opera had clamored for a return to the Greek tragedy; others, on the contrary, had championed the slogan of "progress" and of the consolidation of all the arts under a single formula. Yet what all of them desired, in fact, was merely to substitute one set of symbols (without which there can be no opera) for another which, in their opinion, had become obsolete and meaningless. At the same time, they wished to assert this "truth" in yet another fashion—by providing it with an inner meaning, a sense of inner satiation, a sincerity of feeling that was to take the place of mere superficial loveliness. Mussorgsky had borrowed these theories from Dargomyzhsky, Cui and Balakirev, and yet all of them—*horrible dictu!*—had in this attempt fallen involuntarily under Wagner's influence. By way of a personal contribution, however, Dargomyzhsky had discovered yet another meaning to musical "truth," that of seeking to identify and depict the hidden, inner musical modulations of human speech.

VI

Dargomyzhsky's reconciliation with the "Balakirev Gang" was partly due to their mutual acquaintance with the Purgold family.

The Purgolds were Germans from Thuringia, who had done extremely well in the new country of their choice. One of the two brothers had risen to the rank of an Active Secret Councillor. He died as President of the Court of Administrative Appeals leaving a large fortune and an equally large family of ten children, all of whom resided together with their innumerable governesses, nurses and servants, in a luxuriously appointed apartment on Mokhovaya Street, under the supervision of the second brother, a convinced bachelor who was known affectionately to his family and friends as "Uncle O."

Though he too held the rank of a Secret Councillor, he was at heart an artist and a Bohemian. As a young man, he had been a friend of Glinka's; he was also a life-long friend of Dargomyzhsky's, who lived in the same house as the Purgolds. There was thus a constant coming and going between the two households. "Uncle O" was a great amateur of music and of the theatre. He even wrote plays himself— light-comedy sketches on the subject of everyday life in the Purgold family, entitled, for instance, "Auntie's Arrival" or "The Goose Stuffing Has Given Out," which were performed at their home, each member of the family acting his own part. These skits were usually accompanied by musical numbers, most of which were written by Dargomyzhsky. Even in the country, the Purgolds continued to share a house with the old composer, which was a cross between Turgenev's *Nest of Gentlefolk* and German *Gemütlichkeit*.

The Purgold children—the boys as well as the girls—were all very talented. But as soon as one of them departed from the family circle and started to live his, or her own life, this talent seemed to vanish. Only the two youngest girls were endowed with durable gifts: *"Nadia"* played the piano and tried to compose, and *"Sasha"* sang.

They were very different. With pretty, somewhat doll-like features, Sasha was all movement, impulsiveness, restlessness, grace. Seemingly cheerful, merry, bubbling over with contagious laughter, sentimental and often in love, she was inclined to sadness and melancholy when alone. Nadia, or rather Nadiezhda Nikolayevna (as she was more often called even by those who knew her well) was more reserved and aloof than her sister. "What a wonderful Greek profile!" old Dargomyzhsky would exclaim. Actually, there was about her a little of that puritan severity which, though charming in a young person, may turn into bitterness with the years.

Though many Russo-German families in St. Petersburg made a point of dabbling in music as a matter of fashion, the Purgolds' friendship with Dargomyzhsky raised their interest in this art to a somewhat higher, non-amateurish level. It could hardly have been otherwise. At the age of six, whenever there happened to be no music in the Purgold apartment, Nadia would lie down flat on the floor and listen to the singing of Dargomyzhsky's pupils or to his own oddly attractive croaking in the apartment below. As "Uncle O" was generous with money, both she and her sister were given a thorough musical education, with first-rate teachers. At one time, Nadia took piano lessons with Mussorgsky's teacher, the famous Herke. But their real and principal mentor was Dargomyzhsky (even though, at first, he, as a Populist, shared the view commonly accepted by the greater part of Russian "society" at the time, that music should play in a young gentlewoman's life only a decorative part).

The Purgolds made the acquaintance of the "Balakirev Gang," however, not through Dargomyzhsky, but through a friend of the elder son, the young chemist-composer Apollon Gussagovsky. Presently, all of them, Balakirev and Cui, and later Mussorgsky and Rimsky-Korsakov became *habitués* of the Purgolds' hospitable home.

Mussorgsky had immediately made a strong impression on the two sisters. They met at a rehearsal of Dargomyzhsky's *Stone Guest* in the old man's apartment. They had been warned by their host that this time, they would be singing together with "the composer Mussorgsky" and they were a little nervous, for Modest's fame, both as a musician and as a jester, was already fairly well established. They never forgot his appearance that first night. Well-built, with expressive hands, his hair carefully brushed back from his forehead, he had an oddly expressionless face and his rather prominent eyes seemed also somehow leaden, vacant. His speech had a peculiar characteristic: Instead of raising his voice while talking, as most people do, he would on the contrary lower it to a half-whisper, as if he were talking to himself. There was something mysterious about him. But his singing enthralled them, and the very simplicity and feeling with which he sang belied his rather affected mannerisms.

They soon became close friends, seeing each other constantly, at the Cui's, at Mrs. Shestakova's, at the Stassov's country house in Pargolovo. Eventually, the Purgold girls became an integral part of the group, which they laughingly referred to as "the robbers' gang." Now they felt that their life had acquired that special meaning, that special exalted flavor which is to be found in the lives of all those who do not merely exist, but who uphold an idea, a creed. Nadia and Korsinka, in particular, shared the same high ideals of truth and honesty, even though in the beginning, their comradeship hardly foretold what was to become a life-long companionship. Sasha, for her part, had been immediately drawn to Mussorgsky and was in despair because he did not seem to reciprocate her feelings.

The Purgolds' "Tuesdays" usually started with the performance of the latest "hit"—one of Dargomyzhsky's more recent compositions, or a piece of declamation, or something quite special, such as a "quadruple concerto" (four hands on two pianos). With the arrival of the "Balakirev Gang" their compositions began to be performed, too. The girls had fallen immediately in love with their music and ideas and spared no effort to publicize them, by playing, singing or re-arranging their compositions, or by accompanying the authors when they themselves chose to sing them, or simply by arguing and seeking to convince the "un-initiated," especially the bemedalled and stuffy-looking high officials from

among "Uncle O's" friends. Sometimes these were won over
by their enthusiasm, although they kept grumbling that they
just couldn't understand this "so-called music." The Purgolds
thus provided the musicians with the opportunity to become
well known at last, beyond their own narrow circle. Their
feelings toward Dargomyzhsky changed accordingly. As they
got to know him better in the cozy and relaxed atmosphere
of these reunions, their initial hostility and antipathy toward
him changed to respect and, eventually, even to affection.

In the spring of 1870 the two sisters went abroad. They
took with them Mussorgsky's *Seminarist* (which the Russian
censorship had refused to clear for printing) to have it published in Leipzig. This provided the pretext for the beginning
of a correspondence that was to continue throughout their
absence. At first, Modest made a point of writing to them
jointly, so as not to single out Sasha (whose feelings he suspected). Prussia was just then on the eve of her war with
France and Modest in his letters openly made fun of the
Germans—which was not very tactful considering that the
Purgolds were themselves of German origin (even though,
like many Russianized Germans, they felt perhaps more Russian than their Russian fellow-citizens). "You must be surrounded," he wrote, "with the tragic picture of military
preparations . . . The *Vaterland* is threatened, therefore the
Vaterland's sons must enflame themselves with homicidal zeal
—enflame themselves to the point of self-immolation." Sasha
had asked him to advise her which German songs she should
study. He now replied: "I have great doubts about German
music in general . . . German men and women sing like
roosters in the belief that the wider they open their mouths
and the longer they hold their notes—*portamento*—the more
feeling they display . . . You know for yourself: the greatest
German geniuses, Beethoven, Weber, Schumann (each in his
own way) were poor vocal composers . . . This is a people of
theoreticians in music who with nearly every step slip into
abstraction. You, who were educated on the Russian soil of

realism, will not (I hope) fall for the German roosters' *Sehnsüchte*."

When the two sisters returned to Russia, smuggling in the forbidden copies of the *Seminarist*, they found themselves right away in an atmosphere of conflicting emotions. Nadia was keeping a diary at the time, to which she confided all her secrets. In it she referred to her friends not by their real names, but by nicknames of her own invention which were meant to stand for that which she regarded as their main characteristic. Thus Rimsky-Korsakov figured as "Sincerity," Mussorgsky as "Wit," Balakirev as "Strength," Cui as "Spite," etc. This diary reflects the emotional stress from which the two sisters were suffering at the time—Nadia, as her feeling of admiration for Rimsky-Korsakov slowly changed to love, and Sasha because of her unrequited love for Mussorgsky. Though the latter was careful never to give her any reason for hope, she was terribly jealous of everyone, even her own sister. She never suspected that her real rival was no other than "that old woman," Nadiezhda Petrovna Opochinina.

VII

Mussorgsky had left his "home shores" far behind and was now sailing bravely toward those "uncharted shores" about which he spoke so often. Already new horizons were opening up before him—the little *muzhik*, the children's world, Russia itself. He felt even slightly dizzy when he paused to consider the vastness of the tasks ahead. And yet he was still quite unknown except to a "limited circle of unlimited people" (as he himself liked to put it). The public at large ignored even his name. This was actually not surprising considering that it was only recently that after many years of silence another of his works, his mixed choral-orchestral piece entitled *The Route of Senacherib*, had been performed in public for the first time.

For some reason Mussorgsky was much attracted to hebrew themes, to the Bible, and this hebraic strain, grandiose and somehow especially human, was to reappear in many of his works, starting with his *King Saul* and his marvellous *Hebraic Song* and ending with *The Route of Senacherib*. For the latter, he chose another of Byron's *Hebrew Melodies* in his own translation. When it was finished, even Balakirev approved it and Modest promptly dedicated it to him. Mili agreed to include it in the program of a concert of his Free School, but it did not have much success. Actually Modest himself did not expect much of this concert. More important to him now was the fact that his compositions were at last beginning to appear in print. Until the age of 28 only one of his works had actually been printed: his childhood *Polka*. Now, the publisher Iohansen bought from him two of his songs, *Lovely Savishna* and *Gopak*.

As if to compensate for his artistic success, something unpleasant happened to him in civil life. He had never been much of a Government official, and finally the Department of Engineering decided that they could dispense with his services. He found himself once again—though this time involuntarily—a free man. Hitherto he had lived with his brother Filaret, where he suffered no privations. Now, however, he felt that he could not any more abuse his brother's hospitality, since he himself could not contribute anything. He went to the country, to their farm at *Minkino*.

This stay in the country was fruitful. It is there that he completed his *St. John's Night on the Bald Mountain*, a piece that had long been on his mind. It took him only twelve days to complete. He wrote it straight off the cuff without previous draft and immediately imparted the good news to his friends and in the first place to Rimsky-Korsakov, with whom he found it especially easy and pleasant to talk about music. For with Korsinka he did not feel shy as he did sometimes, even now, with Mili or Cesar. He had strummed a few excerpts of this *St. John's Night* to Korsinka before leaving St. Petersburg. Now he informed him that these parts

were especially good: "In the 'Unholy glorification,' for example," he wrote, "there is a little bit for which Cesar will
sentence me to the Conservatory. It is in B minor—the
witches are glorifying Satan—and is, as you can see, harsh,
barbarous and dirty. In the 'sabbath' there is a rather original
alternating call on a trill of the strings and of a piccolo in
B flat. The whole plan and form of the composition is rather
unusual. In 'Satan's cortège' I cleverly avoided the march
clichés à la Liszt's *Hungaria*." And he concluded with some
self-satisfaction: "The general character of the piece is hot,
it doesn't drag, the transitions are tight and without any
German-like approach, which is most refreshing..." He
hoped to look through the whole score together with Korsinka, who already then had a reputation for his knowledge
of orchestration; at the same time he made it clear that he
did not propose to change anything, whatever the shortcomings. Then, at the very end of the letter, as if remembering
suddenly that his correspondent was himself a composer and
that, be it merely out of courtesy, he should not talk only
about himself, he added: "Please, dear Korsinka, do *Sadko*
... I wouldn't nag you to write something on that subject,
weren't I convinced that you will produce something good."
And to Professor Nikolsky he described the acute tension
under which he himself had worked; he hadn't slept nights,
he said, "something so surged up within me, that I simply
didn't know what was happening to me, or rather I did know,
but one shouldn't, for otherwise one might become conceited."

He awaited anxiously Mili's reaction. He considered this
piece his major work and was very disappointed when Mili
reacted most coolly. He began to understand Korsinka, who
claimed that, though it was most pleasant to spend an evening in Mili's company, it was even more pleasant to spend
it without him.

Having completed *St. John's Night,* Mussorgsky went on
to other things. He started transcribing Beethoven's quartets

for the piano, to be performed at the Opochinins' that winter. Then he suddenly remembered his early *Intermezzo in Modo Classico,* about the *muzhiks'* encounter with a group of peasant women in the snow, and having set it to orchestra, dedicated it to Borodin (who was, for some reason, looked upon as the greatest "classicist" of them all). At the same time, he continued to compose *romances,* all of them excellent pieces.

Returning to St. Petersburg that autumn, he felt like a wild horse just escaped from a corral. Everything fascinated him; everything thrilled him. His friends had welcomed him warmly; now he was invited everywhere, everywhere he played the piano and sang—at the Stassovs', at Liudmila Ivanovna Shestakova's, at the Opochinins', and everywhere he was warmly applauded. Indeed, it was hard not to applaud him, for all his more recent compositions, and especially his songs, *The Urchin, On the Don a Garden Blooms, Gathering Mushrooms, The Magpie, The Seminarist, The Classicist, The He-Goat,* all revealed an acute feeling for truthfulness and a keen eye which seemed to confirm Rimsky-Korsakov's words, when he thanked Mussorgsky for "having ceased to mope." For all his poverty and occasional poor health, their author was clearly in good form and happy—because he was surrounded by friends, because his music was beginning to be understood and appreciated, because he was not alone in following this new path in music, because there was also Stassov, huge, kind, watching his every step with adoring eyes and finally because, for the first time in his life, he was in love and, what is more, his love was reciprocated.

VIII

Dargomyzhsky wrote his *Stone Guest* with amazing speed, as though he felt that he had no time to spare. Nadia Purgold joked that he kept producing every scene like a conjurer pulling rabbits out of a hat. His recitatives were unusually stark, without the usual operatic "plumage," but the music, try as he did to adapt it to the text, was of much poorer quality than Pushkin's verse, notwithstanding some daring innovations. Perhaps he was just a little too old for his subject. Though he had as yet heard no part of it, Balakirev was frankly skeptical and called it "A castrated 'Don Juan.' " "I don't doubt," he wrote, "that there may be a few unusual passages in it, but I am equally convinced that the actual substance—that which should be in it—will be lacking."

Nevertheless, excerpts from *The Stone Guest* were now played at the Purgolds more and more often and were generally well received. Sasha Purgold sang the parts both of *Anna* and *Laura,* Mussorgsky those of *Leporello* and *Don Carlos,* Dargomyzhsky himself anything and everything. Even Stassov, overcoming his long-standing antipathy for the old man, had changed his attitude.

One day, Balakirev remarked to Mussorgsky: "Why don't you write an opera to a Gogol subject, to his *Marriage,* for instance?" Actually, Balakirev said this more as a joke. "Yes, yes! Please do!" begged Cui. Modest was somewhat taken aback. To say the truth, he himself had long wanted to compose an opera on a Gogol theme, but was hesitating between various possible subjects. Moreover he wasn't sure: should he entrust the writing of the libretto to someone else, or should he himself undertake to write it, as he had done with the words of his songs? "Ours is indeed a blessed little circle," he would say, "a text is lacking? So what? Off we go and write it ourselves, and not badly too!" Now he had a sudden inspiration: Why not do as Dargomyzhsky was doing with his *Stone Guest*—compose the music to Gogol's own words? The challenge was great, for Gogol's *Marriage* is a farce and is, furthermore, written in prose.

On June 11 he settled down to the task. By the end of the month he had already completed the first scene, after which he departed for the country to stay with his brother, at the latter's estate of *Shilovo,* in the Government of Tula. Here,

rather than open up the main house, he settled down in the
izba of one of his brother's tenants, from where he presently
wrote Cui: "My dear Cesar: greetings! Here I am living off
green fodder *en forme et matière*. I live in a hut, drink milk
and remain all day in the open air, being driven back to my
room only at nightfall. Almost on the eve of my regretful
departure—regretful, because I did not see you—I finished
the first scene of *Marriage*: The first act consists of three
scenes . . . Guided by your and Dargo's remarks, I have been
able to extract all that is needed from them . . . This will be
a first experiment with an *opera dialogué* . . . Now, contrary
to my custom, I'm composing without a piano, for there is
no such instrument here . . . As I don't know whether Korsinka is still in town, or whether he has sailed away to the
chilly shores of Finland taking *Antar* with him (Rimsky-Korsakov was just then working on a symphony inspired by one
of Senkovsky's fairy tales) I beg you, my dear, to read out
aloud this scrawl to him, if he is interested . . . I am trying
to underscore as much as possible those changes of intonation
in the dialogue that originate in the most trivial reasons, for
this, I believe, is the secret of Gogol's humor." A few days
later, having for some reason or other forgotten to mail this
letter, he added that he had completed the first act which
consisted now not of three, but of four scenes. "It rained for
three days in a row," he wrote, "and I worked without a
break so that you might say that we, I and the weather, were
at one."

In another letter, to Liudmila Ivanovna Shestakova, he
went on to elaborate upon his favorite theory, namely that
art did not consist of depicting something "beautiful," but
that it had to picture something *real* and serve as a means of
communication between people: "I keep observing typical
peasant women and *muzhiks*—this insight may come in
handy some day. How much freshness, uncorrupted, there
is in the Russian landscape, oh, how much! And how much
beauty and splendor. I have depicted a minute part of that

which life has given me in musical images for the benefit of
those who are dear to me, and I have shared some of my
ideas with those who are dear to me.—If God grants me life
and strength, I will do so on a larger scale." It can be concluded from this letter that he regarded *Marriage* merely as
an experiment, which he needed to undertake in order to
achieve something else, an act of self-discipline which was
to precede emancipation. And he was worried lest he fail in
this experiment. "All this is desirable; it doesn't exist yet
but should come into existence. It's frightening! Frightening because that which has to be may never be, for it isn't
yet there." Aside from these fears which could be compared
to the anguish of an expectant mother over the fate of her
yet unborn child, he was also the victim of fatigue from over-
work—the usual state of mind of the artist after a fruitful
spell of work. He complained about this in a letter to Rimsky-Korsakov in which he also said that upon his return to
St. Petersburg, in August, he would await his friends' verdict
like a prisoner in the dock. "I say only this," he added, "if
you can completely renounce the operatic traditions and if
you can picture to yourself a musical conversation on stage,
a quite ordinary, ingenuous conversation, then *Marriage* may
be considered an opera."

IX

His friends' "verdict" was handed down not in August, but
in the fall and was generally kind. As his brother's family
had now left St. Petersburg for good, the Opochinins suggested that he come and stay with them, at their apartment
in the Mikhailovsky Palace. *Marriage* was first performed with
much success at Dargomyzhsky's, and later again at the Purgolds', although he had already sung excerpts at the Opochinins', at Liudmila Ivanovna's and in many other friends'
houses. Stassov was, as usual, vociferously enthusiastic. But
even his other friends were very much struck by the novelty,

daring and freshness of his recitatives. Even Mili roared with laughter, wiping his eyes with a bright-colored handkerchief. As for old *Dargun,* he laughed so much as he sang that he kept losing his place. Slapping Modest on the shoulder, he said to him: "Good for you, my boy! You've gone even further than I!" (behind Mussorgsky's back, however, he hinted that the latter had gone too far). Liudmila Ivanovna Shestakova even ventured to use the word "genius," in speaking about Mussorgsky's work. The latter blushed deeply. "I don't understand the meaning of that word," he protested. "Liudmila Ivanovna, my little dove, don't! Please don't! You've given me a cold sweat! I am not a nasty man, why do you punish me? Why these adjectives, which seek to raise my modest personality to the height of some Mt. Olympus? I don't want to climb mountains—I'm lazy, I dread fatigue. ... Let others judge me as they think fit!"

Not only Liudmila Ivanovna, but also Stassov was now beginning to use big words when speaking of Mussorgsky's talent, so that even she, toning down her own enthusiasm, once remarked to him: "Why do you court and flatter Mussorgsky? This is unworthy both of you and of him." But Stassov wasn't courting or flattering. He had simply put his faith in Mussorgsky, completely, without restraint and was now merely trying to show that he had done wisely. Modest had only to strike a first chord on the piano for Stassov to utter in an audible stage whisper a powerful "Ooph!" and when Mussorgsky began to sing, this was echoed by an equally audible "Ah!" until the others complained that they couldn't hear what was being played. It was both comical and touching.

But despite his friends' enthusiasm, both they and (which was even more important) the author himself realized only too well that *Marriage* was merely a first step along the path to something different, something "real," that it was, actually, more of a curiosity-piece than anything else. The hour of creative emancipation had struck; his talent was now fully mature.

And he began to cast about for a theme for another opera, as realistic as *Marriage,* though not necessarily as comic, but which would provide a full scope to his inventiveness . . . He thought about Pushkin, about his beloved Gogol, about Russian history generally, but just couldn't make up his mind. Stassov kept looking around for a libretto too. To his life-long regret, however, the subject for Mussorgsky's greatest masterpiece was provided not by him, but by old Professor Nikolsky. Like Modest, the professor fancied the somewhat obsolete manner of speech of the Russian medieval chronicles, which he would interlace with the jargon of contemporary St. Petersburg officialdom. They would spend hours together, hunched over a bottle of wine in one of the pubs, talking. In time, Nikolsky became his younger friend's principal authority on the subject of "earth-bound Russianism" (as Mussorgsky called it) generally and Russian antiquity in particular. And it was Nikolsky who first drew his attention to *Boris Godunov* and who drafted the first outline of this opera. At his suggestion, Liudmila Ivanovna presented Mussorgsky with her own copy of Pushkin's drama, to which she appended some blank pages for the libretto. Modest was immediately won over to it: The subject for his new opera had been found.

CHAPTER TEN

STASSOV AND THE "MIGHTY HANDFUL"

I

These were the best times of Stassov's life, his second (though by no means last) youth. Far behind him now were his years of friendship with Balakirev, those years of solitude *à deux,* of expectancy. He was now surrounded by young men of talent, of genius even, who had joined his circle in growing numbers.

The musicians had come first: they had been followed by the sculptors, the architects—all of them equally wedded to his ideas. Gathering at Mili's apartment; or at *"Liudma"* Shestakova's; or at the Cui's, or in his own house, they would talk about music, about poetry, about art, or perform their latest compositions. Sometimes the guests would stay on long after midnight and as Stassov, oil-lamp in hand, led them down the broad staircase, they would continue to argue until by the time they reached the entrance hall, the wick would have burnt out and he would have to grope his way back upstairs in the dark. Sometimes they would spend the whole night escorting one another home, occasionally dragging their host along with them, only to return in a bunch to his house at dawn, for breakfast.

Meanwhile, the war with the press continued—to Stassov's delight (for he was a master of invective and polemics)—which he engaged in without restraint. Gradually he found his own eyes opening to the "sacred revelation" of his young friends' work (though they themselves were apt to refer to it somewhat irreverently in culinary terms: "I cooked up . . ." or "I mixed . . ." or "I baked . . ."). His own talents were perforce confined to the one gift of enthusiasm; to their miraculous concoctions he could add nothing but a pinch of spice here, an aromatic herb there.

The trouble was that there was so much to do and the days were so short. He had to argue with his friends, persuade them, lose his temper, praise them and at the same time keep up with his duties at the Public Library, his "baby," which he visited daily, even on Sundays. Then he had to pursue his own research work, or delve into some problem of art history, or write a monograph on the subject of Russian ornamental design, or check the galley-proofs of his latest article or review. Then he might want to attend the opening of some new art exhibition; or visit the painters Ilia Repin, Kramskoy or Vereschaghin in their studios or get a residence permit for a young Jewish boy, a protégé of the sculptor Antokolsky; or call on the beautiful Baroness Anna Ghinsburg to request a subsidy for a promising young pianist; or drop in for a short while at *Liudma* Shestakova's to hear Mussorgsky's latest song; or attend opening night at the Aleksandrinsky Theatre and then go on to Ciniselli's circus (he had always loved the circus for its bright and garish colors). Virtually the only time when he could concentrate on thinking up the subject of a new opera for his friends, or the theme of a new symphony, or the words for a new song, was late at night or early in the morning. And yet even when he lay down to rest after such a full day, he found it difficult to relax, his heart continued to pound and he would hearken to its beat with a feeling of sudden, superstitious fear. He just couldn't bear to depart from this life, which was still so imperfect, where there was still so much unhappiness, so much untruth, but which he loved nonetheless, with a burning, pagan passion. And then there were still countless other minor worries: a bouquet of flowers to be sent to a performing artist, a program to be drawn up, a review to be written for the papers. He so overwhelmed his friends with his solicitude that eventually they became used to it, they took it for granted. "Who sent the flowers? Why, Stassov, *of course!*"

They were apt to overlook what it cost him in terms of thoughtfulness, concern, money even. Reassuring them, comforting them, exclaiming in sympathy, commiserating with them, edging them on, "jacking them up"—he was always there. And when days of sadness came, days of sickness and of death, he was still there, ever attentive, never forgetful. And when death was followed by oblivion—even among the closest friends and relatives of the departed—he alone would remember and remind, organize the funeral, erect the memorial, write the obituary, organize commemorative concerts and publish posthumously the deceased friend's works.

Who was he? What was he? The gadfly on the chariot-wheel exclaiming: "See what a dust I raise?" The drone living off the labor of the work bees? Perhaps, but then his one concern was that the chariot should not bog down in its tracks. His enemies claimed sometimes that for all his talk he was not even the leader of his own orchestra, that he merely swung the baton while his musicians played according to their fancy! But that too, was unfair. True, his gift of sociability was perhaps greater than the quality of his mind, but what of it? It was he who held together all these capricious, touchy, often uncongenial individualists. His greying bushy beard trembling like the panache of an old-time captain summoning his troops into battle, his voice would sound out, bracing, encouraging, like a trumpet signalling the assembly. Without him, all would have collapsed, their ways would have parted and they would have scattered prematurely, as they did scatter later, when the time came for them to do so.

Neither was he alone in creating the theories which the Balakirev group now propounded. Indeed these theories: nationalism in art, the respect of the folk song, realism— were not absolute truths for all times. But in *his* time, as far as *his* friends and contemporaries were concerned, they embodied the truth, the message, the creed which enabled them to live and create. Those who followed a different course—

however talented—those who professed to believe in a "universal art," in an art "for all mankind" (like Tchaikovsky, Rubinstein and Serov) suffered from an arrested development and withered. In fact if one judges a tree by its fruit, then one can truly say that the fruit that grew on the tree of Russian national art flashed and sparkled like the golden apples in the gardens of the Fire-Bird, about which Mili Balakirev was now about to compose an opera.

II

"Mili the Czech," as Mussorgsky called Balakirev since the latter's visit to Prague, led a strange existence that winter of 1867-1868. Putting on his formal frock-coat and picking up his cane and scarlet gloves, he would disappear all of a sudden on some mysterious errand. At the same time, exotic-looking people began to frequent his lodgings with whom he would converse in poor German or else simply by signs.

These were the "Little Slavic Brothers" or *Bratushki* (as they were popularly known) who had assembled in St. Petersburg following the establishment of the "Slavic Committee." For the Balkans and the Slav territories of the Austro-Hungarian Empire were beginning to stir and their representatives looked hopefully toward Russia where the pan-Slav movement had encountered sympathetic support in the highest bureaucratic circles. On arriving in the capital, the "Little Slavic Brothers" had very naturally hastened to seek out one who had gained fame throughout the Slavic world with his production of *Ruslan and Liudmila* in Prague.

Besides Russian folk songs, Balakirev was now attentively studying also the indigenous music of the other Slavic peoples, as well as of the Hungarians (which he regarded as kindred in origin and spirit to the Slavic songs). He would sometimes ask his bearded, fanatical-looking visitors to sing to him, which they would do very earnestly, though at times out of tune. As a result of this fascination with Slavonic folk-lore, Balakirev composed an *Overture on Czech Themes* and brought several interesting Serbian melodies to Rimsky-Korsakov's attention, which the latter very quickly and quite cleverly adapted for his *Serbian Fantasy*.

On May 12, 1868, a festival concert was planned in St. Petersburg's Town Hall under Balakirev's direction. The program was to include samples of the music of the various Slavic peoples, such as Glinka's *Kamarinskaya*, Dargomyzhsky's *Little-Russian Cossack Dance*, Rimsky-Korsakov's *Serbian Fantasy*, Balakirev's *Overture on Czech Themes* and many others.

The rehearsals did not proceed without hitches though these were not of a political nature. The copyist, in his haste, had made a number of errors in the *Overture on Czech Themes*. Because of that, the first violinist lost his place. Balakirev flew into a temper and began to berate him: "You don't understand the conductor's gestures! Your place is not in an orchestra but in a . . . . ." The violinist took offense and walked out, and the orchestra refused to rehearse. However, the matter was settled, a new first violinist was found and the concert took place after all.

It was a great success. The audience included many professors, high officials and Guards officers. The dark eyes of the visiting Slavs glowed. The stodgy Czechs, forgetting their customary restraint, shouted: *Slava! Slava!* which the Serbs echoed with cries of *Zhivio!* The Bulgarians clapped so loudly that their applause resembled the explosion of hand-grenades. Balakirev was presented with a number of bouquets. Next day, in reviewing the concert in the *Gazette de St. Petersburg*, Stassov made this rather unfortunate remark:

"Pray God that our Slavic guests remember forever how much poetry, feeling, talent and ability there is in this small, but already mighty handful (in Russian *"Moguchaya Kuchka,"* literally: "Little Heap") of Russian musicians." The "Russian musicians" themselves were not too pleased with this expression, particularly the modest, publicity-hating Rimsky-

Korsakov, who thought it tactless. But it was colorful and it
stuck. The journalists seized upon it in their turn and lam-
pooned it mercilessly; the public started whispering unfriendly comments. . . The Balakirev group had received
their nickname. They were to remain the "Mighty Handful"
or even simply "the Handful" forever after.

III

Then Balakirev had a brain storm: Why not invite the celebrated Berlioz, who was regarded commonly as the greatest
conductor of his day, to direct a series of concerts of the Imperial Musical Society in St. Petersburg? The Grand Duchess
not only agreed gladly but even honored the old gentleman
by inviting him to stay at her Mikhailovsky Palace. For his
six concerts Berlioz was to receive 15.000 rubles, a large sum
of money in those days.

Berlioz had been in Russia once before, in 1846. He had
made that first trip by sleigh and had complained bitterly
of the ruts and bumps in the hard-frozen snow. His concerts
had been a roaring success though, and had temporarily
saved the composer, forever out of funds, from a very involved
financial predicament. He had retained glad memories of that
cold country where he had been welcomed with such warm
enthusiasm. He had felt at the time that only in Russia did
things of the spirit play such an important part in people's
lives, only there did they literally live for art, breathe art.
And then, when talking to him, the Russians displayed such
wonderful sensitivity, such admirable idealism. It seemed to
Berlioz that, contrary to what he had experienced in the
Western world: money madness, intrigue, prejudice, ignorance—in other words, all that which stifled him at home—
simply did not exist in Russia. In this he shared the illusions
of many foreigners, but it was true only in part. The Slavic
soul is prone to fall an easy victim to the hypnotic effect of
art and it had also succumbed to the magic spell of Berlioz's

baton. But Berlioz did not realize that many of the people he found so charming and congenial were quite different in everyday life and that outside the concert hall or his Palace home, there stretched a vast, slumbering, prejudice-ridden land.

According to Balakirev's plan, Berlioz's concerts were to alternate with the I.M.S.'s regular concerts under his own baton. Mili also took it upon himself to do all the rough preparatory work and to act as interpreter between the guest conductor and the Russian musicians. The programs included both classical works (mostly Beethoven symphonies, with the exception of the last part of the ninth, which Berlioz refused to perform, notwithstanding his professed admiration for Russian choir-singing) and the maestro's own compositions.

The first concert was held on November 16, 1868. Its success surpassed all expectations, overshadowing even Liszt's past triumphs. The press comments were enthusiastic. The I.M.S. gave a banquet in Berlioz's honor and he reciprocated with a reception for his friends and admirers at the Palace.

And yet despite this triumph the old man was sick, gloomy and crestfallen. Balakirev visited him frequently, sometimes in the company of Stassov. Often they would find him stretched out on a couch, groaning gently, incapable of the slightest movement. Stassov would soon cheer him up, however, re-awaken his interest in, and zest for life and urge him to get up and they would drive off to a restaurant, or to the opera, or to his brother Dimitri's.

Before departing for Paris, Berlioz made Balakirev a present of his ivory baton, which the latter was to cherish all his life as the supreme investiture of a genius.

IV

It was not by mere accident that Stassov had coined the words "Mighty Handful." There was indeed something powerful, "mighty" about the group's rapid growth and development.

And yet despite the fact that Mili had reached the peak of his power and was now the virtual dictator of the St. Petersburg musical world, Stassov knew deep down in his heart that his downfall was near.

For although a veritable "eagle" in all things musical, Balakirev's behavior in everyday life was becoming more and more disconcerting. His reactionary ideas and his misanthropy were now aggravated by the proverbial Russian laziness. He had always loved a game of cards, but in the past this had not stood in the way of his work. Now, however, he found it increasingly difficult to finish his compositions. Even Rimsky-Korsakov complained that Mili took no account, either of his own time, or of that of others, which was especially true in Rimsky-Korsakov's own case, for Mili looked upon him somewhat as his personal property. Rimsky-Korsakov resented it all the more since he himself was always fearful of wasting a minute.

Following his masterpiece *Sadko,* the latter had written yet another symphonic poem, *Antar,* on the subject of an oriental fairy tale by the Pole Senkovsky, which was also quite outstanding. In conversation he kept reverting to his favorite subject—the theory of music. For though still a beginner, he was by now the only real musical theoretician of the group. True, as far as creative originality was concerned Mussorgsky could eclipse them all any time. Even Balakirev agreed with this, despite his objections to Modest's realism. What Rimsky-Korsakov lacked was passion, feeling. Stassov would say so to his face. "But don't worry!" he added reassuringly, "The time will come when something or someone will pick you up and make you go and when that happens, you will sing like a bird! What a blaze that will be! God knows, you have all the gunpowder you need right there, within you!"

For Borodin Stassov had the warmest of feelings, even though much about "that chemical gentleman" (as he called

him) irritated him. For one thing, Aleksander Porfirievich
was terribly conservative. It seemed, at times, as if he would
best have liked the whole world to stand stock-still, con-
gealed, so that he himself might continue his laboratory
experiments in peace or be allowed to stay at home with a
"teeny-weeny cup of tea," as he called it. It was even more
difficult to get him to sit down and compose than Mili. And
yet his *First Symphony* was progressing, if slowly. Stassov had
a fatherly feeling for it. There was something very powerful
about it, something primeval, like the full-chested breathing
of a *Bogatyr*—those knight-errants of the ancient Russian
epic sagas. And also something genuinely oriental, more
genuine even than in Glinka! About that time, the Board
of Directors of the I.M.S. decided to revert to a method which
they had—in a somewhat different form—once before un-
successfully tried out on Mussorgsky. They had long faced a
dilemma. While on the one hand they wished to encourage
young talent, they believed that they had no right to foist
upon the public works of an inferior or amateurish quality.
They therefore suggested the following plan: Young composers should submit their latest works to them; these would
then be performed at a general rehearsal in the Concert Room
of the Mikhailovsky Palace after which, depending upon their
reception by this select audience, they would either be performed in public, or returned to their authors. In other
words, it was no longer the composer himself who had the
final say as to the merits of his product—as had been the case
with Mussorgsky—but the Board of the I.M.S.

Balakirev was so eager to perform Borodin's symphony,
that he presented it to the I.M.S. on these terms. This almost
turned out to be a fatal mistake. For the Board had every
reason to look upon Borodin as just another beginning
dilettante, who should be judged with the greatest circum-
spection. To make matters worse, time was so short that the
instrumental scores were copied out hastily and with errors,
so that the piece, difficult enough as it is, sounded quite

awful. Nevertheless Balakirev, who had reserved himself the
final say in the selection of the program for the public concert, insisted that his friend's symphony be performed there
too.

The public concert was scheduled for January 4, 1869. The
unfortunate try-out at the Palace had been followed by rehearsals, during which the symphony began to appear in a
somewhat better light. Indeed, Kologrivov—one of the directors of the Society who sympathized most with Balakirev's ideas—reported to Balakirev joyfully, that the symphony
was meeting actually with approval; even their arch-foe
Zaremba, Director of the St. Petersburg Conservatory, had
been forced to admit that the author was not without talent.
But Balakirev was worried to death. What he feared most was
not so much the public's reaction, as that of the professional
musicians and critics, who were often even more prejudiced
and narrow-minded than the public.

The first part of the symphony met with a cold reception:
there was a little clapping and then silence. Balakirev moved
on hastily to the *scherzo.* The latter went off to a merry start
and when it ended, the author was called out and the movement was repeated. After the *finale,* the author was again
called out. This meant success!

Old Dargomyzhsky, vice-president of the St. Petersburg
branch of the I.M.S., had also been worrying over the fate
of Borodin's *First Symphony.* He was suffering from an acute
attack of aneurism and was thus unable to attend the concert.
He begged his young friends, therefore, to drop in to see him
afterwards to tell him all about it. Only General Veliaminov
came, but not being a musician he was unable to describe
everything in detail. The old man stayed up, hoping that the
others might drop in after all. And they nearly did; in fact,
they actually drove up in a noisy gang to his front door, but
at the last minute they hesitated to disturb him. Dargomyzhsky died in his sleep a few hours later, at 5 a.m. In his
testament, he begged Cui to complete *The Stone Guest* and

Rimsky-Korsakov to orchestrate it. He thereby publicly acknowledged his affinity with the Balakirev Group!

His young friends were not overly chagrined at his passing. Such is the egoism of youth that Mussorgsky alone seems to have genuinely mourned this cantankerous old man. Dargomyzhsky had once shown him something he had written in the album of a friend: "To become a real artist, one must love virtue, art and women; patiently bear with the indifference and partiality of the critics; despise luxury, the social amenities, the insults of the press, envy . . . I do not know, dear Baron, whether you are able to do all this—I am not!" and Dargomyzhsky had chortled merrily at this witty epigram which could easily have been used by way of an epitaph for him. Actually, Mussorgsky wondered whether it was not a good thing that *The Stone Guest* would be performed only after its author had already "rejoined his ancestors," as he put it. For all that he was a revolutionary innovator, Dargomyzhsky remained nonetheless "a man of the 'forties"; he might well not have stood up to the indignation his opera was bound to provoke. Quick to "sour" at every expression of disapproval, he might even have been discouraged from composing for ever . . .

V

Borodin was so overjoyed at the success of his *First Symphony* that he promptly started work on a second. For his part, Stassov, as a connoisseur of ancient Russian epic literature, welcomed the epic form Borodin's talent was taking. All the latter now wrote seemed to assume a broad, powerful, plastic form. His melodic gifts were extraordinary; to all those who heard his songs it was clear that his creative talent extended also into the vocal field. Stassov liked especially *The Sea*; he considered it the greatest song that had ever been written and was overjoyed when the author, touched by his enthusiasm, dedicated it to him. But Borodin's other songs:

The Queen of the Sea, The Sleeping Beauty, The Song of the Dark Forest,—about a dozen all told—reminded him of Glinka and of *Ruslan and Liudmila,* and he began to wonder whether his friend's vocation lay not in the operatic field after all; whether Borodin, not Cui, was destined to become Glinka's successor.

Borodin had himself thought of writing an opera. He kept searching for an appropriate subject, but he was scared by the endless labor involved in this form of work and for which he simply lacked time. Balakirev had suggested to him *The Czar's Bride,* a drama in blank verse by the Slavophil poet Lev Mey, devoted to the rising of the Free City of Pskov against Czar Ivan the Terrible, and in the beginning Borodin had found the subject to his taste, but he lost heart after writing only a few scenes; Ivan the Terrible's Russia, steeped in blood, a Russia of oppressors and oppressed, somehow repelled him. He was not a Meyerbeer, he had no taste for a Russian St. Bartholomew's night.

Stassov had something very different in mind, namely *The Saga of Igor's Host* (in Russian: *Slovo o Polku Igoreve*). What better source of sublime inspiration could there be, he felt, than this wonderful epic poem, the most beautiful in Russian literature, about the most beautiful period of Russian history? For this was a period of hope and power when Russia, though faced already with many a hard test, had not yet been sullied by the Mongol yoke; when her princes were still noble and chevaleresque; when the great menace of the Tartar invasions was just beginning to loom over the horizon.

In April 1869, just before Easter, he submitted to his friend the detailed scenario of an opera entitled *Prince Igor.* Borodin was thrilled. It was as if the whole opera, in its broad outlines, lay there at arm's reach. "The subject is very much to my taste," he exclaimed, "but will I have the strength? I don't know . . . But then: 'Nothing ventured, nothing have.' I'll try!"

Actually, what he was thinking about was not so much the

purely technical difficulties inherent in opera-writing as it's incompatibility with his other activities: his laboratory, his courses and lectures, his civic responsibilities—all of which, he knew, he would have to give up in order to do justice to this new assignment. But the technical difficulties were there, too. First of all there was the question of the libretto. Like the other members of the group, it never entered his mind to enlist the services of a professional writer; he intended to write his own lyrics. He had felt right away an unusually strong attraction to the theme. For one thing, as Stassov had rightly noted, there was something of the ancient Russian *Bogatyr* in Borodin. Moreover, Igor's imprisonment by the Polovtzi, a nomadic Asian people, gave him the opportunity to evoke through his music that which, unknown to himself, lay dormant in him—that Oriental streak which had come down to him from his Caucasian father. However, though in itself an admirable epic poem, *The Saga of Igor's Host* lacked material for a full-length libretto. All it actually said was that one Igor Sviatoslavovich, Prince of Putivl', had called together his relatives, the princes of Southern Russia, to fight the Polovtzi; that his campaign had opened under bad auspices; that Igor had been taken captive and that his wife, Princess Yaroslavna had long lamented his absence. This was harldy enough.

But Borodin was not dismayed. He settled down to work diligently. He visited Stassov at the Public Library, borrowed —on the latter's indications—a pile of books, surrounded himself with source material, steeped himself in the study of history, ethnography and folk music. Then he went on to study various turco-mongol folk songs and even discovered some ancient tribal songs among the few descendants of the Polovtzi who had survived in Hungary. By the autumn of 1869 he was able to write to his wife with a note of good-natured triumph that "the chemists were satisfied with the paper I read out to them in the Imperial Chemical Society, while the musicians were blessed with the first excerpt from *Igor, "Yaro-*

slavna's dream," which is really quite lovely." What these "musicians" did not know, however, was that his enthusiasm for *Prince Igor* and for his musical work generally was even now already a thing of the past, that he was again completely captivated by his laboratory work, that he had even built himself "a teeny-weeny lab" in his own apartment and that it was so cozy, with its workbench, its gas-duct, its comfortable furniture, that he would spend far longer hours there than at the piano.

When Stassov realized that *Igor* was not progressing one bit, he was so disappointed that he offered the scenario to Rimsky-Korsakov, but the latter was now already working on another opera, on the very subject which Borodin had rejected, namely Lev Mey's *The Czar's Bride* which he rechristened, *The Fair Maid of Pskov* (in Russian: *Pskovityanka*).

Perhaps from a feeling of disappointment (not in the subject of *Igor,* which he continued to regard as made exactly to his measure, but because of his inability to successfully master the long and arduous task of writing an opera) Borodin now felt prompted to resume work on his *Second Symphony.* Not that he found this proposition easy either; indeed the period of "confinement" was almost as long. Yet five years later, his *Second Symphony* saw the light of day (*Prince Igor* took another 13 years). Meanwhile, all that which he had planned to picture in *Igor* was now evoked in his new symphonic work: the heroism of the ancient Russian princes, the *Bogatyri* patrolling the endless steppes, their struggle against the nomadic tribes, their triumphs, their defeats. When he heard the first excerpts, Stassov was in rapture; he christened the *Second Symphony* "his" symphony, "the Bogatyr Symphony," "the Leonine Symphony" or just plain "the Lioness."

Gradually Borodin's and Rimsky-Korsakov's friendship grew ever closer. Their rapprochement, like Rimsky-Korsakov's growing intimacy with Mussorgsky, increased apace with an ever so slight cooling-off in the relationship between Rimsky-Korsakov and Balakirev which sensitive Stassov did not fail to notice. Borodin's relations with Modest and Korsinka were simple, comrade-like, with a subtle note of respect on the part of the two younger men. They talked to one another like technicians, like fellows of the same guild, understanding each other intuitively and sharing their plans and projects fully. Korsinka was a frequent visitor in the Borodin home where he would stay up talking to his host until all hours, sometimes even remaining overnight. Borodin, in his turn, like Stassov and Mussorgsky, would visit Rimsky-Korsakov in his tiny room where most of the space was taken up by a grand piano.

Presently, rumors about Borodin's new symphony and about *Prince Igor* began to spread in the musical world of St. Petersburg. Wherever he went, Borodin would be invited to perform excerpts from his opera, especially the unusual oriental dances. In general, the Balakirev group was becoming fashionable. Like the ripples produced by a stone dropped into a pond, their fame was beginning to spread even beyond the strictly musical spheres of the capital. Konstantin Makovsky, a popular painter in his time, and his whole family literally raved about this new school of music and spared no effort to lure its representatives to their parties. After refusing several of these invitations, Borodin at last agreed to visit them and Makovsky's wife—an artist in her own right—painted his portrait, while Dargomyzhsky's *Stone Guest* was performed in extenso in the Makovsky home.

Balakirev heard about Borodin's new symphony from Rimsky-Korsakov who played a few excerpts to him. Mili had been carrying a grudge against Borodin (as he was against all his former friends) but now, upon meeting him at Liudmila Ivanovna Shestakova's, his attitude suddenly changed, his face lit up with a smile, he gazed at him with loving eyes, became sentimental and then, as if he knew of no other way of showing his feelings, walked up to him, seized his nose between two fingers and kissed him on the cheek. Borodin later joked that Mili had "forgiven him" his symphony.

VI

And yet the life of the members of the Handful was not all a bed of roses even now. For one thing, the newspaper war around them continued. With the exception of Cui and Stassov, all the music critics had joined forces against them. Both Cui and Stassov were talented writers and effective fighters. But Cui, though the more intelligent and subtle of the two, lacked "heart," he had too much cunning and too little conviction and so, despite his intelligence, he made many slips; Stassov sensed about him even a "whiff of treachery." This ambiguous event came more particularly to the fore on the occasion of Rimsky-Korsakov's first venture into the field of newspaper polemics.

Edward Napravnik, the young Czech conductor of the Mariinsky Theatre, had just staged his opera, *The Niznii-Novgorodians*. Napravnik was a good musician, he was hardworking, conscientious and the orchestra respected him; he had always been most correct with Cui; moreover, he was an influential man. But he hadn't the slightest trace of fire or inspiration, and this defect showed throughout his work. Cui was admittedly in a difficult situation. What was he to do? To praise Napravnik would have been tantamount to betraying his friends' and his own principles. To criticize him might well have led to a quarrel or even a complete break with the highly respected conductor. Cui did neither, or rather he did something else; he suggested that Rimsky-Korsakov try his pen at musical criticism in his stead!

Korsinka was flattered; he had always resented being taken for a mere amateur. Now he was naive enough to accept Cui's offer and in complete honesty undertook to tear Napravnik's opera to pieces, thereby acquiring an enemy for life.

The atmosphere grew tense. Stassov accused his opponents

of being "musical liars." The critic Famintzin sued him in court for libel and won his case, though not on the count of libel, but on that of the use of abusive language in the press. The Handful promptly hailed this as a victory. In his polemic ardor, Serov went so far as to contend that "any second violinist in a provincial orchestra could swing a conductor's baton with greater success" than Balakirev.

Then Mussorgsky leapt into the fray. Wisely refraining from following in Rimsky-Korsakov's steps, he decided to strike out at his foes with the weapon he wielded best—that of composition. He wrote a musical satire entitled *The Penny Paradise* in which, with biting humor, he proceeded to lampoon in turn each of the critics hostile to their "blessed brotherhood."

VII

At least one of their most vitriolic opponents was not to survive the controversy, Aleksander Serov, the "tiny titan," died on February 24, 1871, at the age of fifty-one.

To Stassov, his passing was a severe shock. Though he had long regarded Serov as a harmful influence in Russian music, the latter was nevertheless his "favorite foe" to whom he was tied by indissoluble bonds. Serov's widow, Valentina Semionovna—a strong and impassioned woman—was now pitiful to behold: lost, crushed by sorrow. Stassov hurried over to see her; she seemed touched by his visit and sympathy. She received him in the modest dining room of their small apartment and immediately broached the subject of how best to perpetuate her late husband's memory. Stassov thought that the best way would be to publish his works. He undertook to request an Imperial grant of 3.000 rubles and offered her his services as editor. In this capacity, he said, he would publish everything his opponent had ever written, including even Serov's violent attacks upon his own person. Serov, he said, was a personality great enough to be responsible before posterity for his words and actions.

But even as he gave her these assurances, he couldn't help reflecting upon his late friend's countless errors. *"Ma position,"* Serov used to say, *"c'est l'opposition."* And he spoke the truth. He was opposed to everything, to the good as well as to the bad and—alas!—sometimes even to the great. To only one man was he unwaveringly loyal, namely to Richard Wagner, never realizing that, whatever his merits, Wagner was basically alien to Russia and his impact on Russian music could only be insignificant. Serov had spoken about Borodin's First Symphony as "the homespun product of a beginner." When Balakirev was dismissed from the I.M.S., he had proclaimed that "the downfall of Balakirev and his party is logical and fair." In the end, he had lost not only his judgment but even his sense of morality. But even admitting this serious defect one couldn't deny that he had been one of the foremost Russian musicologists of his day.

Later, in the hushed semi-darkness of the bedroom, as he stood gazing intently at his former friend's lifeless, waxen face, Stassov noted that, as is often the case, death had erased the accretion of years of life and toil. Despite his grey hair, despite the wrinkles in his face, this was again the old Sasha Serov, his childhood friend. But Stassov had also some bitter thoughts. How selflessly had Serov pursued his vocation, only to be cut off in his prime; how abundant had his talent been. And yet his vociferous activities had been largely fruitless; his gifts, however attractive, had served a cause that was basically negative. "One God and one music," proclaimed Anton Rubinstein Serov's credo could be seen as a transcription of this slogan: "One Wagner and one music—*his* music!" But Serov's betrayal of his Russian patrimony was bound to bring redemption: for the "universal" music of the Rubinsteins, the Tchaikovskys and the Serovs was stamped from the very beginning with the curse of impotence and sterility.

CHAPTER ELEVEN

AT THE PINNACLE OF FAME
(Boris Godunov)

> *" 'Ist doch—rufen sie vermessen—*
> *Nichts im Werke, nichts getan!'*
> *Und das Grosse reift indessen*
> *Still hinan."*
> FEUCHTERSLEBEN

I

In every group or party there are certain individuals who remain, as it were, on the periphery, astride the dividing line between that particular group and its neighbor. Although they are regarded inevitably with some degree of suspicion, they are nevertheless tolerated because they serve as a contact with the outside world. Occasionally—and this too is inevitable—they betray their groups and go over to the neighbors, whose convictions they may long have shared in secret. They are then condemned by their former associates, while their erstwhile enemies welcome them joyfully, like prodigal sons returning into the fold.

Rimsky-Korsakov had always been set apart by the enemies of the Mighty Handful; the enemy critics—even Serov, even Laroche—often paid him compliments. It did not come as a real surprise to anyone, therefore, when Azanchevsky, Director of the St. Petersburg Conservatory, invited him in the summer of 1871 to teach practical composition and orchestration at that institution, so suspect, of course, to Stassov and his friends. Wasn't this an admirable answer to those who reproached him, Azanchevsky, for being a reactionary? A tangible proof of the Conservatory's willingness to open its doors to all serious musicians, however daring, however revolutionary? Actually, what Azanchevsky secretly hoped was that Rimsky-Korsakov would "come to his senses" within the Conservatory's hallowed walls.

Rimsky-Korsakov himself, however, was hesitant. What was he to do? His friends advised him to accept the offer, especially Balakirev, who had his own ideas and ethics in regard to politics in music. The main thing, he believed, was to have one of his own men in the enemy camp. Who knows? One day it might be possible to take over the Conservatory altogether.

Rimsky-Korsakov had by that time gained general recognition—and justly so—as a master of orchestration. His fame rested essentially on his two colorful and fascinating tone-poems: *Sadko* and *Antar,* which sparkle in all their untarnished glory to this day. But all this enchanting music had been written largely by intuition; he had scant knowledge of musical theory; he was incapable of harmonizing even the simplest choral piece. He had never yet written any counterpoint; he had but the vaguest notion of the fugue; he didn't even know the terminology of the various chords and intervals and had never conducted in his life. In fact, he still looked upon himself as a dilettante. While accepting Azanchevsky's flattering proposal, therefore, he carefully concealed his ignorance, being determined not only to teach others, but to brush up on musical theory himself.

He was working on his *Fair Maid of Pskov* at the time. He had immediately sensed that this drama, which before him had already attracted the attention of Mussorgsky and especially of Borodin, had definite operatic possibilities. But he had also realized how difficult it would be to write a libretto, since the prologue takes place fifteen years before the opening of the first act and quite a few of the *dramatis personae* who appear in it, are either never seen again, or if they are seen, re-appear considerably aged. In the end, Rimsky-Korsakov—who, like all the other members of the group, insisted on writing his own librettos—resolved the problem by dropping the prologue altogether and blending its contents into the opera proper.

In the summer of 1868, an eccentric fellow composer by the name of Lodyzhensky invited him to his country estate in the Government of Tver', where the Borodins were already staying. Oddly enough, it was this chance invitation which provided Rimsky-Korsakov with the incentive for fruitful work. He was living alone at the time in the large official residence of his brother, the admiral. His life was uneventful, and he was beginning to feel bored. Now, upon receiving Lodyzhensky's invitation, the very thought of living in a remote part of the country, in the very heartland of Russia, overwhelmed him suddenly with such a feeling of obsessive love for his motherland, his people and their history and, conversely, with such an urge to start work on his *Pskovityanka* (as he planned to call the opera) that hurrying over to the piano, he improvised then and there the theme of the crowd acclaiming the Czar.

Upon his return to St. Petersburg, in the fall, he completed the first act and shortly thereafter Balakirev borrowed a first choral excerpt for a concert of the I.M.S., which already included Rimsky-Korsakov's earlier *Serbian Fantasy*. Mili wanted his young friend to conduct both pieces himself, but Rimsky-Korsakov's superiors in the Navy objected to his appearing on the podium in uniform (Russian officers were not allowed to wear civilian dress, not even off duty).

The opera progressed but slowly; indeed, he completed it only three and a half years later. For one thing, his naval duties kept him fairly busy. Then he was also orchestrating *Antar*. Finally, the orchestration of Dargomyzhsky's *Stone Guest* took up much of his time.

The writing of *The Fair Maid of Pskov*, coincided with the blossoming of the composer's first (and only) love—for Nadiezhda Purgold. He was thus able to put into this work all the freshness of his still unexhausted—if not too powerful —lyrical talent. He also reflected in it most of the moods and beliefs common to the members of the group, saturating the score with bits of folklore and folk-song (some authentic, others of his own invention). The main accent of the plot rested on the love story of Olga and of Tucha, the dashing champion of the Free City of Pskov's freedom. But true to his times, he also assigned a prominent part to the people, through the device of mass choral numbers. The result was admirable and in its amended version (which Rimsky-Korsakov wrote himself) *The Fair Maid of Pskov* has survived in the Russian operatic repertoire to this day.

While work was in progress, the composer showed excerpts to his friends and it was of course also performed at the Purgolds, first in parts and then *in extenso*. They all loved it. How could they have not loved it? Wasn't it a "model opera" of sorts, a compendium of the beliefs they all professed, the very embodiment of their creed? Not that they were blind to its shortcomings. "The music," wrote Borodin to his wife, "is incredibly beautiful but—as Stassov aptly remarked—it is a little cold, a little passionless; with the exception, I must add, of the scene of the *Veche,* which is marvellously good!" Cui who, at the time, was busy working on his romantic *William Radcliffe* (on a theme by Heine) also approved; one reason being that Korsinka was helping him orchestrate his opera, which was something Cui himself never had any taste for, indeed was incapable of doing. Mili's approval lacked enthusiasm. His favorite pupil was obviously escaping his grip. Alone Mussorgsky was unqualifiedly enthusiastic. At the Purgolds, he had been the first to sing Ivan the Terrible's part, but then he was always willing to sing any part for which there were no other volunteers. He also sang the entire opera, from beginning to end, to Eduard Napravnik, the conductor, one evening in the painter Lukashevich's apartment. Napravnik liked neither the opera nor its author. But Lukashevich wielded considerable influence with the Director of the Imperial Theatres, Ghedeonov, and his insistence, and especially the goodwill of Grand-

Duke Constantine, the head of the Navy, settled *The Fair Maid's* fate. The Mariinsky Theatre accepted it for production.

Actually, for all its merits, *The Fair Maid of Pskov* had no real artistic or historic value even in those days. It was doomed to pale before another opera, on a contemporaneous theme, which was being written at that very same time, in that very same room, down the corridor to the left, off Panteleymonovskaya Street.

II

For in the autumn of 1871, Mussorgsky and Rimsky-Korsakov had taken a room together, living there until Korsinka's marriage the following spring.

The history of music knows few such examples of two composers living and working together. Actually even with them, the system worked satisfactorily only because they adhered to a set of strict rules. Thus, in the morning, Mussorgsky used the one piano, while Rimsky-Korsakov copied his notes and wrote his orchestrations. At noon, Modest departed for his office and Korsinka took over. Twice a week, the latter was away all morning teaching at the Conservatory.

Mussorgsky was the more hardworking and dedicated of the two. "You couldn't have tempted him out of his lair with all the sweetmeats in the world!" said Stassov. Korsinka for his part, spent every free moment of his day at the Purgolds, with Nadia. Hardly anyone visited them in their "lair." Occasionally, when he happened to be passing in the neighborhood, Borodin would drop in for a chat. He found that their living together was having a beneficial effect on both. "Modest," he wrote to his wife, "has improved the recitative and declamatory aspects in Korsinka's work while the latter in his turn has eradicated Modest's tendency towards awkward originality, has rounded off his harmonizations, simplified his orchestrations, corrected the absence of logic in the structure of his musical forms; in other words, he has made Modest's work incomparably more musical!"

Their only regular visitor was Stassov. He would drop in on them early in the morning, on his way to the Library, and would usually find both young men sound asleep. Whipping off their blankets, he would squirt cold water over their faces, stand by holding their dressing gowns while they washed and then, after they had pulled on a few clothes, would sit down with them to share their morning tea with Swiss cheese (which they all "adored"). After which Modest and Korsinka would play their latest compositions to him.

Although they were both devoted to Stassov, their attitude toward him was quite different. In Rimsky-Korsakov, there was always a note of reticence, as if he were withholding something; throughout his life he was to approach people with the same circumspect caution. Stassov's friendship with Mussorgsky, on the other hand, had become immediately as enthusiastic as that which had existed once between him and Balakirev. Although there could hardly be two individuals less alike than Mili and Modest, the pattern of their friendship with Stassov was much the same. As he had done with Balakirev, Stassov made Mussorgsky a present of his photograph (a reproduction, this time, of one of Repin's portraits) which Modest acknowledged in enthusiastic terms: "Your energetic and perceptive gaze impels me towards all sorts of good deeds . . . You gaze into the distance, you seem to sense something lying far ahead, every little wrinkle in your face shows strength and an awareness of what is right . . . And it is that which is so good in you, so alive, so forward-looking and far-seeing, which impels me to do all these good deeds." Years ago, Balakirev had thanked him in very similar terms, he too had claimed that Stassov's portrait prompted him "to write better."

In due course, Stassov introduced Mussorgsky to his painter friends, of the so-called Itinerant (in Russian: *Peredvizhniki*) group. The latter had been formed in 1863 by thirteen

students of the Academy of Fine Arts—all of them candidates
for the Gold Medal—following their refusal to paint, for
their final competition, a picture on a subject called *Alone
in Walhalla*. They had walked out and had established a
"Fraternity of Itinerant Exhibitions" which travelled from
city to city and professed the very same populist and realistic
creed that was so dear to Mussorgsky's heart.

The members of the various "worlds" with which Stassov
associated as a rule intermingled but rarely, but there were
exceptions and Mussorgsky was one of them. He had been for
many years already a close friend of the painter Mikeshin to
whom he had even dedicated one of his songs. He now struck
up an intimate friendship with Stassov's protégé, the young,
merry, sturdy and brilliantly talented Ilia Repin. Stassov
used to refer lovingly to Repin, Mussorgsky and the young
Jewish sculptor Antokolsky, as "my trio." Modest took great
pride in belonging to this little group, though he somewhat
under-rated his own part in it.

Lean, passionate, with a youthful exuberance that was both
amusing (for he spoke Russian with a most extraordinary
accent) and charming, Mark Antokolsky specialized in sculp-
turing portrait figures of Russian Czars and statesmen. He
was popular with his artist friends—who in their relations
with him showed none of the antisemitism they sometimes
felt against other Jews (most of whom, incidentally, were
pub-owners, i.e., "exploiters) of their acquaintance. To them,
he was just another hard-working artist like everybody else.
Indeed the very fact that this young Jew from inside the no-
torius "pale" had become a Russian artist, that he was now
serving the cause of Russian art and was thus helping to
glorify the Russian name, seemed to them living proof of the
spiritual vigor of their country.

Closer even than with Repin was Mussorgsky's friendship
with the young architect Victor Hartmann. To Perov (another prominent member of the Itinerant group) he felt more
of an artistic than a personal affinity, since Perov too, was a

genuine realist. As for Kramskoy, the leader of the group, he literally overwhelmed Mussorgsky by the power of his intellect. "It is high time," Kramskoy preached, "that the Russian painter learn to stand on his own feet. He doesn't have to cling to a nurse's apron-strings. The time has come to create a Russian school of painting." One would have thought that this was Mussorgsky himself or Stassov speaking.

Which is why Stassov felt that the Itinerants were the blood brothers of the Mighty Handful, and why he put so much—perhaps too much!—hope in them. Not that they lacked talent (Repin was enormously gifted) or lacked the roots of Russian folk-song on which the Russian school of music had grown: The Itinerants were uncouth and parochial and remained a school of strictly local significance, compared to the musicians of the Mighty Handful.

In those days, however, nobody realized this state of affairs, last of all Modest with his narrow and uncompromising esthetical opinions. As they sat in one or the other's studio, drinking vodka, eating sausage sandwiches or sending to the neighboring pub for beer and crawfish, they would hold forth a little tipsily on elevated subjects and shower one another with compliments.

Aside from their ideological affinities, Mussorgsky's *rapprochement* with the painters may also have been facilitated by a noticeable cooling in his relations with Balakirev and the rest of the group, with the one exception of Korsinka. It irked him that both Mili and Cui should, out of habit, continue to regard him with condescension whereas among his painter friends he had come across people who sincerely admired his music (even though they did not always understand it).

"Why is it?" Mussorgsky exclaimed once in a letter to Stassov "that when I listen to your conversation, to the conversation of the painters and sculptors not excluding even the monumental Misha Mikeshin, I am able to follow the pattern of your thoughts, your ideas, your aims, and that I so seldom hear anything about technique? And why is it that when I listen to our musical brethren, I hear hardly a live thought, but instead mostly primitive chatter about technique and the ABC of composition? How often, in a roundabout way, have I brought up subjects on a higher level with my musical brethren, and the result? Either a rebuff, or else confusion or more often still incomprehension! Why is it that Antokolsky's *'Ivans'* (*Ivan III* and *Ivan IV*) and especially his *'Yaroslav the Wise,'* why is it that Ilia Efimovich Repin's *'Volga Boatmen,'* his *'Village Procession'* and Perov's *The Huntsmen* are so impressive that when one sees them for the first time, one feels like crying out: 'You are just the ones I wished to see!' And why is it that all that which is done in music, for all its many excellent qualities, is so much less alive?"

To his painter friends he now confided all that was most dear to him, his innermost thoughts. As he worked on *Boris,* he kept re-reading the Russian historians, especially Soloviov. "History," he wrote, "is my nightly bed-companion and I relish it and delight in it, despite weariness and a gloomy morning at the office!" and he would disclose to Repin: "It is the people I want to depict: I see them in my sleep, I think of them while I eat, they haunt me when I'm drinking, the people with their simple, unsophisticated ways. And what a richness there is in the people's speech. What an inexhaustable mine you have there, as soon as you seize hold of all that is real in the life of the Russian people! Just stir it up— you'll dance for joy!—if only you are a genuine artist!"

III

Such was the setting, the framework for the creation of *Boris Godunov,* Mussorgsky's masterpiece. He realized himself that this was the acme of his creative career. Later, recalling these times, he wrote: "I lived by *Boris* and in *Boris;*

and the time I spent with *Boris* is etched in my mind in indelible ink!"

As he read and re-read the copy of Pushkin's *Boris Godunov* which "Liudma" Shestakova had given him, his enthusiasm never waned. And yet he knew that it would not be so easy to produce an opera on this out of all subjects.

For Pushkin had written his *Boris* during a period of infatuation with Shakespeare. Like Shakespeare's chronicles, Pushkin's drama consists of a number of brief, disconnected scenes, whose only link is chronological. This was all very well in Shakespeare's time, when the changing sets could be indicated by a single poster inscribed alternately: "A forest" or "A hall in the castle." And today, this quick change has again been made possible by the use of the revolving stage. But in Pushkin's or Mussorgsky's times it was possible only by a tour de force. On the other hand, Pushkin had not written his drama for the stage. So, Mussorgsky had first of all to make cuts in Pushkin's text and to confine his own contribution—as far as the story went—to a little "padding" here and there for the sake of continuity without, as yet, engaging in any major alterations.

In due course still other problems arose. Pushkin had been inspired largely by the historian Karamzin's version of the subject. According to Karamzin, Boris Godunov ascended the throne of the Moscow Czars after murdering the Czarevich Dimitri. His subsequent remorse made him powerless to fight the Impostor who later rose up against him under his victim's assumed name. Though this theory was already strongly contested at the time, Mussorgsky endorsed it. His instinct told him rightly that Pushkin's characterization of the Czar was inadequate for the stage. He therefore proceeded to soften Karamzin's image so as to make Boris appear more attractive, more sympathetic from the performer's point of view, thereby also increasing the intensity of the whole drama. Thus, for instance, he introduced the very effective scene of the Church chimes and added, almost in its entirety, the scene of Boris' death, which became thus the culminating point of the opera.

Stassov kept supplying him with source material from the Public Library and suggested additions and changes. He searched for and unearthed the text of an ancient folk song, *As It Happened in the City of Kazan* which Pushkin had merely mentioned without quoting; he also found an appropriate text for the song of the innkeeper's wife. As a result of all this research, and egged on and encouraged by Stassov, Mussorgsky became increasingly bold and independent. For once the libretto, instead of preceding the writing of the music, proceeded apace. Modest realized only too well, of course, the relative value of his own amateurish verses as compared to Pushkin's immortal lines, but what could he do? After all, it was only thanks to these changes, however clumsy, that the opera could exist at all.

He had come far since the days of Dargomyzhsky and of his own *Marriage*. His purpose was no longer to reveal the hidden musical undertones of one word or even one sentence. His music was now an "autonomous" entity, linked to the word, of course, but only indirectly, more by meaning than consonance. Pushkin's words were for his taste too saturated with philosophical meaning and lyrical feeling to serve as a good musical medium. They constituted an unnecessary burden, which Mussorgsky was so bold as to discard. From now on it was not the music that would serve the word, but the word that would be subordinated to the music.

As a result of all these changes, Pushkin's 23 scenes were cut to 7 and his countless personages were reduced to 14, to which Mussorgsky added 5 others of his own invention. He had begun to write the opera in October 1868; by early November he had completed the first scene of the prologue.

This scene is set in the *Novodevichy* monastery near Moscow. As in Pushkin, the people, goaded on by the Bailiff's stick-swinging henchmen, beg Boris with mock-lamentations to accept the throne, vacant since the death of his brother-in-law, Czar Feodor. But Mussorgsky prolongs this scene somewhat through the introduction of a few colorful episodes of his own invention. In the end Boris refuses the throne and the curtain drops against the background lamentations of the crowd.

The second scene of the prologue was ready ten days later. This is the famous magnificent "Coronation scene," with the wonderful chiming of the carillon and the *Slava* ("Glory") for which Mussorgsky utilized an old Slavonic tune from an ancient anthology by the Czech musicologist Prac, which had already been used by Beethoven.

Act I begins with the scene in the monk Pimen's cell, in *Chudov* monastery. His soliloquy *One last story shall I tell* is taken verbatim from Pushkin. The music accentuates to perfection all the nuances of this piece, and the weirdly simple, monotonous phrasing of the accompaniment gives the listener an impression of mystery-laden timelessness. The *duo* of Pimen and the young novice Grigori departs from Pushkin's text. The music of this scene is full of penetrating charm. Grigori awakens with a cry, as after a nightmare. His prophetic dream, coming after Pimen's story suggests to him that he assume the part of an Impostor. It is probable that Mussorgsky wished intentionally to give the Impostor's role an unreal, fantastic touch. For wasn't the pseudo-Dimitri's whole career one short-lived, incredible dream?

The second scene of the first act is that of the inn: The Impostor is making his way to Lithuania in the company of two run-away monks, Varlaam and Missail. The Bailiff's men, who have a warrant for his arrest, catch up with him, but he escapes through a window. Here again, Mussorgsky sticks closely to Pushkin's text, adding only the comic skits of the monk Varlaam.

By the following spring, the first scene of the second act, *The Czar's Chambers in the Moscow Kremlin*, was ready. Mussorgsky thinned out Pushkin's text, added much of his own and for better scenic effect, introduced the episode of Prince Shuisky's visit and the latter's report on the appearance

of an impostor in Lithuania. Then he added the scene in Red
Square and, finally, the grandiose death scene of Boris. He
also transferred to this death scene Pushkin's story about the
body of the dead Czarevich appearing miraculously in a
vision to the Patriarch, with the difference that in Mussorgsky's opera the story is told by old Pimen.

Meanwhile, the orchestration had proceeded apace. Barely
a year after he had started, in the summer of 1869, the first
version of the opera was completed.

True to habit, Mussorgsky had not kept his progress secret;
he had from the outset played and sung excerpts from *Boris*
to his friends. Even Dargomyzhsky had lived to appreciate
his young pupil's first wonderful achievements. Most often
these excerpts were performed at the Purgolds', where they
soon became a feature of their musical evenings. Most of
those who heard *Boris* liked it, even though they hardly
appreciated its real significance. The one exception was
Balakirev who, to Mussorgsky's great disappointment, voiced
disapproval of the opera. Actually, this was not surprising; the
romantic and idealistic Mili could hardly enjoy the colorful
but brutal realism of these scenes. Besides, from the strictly
musical viewpoint, Modest was by now infinitely remote from
Mili's whims and theories, pet harmonies, favorite tonalities
and orchestrations *à la* Liszt or *à la* Berlioz. There was one
thing Balakirev never forgave, namely disloyalty to his doc-
trine. And it was obvious that Mussorgsky was breaking new
ground. As far as harmony was concerned, he was doing
goodness knows what. Through his abusive use of disso-
nances, his savage modulations, he had apparently forgotten
all that which had been so painstakingly drummed into him.
Mili frowned and was so tactless as to criticize Modest even
in front of strangers.

Stassov did not frown. On the contrary, he was enthusiastic.
In fact, he had a positively paternal feeling for *Boris*. Pimen's
story about the Patriarch's vision fascinated him. "It's as
good as Glinka's *Ballad of Finn*," he exclaimed (which was

in his eyes the highest praise). And yet even he was scared by the opera's "extremism" and therefore suggested changes. But Mussorgsky, usually so modest, so obedient, so amenable, seemed now suddenly transformed; he refused to be swayed or intimidated.

IV

However interesting, his friends' reaction was only one of his concerns. He had other things on his mind. For Mussorgsky was by vocation a theatrical composer; he knew that it was only on stage that *Boris* would come to life and sparkle in all its glory. But it was not easy to stage such an opera. For one thing, there was in those days only one opera house in St. Petersburg, the Imperial Mariinsky Theatre; there were no private opera halls. And like state-owned theatres the world over, the Mariinsky Theatre was run by a prejudiced and ignorant bureaucracy. True, its orchestra was conducted by a serious musician, the 32-year-old Czech Napravnik, but he was a conservative; moreover, ever since Rimsky-Korsakov's attack in the press on his opera he bore the "Balakirev Gang" a grudge.

The Director of the Imperial Theatres and the Hermitage picture gallery was, at the time, one Stepan Aleksandrovich Ghedeonov (not to be confused with Borodin's father Ghedeanov). Why he had been appointed to this post, so vital from the point of view of Russian art, we know not for he seems to have had no knowledge or understanding of art. But he took his functions seriously and was fairly accessible, and this was something to behold.

In the summer of 1870, Ghedeonov granted Mussorgsky an interview; he informed him that the coming opera season was already fully booked but promised him that when "those who have the final say in the matter," i.e., the Committee of Conductors (the "Vaudeville Committee" as Cui sarcastically called it), reconvened in the fall, they would invite him to

show them his opera or, in Mussorgsky's own words, "to scare
the wits out of them with *Boris!*"

In the autumn of 1870, the score was formally submitted
to the Mariinsky's Board of Directors and shortly thereafter
Mussorgsky was summoned to appear before the fair eyes
of the committee. Aside from the conductors and leaders of
the Mariinsky Theatre, the seven-man committee included
the conductors of the French and German theatres in St.
Petersburg. Modest played and sang to them the whole opera
in person, after which the members retired to study the score
behind closed doors. On February 10, 1871, they handed
down their verdict: *Boris Godunov* was rejected by 6 votes
to 1 (that of Napravnik!).

The novelty of the music had perplexed the members of
the committee, especially the French and German maestros,
who were accustomed to entertain their audiences during
intermission with uncomplicated little pieces. It was reported
moreover, that one of the committee members, the double-
bass virtuoso Ferrero could not forgive Mussorgsky for making his double basses play chromatic thirds; he could take
much, but such frivolity was really going too far! In all
fairness to the committee, however, one should add that in
motivating its rejection, they made a number of pertinent
observations. Among others they pointed out that the opera
had no feminine roles and that this made it monotonous and
undramatic.

Be it as it may, the rejection of *Boris* was a hard blow to
Mussorgsky; it is always painful for an operatic composer
to be denied the right to stage his work. Moreover, there
was good reason to fear that since he had been too proud
to pay any heed to the criticism of his friends, he would also
obstinately refuse to make changes in his opera by the orders
of a "bunch of conductors." But to Stassov's amazement,
Mussorgsky gave in and undertook to make the necessary
changes, so that, in effect, the initial rejection helped to make
Boris into the masterpiece we know.

In order to introduce a feminine role (that of Marina) Mussorgsky added the entire "Polish scene" (in the castle of Sambor), thereby amending considerably Pushkin's episode at the fountain. The duo of Marina and Grigori seems to have been inspired by the composer's own passion for Nadiezhda Petrovna Opochinina (in whose home he lived throughout this period). Less fortunate was the further introduction of a Jesuit priest, Father Rangoni (inspired, no doubt, by Father Pierling's work on the Impostor). As is to be expected, this Rangoni plays a Machiavellian part throughout the whole Polish intrigue, persuading Marina to convert Grigori to catholicism, eavesdropping at the fountain, etc. But although his part is most interesting in musical terms, it weakens and slows down the action.

Mussorgsky also expanded the part of the innkeeper's wife which now became the second major feminine character and composed for her the rather racy ditty about the drake. Then he prolonged the scene in "The Czar's Chambers in the Kremlin" to include Boris' *arioso,* the tale of the parrot and the humorous songs of the nurse and of the young Czarevich, Boris' son. Finally, throwing out the scene in Red Square altogether, he transferred some of its episodes (such as that of the urchins teasing the half-wit) to the newly introduced scene "Before the Walls of Khromy."

This was the most important of his changes; it was suggested to him by the same Professor Nikolsky who had brought the subject of *Boris* to his attention in the first place (Stassov, already disappointed because it was not he who had recommended the subject to Modest, was literally in despair at having again been late with his suggestions).

The scene—one of the most powerful and original in the whole opera—replaced Boris' "Death Scene" as the *finale:* the mutinous rabble has just captured one of the Czar's boyars to whom they alternately pay mock reverence and flog; nearby, a group of urchins are teasing the half-wit; the run-away monks Varlaam and Missail egg on the populace that seizes hold of some Catholic priests chanting latin litanies and tries to lynch them. All of a sudden, in the midst of this revolutionary pandemonium, there is the merry jingle of the bells of the Impostor's sleigh and the crowd rushes off to acclaim him. Presently, the stage is deserted but for the half-wit who, forlorn in a corner, mournfully intones his heartrending lament over the fate of the Holy Russia. The curtain drops slowly.

Only in this amended form, with mass scenes at the beginning and at the end, with the people bursting in on the action with their group choral effects, did the opera acquire the character which its author had intended to give it at the very outset—that of a grandiose, epic, impersonal folk drama. The plot revolves, actually, around two heroes—Czar Boris, with his private drama and his pangs of conscience, and the Russian people. Mussorgsky pictured this Russian people as he had set out to do: of one piece, massive, without embellishment. Representing it at a time of great historic challenge, he showed it as being ignorant, stupid, submissive, but also as capable of frightening, wild revolt. The climax to this grandiose drama was genuinely Shakespearean.

V

The vexing problem arose again: How was he to stage his opera? *Boris* was now more perfect, more beautiful than ever before, but it was also still more difficult to produce. For one thing, there was the frankly revolutionary scene "Before the Walls of Khromy" which, alone, required what the Professor of Fortifications Cui called a long and persistent "approach operation."

A first point was scored, a first bastion taken when Napravnik agreed to include in the program of an Imperial Musical Society concert scheduled for the month of February 1872, the *finale* of Act I—the magnificent *Slava* for choir and orchestra. It was a success. Then, in April, Mili included—

if somewhat halfheartedly—another excerpt from *Boris* in the program of a concert of his Free School. For some reason, he chose the rather unoriginal but effective Polish scene. The public received it coolly. A few days later the entire opera was performed at the Purgolds' by Sasha Purgold and the author, accompanied by Nadia. Borodin, who was hearing the new version for the first time, was enthusiastic. "How delightful!" he kept exclaiming, "What diversity! What contrasts! How polished and well motivated everything is now!" In general, these gatherings at the Purgolds', where artists and singers met with representatives of the bureaucratic world, were beginning to play an important part in building up interest in *Boris* and in establishing an atmosphere favorable to its subsequent acceptance by the public.

Presently, still another development intervened in Mussorgsky's favor. Inspired, perhaps, by the fashionable Wagnerian theory about "coordination of the arts," the rather muddle-headed Director of the Imperial Theatres Ghedeonov had a sudden brainstorm: Why should an opera be written by only one man? Wouldn't something written by five different composers be five times better or more interesting? He addressed himself to the playwright Victor Krylov, who in due course produced a libretto based on the life of the prehistoric Slavs and entitled *Mlada*. For the music Ghedeonov turned, through Stassov's good offices, to Borodin, Mussorgsky, Cui and Rimsky-Korsakov. Stassov expected his young friends to refuse this offer but to his surprise they accepted. The ballet was to be written by a fifth composer, Minkus, who specialized in supplying ballet music for festive occasions. The result was to be an opera, based on a fairy tale, enhanced by a ballet and combining everything: Slav folklore, ancient pagan mythology, historic melodrama, etc. Cui agreed to write Act I, Rimsky-Korsakov and Mussorgsky took Acts II and III, while Borodin chose Act IV. Ghedeonov obtained a credit of 10.000 rubles for this undertaking and work began. Naturally, this assignment brought the composers into close contact with their "employer"—which was perhaps the secret reason why they had accepted his offer in the first place. Actually, the assignment was a fairly easy one for they all made generous use of their files: Mussorgsky —from his *Salammbo* and his *St. John's Night on Bald Mountain,* Borodin—from his temporarily abandoned *Prince Igor.*

But nothing came of this venture. Ghedeonov had soon spent the allocated credits, no others were forthcoming and *Mlada* remained unfinished.

It is said that in the days of sailing ships, French wine-growers, when wishing to produce an exceptional vintage, were in the habit of sending their bottles to the Indies and back and that this trip, seemingly pointless, had a miraculous effect on the wine's quality: the *retour des Indes* bottles were usually exceptional.

Something similar happened to Borodin: The music he had designated for *Igor* emerged from this "trip to *Mlada* and back" revived, rejuvenated, revitalized. His participation in Ghedeonov's project provided him with the incentive he had so long needed in order to resume work on his opera. Even Rimsky-Korsakov benefited somewhat from this incompleted project: Many years later he was to write his own version of *Mlada* in the form of an opera in the classical tradition.

Although Mussorgsky had completed his portion of the collective assignment and although he too had profited from the experience, he was nevertheless more than any of his comrades embarrassed at having exchanged his life as a free artist for that of an artisan working on commission. He complained bitterly to Stassov. "The moral fiasco of our group," he added, "is impending . . . I told Korsinka and Borodin, that in order to save the integrity of our group, I for one would much prefer to give orders than to bow and listen." Rimsky-Korsakov thereupon suggested that he write a new *Penny Paradise* with themselves as targets, "giving us all a hiding—but lovingly." Modest was delighted with the idea: "If this little thing is a success," he wrote, "then the group is saved, for what Philistines would draw and quarter themselves for their own blunders?" However, this parody was never written. Actually, their rapprochement to Ghedeonov bore little fruit: When *Boris* was re-submitted to the Mariinsky's Board of Directors, it was again rejected, despite Ghedeonov's and perhaps even Napravnik's benevolent attitude.

At this point the Purgolds' gatherings were of decisive help. The painter Lukashevich, Ghedeonov's assistant (who was about to take over the Sets and Costumes Department at the Imperial Theatres) was a frequent guest at the Purgolds; he too had enjoyed *Boris* and was well-disposed toward its author. It was he who had organized its first audition by Napravnik. Now he suggested that a few excerpts from *Boris* be staged at a benefit performance of operatic music. As a rule, the benefit programs consisted only of works which had already been produced. Moreover, the selection of these programs was left "to the discretion of the beneficiary." However, as most of the star singers of St. Petersburg—Platonova, Kommissarzhevsky, Vorobiov, Petrov and many others— were personal friends of Mussorgsky's, Lukashevich believed that it might be possible to interpret the expression "discretion of the beneficiary" in its broadest sense and to smuggle in a few scenes from his still unknown work. The idea was welcomed with enthusiasm and after a few conspiratorial meetings, it was decided to stage three excerpts from *Boris* at a performance planned for the benefit of the director Kondratiev.

Because of the semi-legal nature of the whole project, the soloists, choir and orchestra were obliged to rehearse in secret, in their free time, sometimes even in private homes. This they did under the leadership of Napravnik, who had been won over to the plot. The event was set for February 5, 1873.

"Judgment is at hand!" Mussorgsky wrote to Stassov

shortly before the fateful evening. "With a cheerfulness amounting to recklessness, we gaze into the remote musical distance which beckons to us and the judgment does not scare us! We will be told: 'You have trampled underfoot every law, divine and human!'—'Yes!' we will reply, and we will tell ourselves: 'Just wait and see what follows!' They will croak: 'You will be forgotten soon and forever!' We will answer: 'No! No! No!' "

The benefit performance, which consisted of the first act of Weber's *Der Freischütz* and of three excerpts from *Boris,* "Marina's Parlor," "The Scene at the Fountain" and "The Scene at the Inn," was a tremendous success, the greatest, most unqualified success, perhaps, in Mussorgsky's life as an artist. Petrov was outstanding as Varlaam, Obarinova was good as the innkeeper's wife, Platonova sang Marina's part and Kommissarzhevsky performed that of the impostor. Indeed, it was one of those rare exhilarating and festive evenings, when the audience listens with bated breath and bursts into applause without even realizing it. The Mariinsky Theatre, wrote Cui, had never seen anything like it!

After the performance, the composer was feted at the Rimsky-Korsakov's. The guests included Stassov and also Sasha Purgold who, having overcome her passion for Modest, had married another of the guests, a naval officer by the name of Molas. Toasts were drunk in champagne to Mussorgsky and to an early performance of his opera *in extenso.* When Modest got home, "glowing all over with happiness and elation," he stumbled against something prickly and cried out in pain and surprise. It appeared that Dimitri Stassov's wife had sent him a laurel wreath and he had inadvertently pricked himself with the pin of the ribbon—an appropriate symbol of his short-lived success.

Even those critics who were usually hostile to the Mighty Handful, acknowledged the three scenes from *Boris* though with an air of condescension. Even Hermann Laroche, an extreme classicist and a follower of Hanslick, admitted that he had gone to listen to *Boris* without much hope, indeed with considerable misgivings, but that the composer had surprised him with "quite unexpected flashes of beauty," and that, despite his pretentiousness and affectation, Mussorgsky showed signs of considerable spiritual strength.

This first success made for an atmosphere conducive to the opera's performance *in extenso*. The celebrated singer Platonova was just then about to sign up for another contract with the Mariinsky Theatre. One of the Purgolds' more frequent guests and an old personal friend of Mussorgsky's, she was also on very close terms with the painter Lukashevich, Ghedeonov's assistant. Through him, she now made it known that she would sign the contract only if *Boris Godunov* were performed for her benefit, after which Lukashevich also put personal pressure on his chief. Subjected to this crossfire, Ghedeonov succumbed. Overruling the "Vaudeville Committee," he decided to stage the opera on his own authority.

All this took up a lot of time and in the end *Boris* saw the light of day almost a full year after Kondratiev's benefit, on January 27, 1874.

Meanwhile, the music publisher Bessel had purchased the *Klavierauszug* which, a few days before opening night, Mussorgsky dedicated jointly to his friends in terms strongly reminiscent of Fichte. "I look upon the people," it read, "as a personality inspired by a single idea. This is the purpose which I attempted to achieve in this opera. To you who, through your wise advice and sympathetic deeds gave me an opportunity to subject myself to this stage-test, I dedicate my work."

He thus, for the last time and despite the many past disappointments, voiced his confidence in and expressed his gratitude to the members of the "Balakirev Gang."

VI

The opera was a smash hit. With the exception of the scene in old Pimen's cell, Napravnik had made none of his habitual cuts. Indeed one should give both conductor and management their due: the production was faultless. True, there had been few new expenses, as the sets and costumes were left-overs from a recent gorgeous production of Pushkin's *Boris Godunov* which had been a flop and had soon been dropped. But Napravnik had spared no efforts to bring the orchestra and choir to a high point of perfection. True, Stassov and some of those who had heard *Boris* at the Purgolds, reproached the conductor for having assigned the individual "voices in the crowd" to choral groups, but as this figures this way in Mussorgsky's own manuscript, it was probably done with the composer's agreement.

The public was both thrilled and stunned, especially the students up in the "Penny Paradise," who went literally wild and kept calling for the author. But even the traditional audience of first nights and benefit performances, the so-called "nice society," were captivated, despite their convictions and prejudices and perhaps even against their own better judgment. As one lady put it: "It's a disgrace and not an opera! There isn't even a note of music in it. You cry, you laugh and yet there's absolutely nothing to listen to!" Actually, most of them attributed their own favorable impression of the opera as well as its success to the singers' performances which, with very few exceptions, were first rate, most of the artists having already sung their parts, the year before, at Kondratiev's benefit.

Mussorgsky stood in the wings throughout the performance. Naturally, he was terribly nervous. To make things worse, a small incident now occurred just before the curtain went up, which was to make his anguish even more unbearable.

Four young girls, close friends of the Stassov family (and perhaps even at Stassov's own suggestion) had purchased a laurel wreath, which they adorned with ribbons appropriately inscribed ("Onward to uncharted shores!", "A primeval force arose!", "Glory to thee for Boris! Glory!") and which they planned to present to him on stage. Under the existing rules, this required the explicit authorization of the management. The latter, however, ruled that they would have to present their wreath in private, in the wings, and neither their pleas nor their youthful charm had any effect. When he was informed of this episode, Mussorgsky was in despair. At first he even thought of leaving the building; but presently he agreed to stay, on condition that he did not see the ill-fated wreath until the performance was over. In the end, it was presented to him almost surreptitiously, by one of the stage hands.

The incident caused an immediate uproar. Stassov flew into a rage and threatened to write a protest in the press. For fear that the management might seize upon this pretext in order to drop *Boris* from the theatre's repertoire, Mussorgsky implored him to desist. But the story got into the press after all without Stassov's intervention, together with a protest on the part of the young ladies in question. Whereupon Mussorgsky quite lost his head and wrote a lackadaisical letter to Napravnik in which he said that he too had found it most tactless of them to present a laurel wreath to a young composer on the opening night of his first opera, before he had even a chance to prove whether he was worthy of such an honor. Then, not pausing to think what such a public reprimand might mean to his enthusiastic young admirers, he wrote another letter, along similar lines, to the publisher of the paper that had printed their protest.

All of which, of course, poisoned to some extent his own enjoyment of *Boris'* success. But worse still was the reaction of the critics.

For during the year that had elapsed since their first glimpse of *Boris* at Kondratiev's benefit, the latter had found time to revise their initial favorable attitude toward this work. Now, in tones part-rude, part-ironical and part-didactic, they literally ganged up against Mussorgsky. Famintzin (one of the victims of Modest's first *Penny Paradise*) spoke of his "ignorance of the most elementary rules of musical grammar." Soloviov described the opera as a "cacophony in five acts" and accused its author of "chasing after coarse effects." Still more mortifying, however, was the opinion of the intelligent and talented Hermann Laroche.

The latter, an ardent classicist and admirer of Mozart who, like Balakirev's ex-mentor Ulybyshev, was of the opinion that the decadence of music had started with Beethoven, was understandably disgusted with *Boris*. In an article entitled "An Intellectual Realist in Music" (after the name given to his followers by the brilliant young nihilist critic Pissariov) Laroche voiced surprise at Mussorgsky's "gross schoolboy slips." The opera, he said, was obviously the work of a child, of a beginner who "while claiming to explore the unknown, to venture into the field of chromaticism, has already been exceedingly corrupted." He did not deny Mussorgsky's talent. For example, the song *"As it happened in the City of Kazan,"* he said, had quite a grandiose power, and the *Scene at the Fountain* was full of sensuous charm, nostalgia and poetical inspiration. Indeed, he went on, in Mussorgsky's person, the Balakirev group had at last acquired, not an imitator, but an original and powerful innovator, endowed with qualities which the others lacked conspicuously. Such qualities could have marked them with a stamp all their own, i.e. individuality, inventiveness and independence. Of course, this stamp was a profoundly alien one; in fact he, Laroche, was deeply hostile to it. "With Mussorgsky," he wrote, "what counts most is not completeness of knowledge, scope, breadth of horizon or artistic refinement, but brutal life force." At the same time, Laroche understood that the young composer could no longer be influenced by mere words of good advice. "I look upon his artistic strivings," he concluded sadly, "as a *fait accompli!*"

Another writer, the outstanding philosopher and literary critic Strakhov also saw fit to speak out against Mussorgsky. Though not a musician himself, he regarded Modest as yet another symptom of Russia's cultural backwardness. In a series of letters to Feodor Dostoyevsky's *Grazhdanin,* Strakhov protested against the distortion of Pushkin's text by yet another of those "uncouth realists" who were cropping up everywhere these days in the press and in the world of art. Listening to *Boris,* he said, had given him the same feeling of revulsion as he experienced at the sight of the portraits of the Itinerant group of artists; he felt like saying: "So true and yet so horrid!"

Though unpleasant, such criticism was to be expected; indeed it could be regarded as merely another of those "professional hazards" which are the lot of every innovator in art. Infinitely worse was the unexpected, treacherous blow dealt *Boris* by one whom Mussorgsky had always looked upon as a friend, namely Cesar Cui!

Why did he do it? For what reason? Try as he did, Modest could find no explanation, barring meanness and envy. Although—to quote a remark attributed to Czarina Elisabeth I of Russia in speaking about one of her courtiers—Cui was "excessively averse to wishing anybody any good," and although he may also have resented Mussorgsky's successful intrusion in the field of opera-writing (which he had long regarded as his private reservation) these could not have been the only reasons. For Cui was probably sincere in his dislike of this music, powerful and colorful but lacking "good taste." Cui's own talent was one of those small, elegant gifts that are graced as a rule with more "good taste" than creative power. He was, moreover, a typical representative of "nice" St. Petersburg society, whose prejudices he showed to an ever growing extent. Indeed, he himself had become an "innovator" mainly because he had a good, inquisitive (though superficial) mind and also by accident, because of his meeting with Balakirev to whose ideas he was at first receptive and which he defended with considerable literary brio. But he had no real, personal, creative gift. Because of that, and despite his considerable intelligence, his judgment was constantly wrong. If one were to assess a critic by the number of accurate versus the number of inaccurate forecasts that come from his pen, Cui would have to be placed at the very bottom of the list, for his were virtually 100% wrong. About *Boris* he now wrote that although Mussorgsky's talent was both powerful and original, the work as a whole was "immature." He denounced the "choppy recitative," the "disconnectedness of musical thought" which made the opera "potpourri-like." He found that this was due not to Mussorgsky's "creative impotence," but to the fact that he was "insufficiently self-critical" and that he wrote "with a lack of fastidiousness," "complacently" and "hastily."

Cui's article was of course wind in the sails of the group's opponents. Soloviov dubbed him "the Handful's Brutus." For his part, Mussorgsky was terribly pained and disappointed. To make matters worse, Cui had referred also to the incident with the wreath and, while commenting in ironic terms about its donors, attributed Modest's letter to the editor to his alleged "craving for publicity." "What a horror that article of Cui's!" Modest complained to Stassov. "Shame on him who publicly makes fun of women who deserve only sympathy for their daring and fearless action. And this assault upon the composer's 'complacency.' The brainless ones are not satisfied with the modesty and absence of boastfulness from which I have never departed and from which I shall never depart as long as I live. Behind this insane assault, behind this deliberate lie, I can see nothing. It's as if soapy water had permeated the air, dimming everything in sight." He recalled how Stassov, with "the perception of a woman in love who senses that her beloved one is threatened," had said: "I fear Cui in connection with *Boris!*" And he humbly begged forgiveness for the scene he had made to his friend on opening night. "I was nasty to you but I was not contemptible, I did not contest your devotion. Whatever happens—I cannot part with you, I love you passionately and in your pale face I saw an expression of equally strong love for me."

Actually, the opera was a lasting success only with the radical youth. On their way home from the performance, the students continued singing some of the more "subversive" tunes from the scene, *Before the Walls of Khromy*. (Though they probably did so mainly because these *sounded* subversive.) For their part, the official, bureaucratic circles of the capital became increasingly hostile. During the second performance already, a friend of the singer Platonova came up to her during the intermission and inquired: "Do you mean to say that you like this music so much that you chose it for your benefit?" and when she replied in the affirmative, he exclaimed: "It's not an opera, it's a disgrace to Russia!" and hurried away.

And yet "the disgrace to Russia" continued being played. The first year, *Boris* was performed ten times to a full house. The public was dismayed, indignant but kept going to see it. In due course Napravnik succumbed to his habitual inclination and began to make cuts: thus he dropped the scene *Before the Walls of Khromy* in its entirety, as well as a few other episodes. In this amended form, it was performed periodically for another eight seasons. Finally, after 24 performances, it was dropped from the repertoire. The "disgrace to Russia" had ended. Only thirty years later was its fame to spread throughout the world.

VII

Boris Godunov is in many ways a work of genius; and yet the critics were justified in feeling hurt for Pushkin's sake. But the point was not that Mussorgsky took the liberty of amending Pushkin's text; it was the fact that there was just no congenial feeling between poet and composer. Because of that the music often outweighs the word, overburdening it with emotion. Mussorgsky's personality—powerful, massive, tragic—was in itself in striking contrast to Pushkin's versatile, ethereal, incandescent lightness of touch. Although Pushkin sought to imitate Shakespeare, his drama retains all the clarity, lucidity and balance of the French eighteenth century. Mussorgsky's opera is brighter, more violent, more tragic, closer in spirit to the "savage" trend in Shakespeare. Western audiences were one day to be overwhelmed and captivated by its "barbarism." But the "barbarism" of *Boris* is the barbarism of ancient Muscovy. Garish, colorful, dazzling like the brilliantly-hued cupolas of the cathedral of St. Basil-the-Blessed in Red Square, it is historically authentic. And yet at the same time, how much restraint, how much moderation there is in the effects; how much directness and honesty in the approach; how much refinement and precision in the design! And with all that no trace of the conventional, the vacuous, the banal. It lives and breathes with such intensity as if everything—melody, harmony, orchestration—had only just been discovered, as if they were all brand new. How striking that, with his lack of theoretical knowledge and his relying exclusively on his unfailing creative instinct, Mussorgsky should have been able to build up such a well-integrated, finely finished work of art. What a tribute to Balakirev's pedagogical methods! And yet now even Balakirev was turning against him.

His contemporaries were too concerned with the novelty of *Boris* to quite realize this. All of them, whether friend or foe, accepted it with reservations, with various "buts." The foes said: "The opera is the work of an ignoramus, but the author does not lack talent." The friends countered: "The opera is a work of talent, but the author is an ignoramus." It was all a matter of *nuances*; otherwise, there was little difference between the treacherous comments of Cesar Cui and the fervent congratulations of Rimsky-Korsakov. Modest was too sensitive a man not to notice this situation and consequently he felt deeply hurt. Rimsky-Korsakov himself always claimed that this marked the starting point of his spiritual decay. He now began to shun his former friends, to seek different company, to shroud himself in an aura of mystery, to express himself in a more obscure, florid and unintelligible language than ever before and to resent ever more the abyss which, as he suspected, existed between his own opinion of himself and that held by his friends (with the one exception of Stassov).

And yet in the long run, *he* was right, not they. He was ahead of his time by at least half a century. It is only now that the public is able to appreciate his music. What to his contemporaries sounded like "chopped recitative" seems inspired melody to us. What they regarded as crass errors due to his ignorance, revealed themselves to be daring flights into the future. The author of *Boris* knew, indeed he could not help knowing that he had created "a miracle of perfection." He sensed, indeed he could not help sensing that he was never to write anything better. And yet there he had to stand, now, listening, while "midgets" claimed to teach him how to write music!

Like Christopher Columbus before him, Mussorgsky had discovered an unknown continent. Starting off from the narrow-gauged and false theory of realism, he had created a work of genius which had nothing in common with realism.

VIII

When evaluating the merits of *Boris Godunov* our thoughts must turn involuntarily to that other musical titan, to one who was the complete antithesis of Mussorgsky, namely to Wagner. It is difficult to imagine two personalities more dissimilar than these two men, who were after all contemporaries and who furthermore set themselves the same objective.

To Wagner, the human voice was merely a sort of *obligato* mouthing certain words. His "continuous melodies" are monotonous and poor, so that without an orchestra they would be a mere endless flow of sound. But the orchestra is

extraordinarily, overly rich in content. *Boris* is, above all, a
vocal opera, its recitatives are so saturated with emotion that
they would lose none of their force and expression even without an orchestral accompaniment. The orchestra performs
merely a subsidiary function, it only accompanies the voices,
outlining the atmosphere with a few brilliant, impressionistic,
quick flashes. The *leitmotifs* are treated by Mussorgsky with
greater complexity, finesse and discretion than is the case
with Wagner, whose *leitmotifs* sometimes resemble in Rimsky-Korsakov's own words "a military fanfare"—which is
perhaps the reason why they linger more easily in one's mind.

Both of them wished to stir through the medium of
their operas, the souls of their respective peoples at their
most sublime. Wagner succeeded in doing so to perfection.
Mussorgsky's music is the product of a more personal, capri-
ciously individualistic creative talent. The Wagnerian fad
became a principal current of European musical culture
already in the composer's lifetime. Whereas Mussorgsky's
operas remained long forgotten, unclaimed, unsolicited, un-
wanted. Only at the beginning of the twentieth century,
when the anti-Wagnerian reaction set in, did Mussorgsky's
music come into its own. Its real significance actually lies
not so much in the influence it exercised over a generation
of musicians as in the fact that it was a precursor and that as
such, it was able, when the time was ripe, to freely blend
itself into the panorama of contemporary music, to hold there
a place of honor and to light up the whole scene.

CHAPTER TWELVE

BALAKIREV'S "WITHDRAWAL INTO THE WILDERNESS"

"My wife shall linger on alone."
BYRON

I

"But what has happened to Mili? What has befallen our merry, vivacious, despotic, charming, insufferable Mili." Time and again his friends asked themselves this question, sadly, worriedly and sometimes even with a note of self-reproach.

True, for a long time, young, egoistic and self-absorbed as they were, they had noticed nothing. Mili was rarely seen nowadays? Well, so what? He was probably just busy with his concerts, his Free School, his lessons, who knows? The diversity, indeed the very nature of his work estranged him somewhat from his friends. And then, to be quite frank, they breathed somehow more freely in his absence.

But as time went by it became impossible not to notice that something *had* changed. "Balakirev made the saddest impression on me yesterday," wrote Stassov one day to Rimsky-Korsakov, and the very fact that he referred to their former leader by his surname indicated how very remote the latter had already become to all of them. "Judging by his appearance you would think that he hadn't changed at all: the same voice, the same figure, face, words,—everything is the same except that in fact everything is different and there is a complete reversal of his personality . . . Imagine: every once in a while we would fall silent and this silence would last for several minutes! Then I would try again, talk about this and that, drop one subject, pass on to another, carefully

225

avoiding anything unpleasant—all to no avail: he says a few words in reply and then again silence ... I have known him now for fifteen years and I have never seen anything like it! No, this is quite a different person; yesterday I had before me, not the vivacious, energetic, restless Mili Alekseyevich of the past, but a corpse."

Stassov said as much to Mussorgsky who replied: "What you write about Mili, my dear generalissimus (Stassov had just been promoted to a civil service rank equivalent to that of a general in the army) depressed me, even though I did not personally witness his *icification*. Easily impressed as I am, I had the most horrifying vision: your lines sounded to me like a burial service for Mili's artistic ardor—how terrible if that were the truth and not, on his part, simply a mask! It's too soon, *too disgustingly soon*! Or is it disillusionment? But then: where is his courage, and also his awareness of the *cause* and of his artistic aims which can never be achieved without a struggle? Or was art merely a means, instead of an aim?"

Borodin's impressions of Balakirev were equally sorrowful. He paid Balakirev a visit and at first everything seemed as of old: Mili showed great interest in his new symphony, begged him to play all the finished movements, after which, naturally, he also pressed him to change this or change that. And thereby, as usual, he sometimes demanded the exact opposite of what he had so insistently propounded a few months earlier: Themes which he had then urged Borodin to repeat in their entirety, he now advised to restate only in part; tonalities which he himself had then recommended were now suddenly no longer appropriate—in other words, the habitual Balakirev "tricks" over which one could but laugh good-naturedly. Borodin had come, however, not to listen to advice but to recover the score of his *First Symphony,* which Balakirev had never returned to him, allegedly because Nadiezhda Purgold had wanted to write the *Klavierauszug.* Actually, Mili's plans were more ambitious still: he hoped to re-orchestrate it completely, perhaps even to re-write it altogether. The whole score was marked all over with his comments, such as: "double!" or else "give this to the clarinets!" just where, on Mili's earlier insistence, the clarinets had been replaced by the oboes. But Borodin was used to his friend's eccentricities. What he couldn't understand, however, was why Balakirev now so persistently avoided meeting the other members of the group. Why hadn't he even bothered to come to listen to Rimsky-Korsakov's *Fair Maid*, when his favorite pupil's opera was performed for the first time *in extenso* at the Purgolds? What was the matter with him? And Borodin wrote to his wife in Moscow: "Perhaps it's his conceit which is gnawing at him. He is such a despot by nature, that he demands complete subordination even in the most trifling matters. He is quite incapable of understanding and recognizing freedom and equality. He cannot endure the slightest opposition to his tastes and even to his mere whims . . . And yet he realizes full well that we are all now grown up, that we are standing firmly on our own feet and that we no longer need his guidance. This, evidently, vexes him. More than once he has told Liudma Shestakova: 'Why should I listen to their things? They have by now grown so mature that I am no longer necessary to them, they can do without me.' His nature is such that he positively *requires* adolescents around him, over whom he can fuss like a nurse over a child. Meanwhile, his obvious avoidance of the group, his estrangement from them, his asperity of speech, especially when talking about Modest, have caused many sympathies to cool. If he continues in this vein, he may well become isolated and that, for a man in his position, amounts to moral death . . . Even Liudma who used to be able to put him back in the right mood has lost all her influence . . . Stassov cannot forgive Mili his attitude toward the benefit concert for Dargomyzhsky's *Stone Guest* for which all arrangements had been made and which never came off, merely because Mili kept postponing it for no particular reason.

Liudma herself cannot forgive him his incomprehensible indifference toward *Ruslan* when Mili, after talking her into reserving a box especially for him, suddenly decided for no reason at all to hang around at the Zhemchuzhnikovs all evening and did not even attend a subsequent performance. Modinka (Mussorgsky) is hurt by Mili's unfair and high-handed comments about *Boris* . . . Korsinka is offended by his indifference to his *Fair Maid* . . . In the past, Mili would often be the first to show interest in anything new, however unimportant, even in the embryo stage. Be it as it may, the abyss between him and us is growing ever wider."

This estrangement was not the only symptom of the change that had occurred in Mili. One day Borodin heard a terrible rumor: Balakirev had gone mad! He almost believed it. He recalled that Balakirev had once suffered from an inflammation of the brain and that he was constantly complaining about his headaches. And then that incomprehensible bigotry!

For, oddly enough, strong religious feelings were regarded by the intellectuals of that generation as a symptom of insanity. Mili, who was wont to condemn the "mystical strain" in Mussorgsky, was now himself reneging what they considered the only true faith—materialism—and falling a prey to superstition. At first he carefully concealed this; nevertheless on one occasion—*en passant,* and with seeming reluctance—he admitted to Rimsky-Korsakov that he was in the habit of visiting a remarkable fortune-teller. According to rumor, the latter—a brunette, still young, with large dark eyes—was a veritable sorceress. Although fortune-telling was indeed her profession, she seemed to have a somewhat more than purely professional interest in Balakirev. Her technique consisted in looking into a hand-mirror and describing the appearance of the people she saw reflected in it, as well as their feelings and intentions in regard to Balakirev. As all this took place by candlelight, Mili probably saw nothing but diffuse shapes and shadows which he, however, dutifully interpreted in the light of her remarks. "He doesn't believe in God," Rimsky-Korsakov muttered to himself as he listened to this story, "and yet he believes in the Devil!"

But presently Balakirev began to believe in God, too.

When he embarked upon a religious subject, his atheist friends kept as a rule mostly silent. But he sensed, of course, their disapproval. Even Borodin, for all his broadminded tolerance, felt that this "odd and unexpected swing toward the most fantastic, the most naive type of pietism" (as he put it to his wife) was distasteful and indeed intolerable. Stassov, for his part, did not mince his words. Every time he and Balakirev met he would, says Borodin, "blast Mili with unrestrained machine-gun salvos of reproach" contending that all this religious soul-searching was "bunkum"; that he "couldn't understand how an intelligent man like Mili," etc. etc. Which, of course, had merely the effect of scaring Balakirev off even more. He began to seek other company, to associate with another type of people; he got to visiting a priest of the Old Believer sect whom he regarded as a custodian of all that was most pure and beautiful in Russia's cultural and historical heritage. Even more frequent were his visits to Tertzi Ivanovich Filippov, a high official in the Department of State Control and an ardent connoisseur and collector of Russian folk-songs, of which he knew a large number and which he would himself perform in a high falsetto voice. As Filippov was also extremely religious, the two men had much in common. Filippov's house had the atmosphere of peace and serenity which is traditionally associated with devoutly orthodox persons. Oil lamps flickered beneath every ikon, the air seemed fragrant with a peculiar perfume, a combination of incense and cypress-wood, which Mili found ever so agreeable and which had a most soothing effect on him. Everything about this house was enjoyable: the pleasant, mellow, typically Russian features of the host; the fine leather bindings of his books; the tasty meals he served his guests. Presently, Filippov introduced Balakirev to Konstantin Petrovich

Pobiedonostzev, a professor of canon law and tutor to the Czarevich Aleksander (the future Czar Aleksander III). Pobiedonostzev gave an impression that was far from serene and far from soothing. In fact, there was about him a quality of stern fanaticism which is sometimes found among members of the Roman Catholic clergy. He was, however, exceptionally intelligent.

Strangely enough, even Mili's appearance seemed to have changed. He had always looked much older than his years. To think that he was still only 35! But what had happened to his good looks? Now that he had become a little stouter, although his face had remained lean he seemed even smaller than before. His complexion had always been swarthy, but now his expression had become tense, restless, tortured. Even his fine large eyes had lost some of their magnetic fire. He looked positively oriental.

Presently, his friends heard something even more incredible: Mili had given up music altogether and had taken a minor job with the Warsaw Railroad Co. at 80 rubles a month. Moreover he had done this over a year ago, but he lived such a retired life that for a long time nobody was aware of this development.

The surprising thing about it all was that none of those who had been so close to him found the courage, or were sufficiently concerned to try to approach him, to seek to understand what had happened to him, to help him, be it only financially, as he had on one occasion offered to help Mussorgsky when the latter had lost his job. All of them were in one way or another obligated to Mili, he had played a large and beneficent part in their lives, he had in many cases discovered their talents, he had shared with them altruistically all he knew about music and would have been equally prepared to share with them his last piece of bread, if need be. Of course he had in the meantime provoked and offended each one of them in turn. And in the end he himself had chosen to part company with them. And yet would it not have been possible to overcome this feeling of resentment, to knock at the door he had slammed? In this, the most difficult hour of his life, Balakirev found himself absolutely alone.

We shall never know what actually happened to him. None of his letters of this period have come down to us; he kept no diary. There isn't even any circumstantial evidence, any indirect confession, such as is sometimes provided by creative work, for Mili had given up composing. Fortunately —although this was in itself a sign of weakness and contradiction—he had not destroyed his manuscripts but had stacked them away, neatly—as was his wont—in a secret hiding place.

II

If Balakirev's friends knew little—and cared even less— about his inner, spiritual anguish, they knew hardly more about his everyday existence. They knew of course—and they hadn't been overly surprised to hear it—that he had been unable to retain his position as concert manager and conductor of the Imperial Musical Society. For soon after his appointment, and from many quarters at once, an intrigue had been started against him which, in due course, undermined his position.

In many ways, indeed by the very nature of his talent and personality, by his selfless devotion to art and his personal integrity, Balakirev resembled Liszt. But in contrast to the latter he was bad-tempered. With his olympian serenity, showering compliments right and left, Liszt was universally popular. Outspoken and violent, Balakirev caused everywhere a feeling of irritation. With the prudence and thoroughness of a *parvenu,* Liszt was careful to respect the conventions of the Courts and aristocratic circles with which he associated, whereas Balakirev treated the Grand Duchess Elena Pavlovna as he would have treated a choir-girl of his

Free School. The intrigue was bound to succeed all the more easily in that he had revealed himself to be a fairly second-rate conductor and the beautiful programs he chose for his concerts were often so difficult that attendance soon dropped noticeably. Finally, in selecting his friends' compositions for these concerts, he was apt to base his choice on the merits of certain individual passages, rather than on their significance as a whole. Clearly, as it was pointed out to the Grand Duchess, to become a good conductor, it did not suffice to have a good ear, to understand music and to be endowed with Balakirev's many other outstanding musical gifts.

All this provided her with good reasons to part company with a man of his difficult character. At first, however, she attempted to do so amicably: she suggested that he tour Europe on behalf of the I.M.S. and study Western folk-music. But Mili refused haughtily; he did so, moreover, in such rude terms that the old lady was deeply hurt. Then, after openly flouting the views of most of the I.M.S.'s directors and insulting them, he proceeded to alienate also the orchestra. Most of the players were of German origin. He had always been opinionated, violent and exacting. Now, he not only refused to speak to them in their mother-tongue, but kept making puns in rather doubtful taste about an alleged invasion of Russia by the Germans. The Grand Duchess and the directors started looking around for a replacement.

At first their choice fell on a "teuton"—one of Balakirev's pet bogeys, the German Zeifritz, who had just arrived in Russia. But when Berlioz was invited to give his authoritative opinion on the candidate's merits, he immediately smelt a rat and while commenting favorably on Zeifritz's qualifications, heaped praise on Balakirev himself. Zeifritz's candidacy was quietly dropped. But in the spring of 1869, Balakirev was forced to resign and the young Czech Eduard Napravnik was appointed in his place.

This cruel affront did not pass unnoticed. In the Moscow

Russian Gazette Tchaikowsky wrote that, just as the great eighteenth century scientist Lomonosov could not be dispensed with by the Academy of Sciences of his day whereas Lomonosov could afford to dispense with the Academy, similarly Balakirev could not be "dropped" by the Imperial Musical Society. For his part, Nikolai Rubinstein, Anton's brother, demonstratively arrived in St. Petersburg from Moscow in order to conduct, at a concert of the Free School, Balakirev's *Islamey,* a most difficult piece.

Encouraged by the "Muscovites'" support, Balakirev attempted to fight back. Concentrating all his energy on the concerts of the Free School, he began to collect additional funds and to spend even some of his own hard-earned money. But the odds were too uneven. On the one hand, there was the influential Imperial Musical Society, headed by the Grand Duchess, who spared neither effort nor money and who was supported by the bureaucracy, the Court and the press. The Grand Duchess had even donated funds for the founding of a magazine entitled "The Musical Season," edited by the critic Famintzin, one of Balakirev's arch-enemies, the sole purpose of which was to fight the "Balakirev Gang." The generous distribution of free tickets and the invitation of Italian singers to perform the ever-popular light operatic repertoire also worked in favor of the Imperial Musical Society. On the other hand, there was the Free School—penniless, headed by an impractical, idealistic director of unflinching principles—which offered, furthermore, complicated concert programs. To make matters worse, Balakirev was beset by severe financial difficulties and had therefore to devote more and more of his time to giving private lessons.

Under such circumstances, Balakirev was prepared to agree to compromises which had been unthinkable to him in the past. Thus, he decided to perform Mozart's *Requiem* and, through mutual friends, requested the celebrated Adelina Patti (who was singing with the Italian opera of St. Petersburg at the time) to participate. Patti agreed to sing for the

Free School, only not the *Requiem*, but one of her usual lighter repertoires. Whereupon Stassov wrote his friend a sharply worded letter in which he reproached him for betraying his principles, for agreeing to "beg for alms" from a singer whom he admittedly despised. Actually, nothing came of the Patti concert. Then Balakirev thought of organizing a grandiose mass concert *à la* Berlioz in the Imperial Riding School. Authorization, however, was withheld. Neither did a proposed trip to Moscow materialize, at Tchaikovsky's invitation, which, he had hoped, would provide him with an opportunity to give many lessons in that city.

He had always hated to play in public, regarding it as a profanation of something sacred. And yet now he was prepared to do even that. He had been a successful pianist in his youth; since then he had made considerable progress, if not in his technique, then at least in the depth and maturity of his interpretations. He now decided to give a concert— not in St. Petersburg, which was already satiated with foreign virtuosi—but in his birthplace, Niznii-Novgorod where, he hoped, he would be still remembered. He expected to make a thousand rubles in one evening. The concert was a complete flop, however. He played to an empty house (the box-office returns totaled . . . 9 rubles!). For nobody did remember him any more. Those who had known him as a child had either died or left town; the others had, probably— as elsewhere in provincial Russia—no time for music. Years later, as he recalled that awful evening, he was wont to say with a wry smile: "That was my Sedan!"

After that there was no longer any doubt in his mind that "God's blessing" no longer rested on his music. The signs in the sky were clearly visible to all, he might as well bow to the irrevocable and join the ranks of the ordinary men, with their ordinary, day-to-day, humdrum interests and activities. The church taught humility and resignation; very well then, he *would* be humble and resigned, if not immediately and if not forever.

Of all his friends, only Borodin seems to have understood what was happening to his former mentor. Writing to Rimsky-Korsakov, he remarked: "Let us assume that he has not gone out of his mind; but then is his present condition very much better than insanity? The one thing that scares me is the thought that Mili may end up like Gogol. His pietism is most suspect and forebodes no good. Sadder still is his incomprehensible coolness toward all things musical and toward his own interests. What does the future hold in store for him? I hate to think . . ."

In recalling Gogol's example, Borodin had correctly gauged the depth of Balakirev's tragedy. However, Gogol had burned the manuscript of the second volume of his *Lost Souls* only shortly before his death when, like Tolstoy, he had already given up all creative work. Whereas Balakirev was withdrawing from the world of art at the peak of his maturity and talent; he hadn't died, he was merely giving up all that which he loved best for a life which he himself had, until then, condemned with all the verve of a romanticist. It was like the drowning man who, his forces spent, resignedly sinks to the bottom. His case was simpler and, at the same time, more frightening than Gogol's. The annals of art know few like it, with the one exception, perhaps, of Rimbaud, who gave up his poetry and departed for Africa to trade in elephant tusks and hoard money. Rimbaud also gave up; he too became a faithful son of the (Catholic) church. His destiny was even more tragic, it ended in death without a reversal whereas Balakirev returned to his strivings five years later. But nobody could foresee this turn of events: for all the world, his withdrawal was for good.

Of course, in all this, his financial difficulties played their part. For how could they have been solved by the 80 odd rubles he was now earning doing a job that took up all of his time? True, the money came in regularly, not like the pay for his lessons. He himself claimed that he did not wish to "profanate" music any more, to turn it into a means of livelihood. He wished to perform music for its own sake. But he seemed to want to get away from music for other reasons too, as can be seen from the following episode:

When his Moscow friends heard of his predicament, Tchaikovsky and Nikolai Rubinstein were genuinely alarmed. Russian Art could not afford to lose one of its major and most worthy representatives. Rubinstein offered Balakirev a professorship at his Moscow Conservatory at a salary of 3.000 rubles a year. Deeply touched, Mili thanked him effusively but declined the offer. He didn't have enough knowledge of musical theory, he said; his knowledge of composition was purely empirical, he could not teach others. As if he had been doing anything else all his life! Of course, to accept a professorship in a conservatory the teaching methods of which he had fought tooth and nail for years would have been tantamount to betraying all he stood for. Yet, not many people are capable of remaining faithful to their principles under such difficult circumstances.

The Moscow music critic Kashkin, a friend of Tchaikovsky's and Rubinstein's, obtained at last an interview with the voluntary recluse. Balakirev received him in his tiny flat, filled with dogs, cats and ikons. He carefully avoided mentioning any of the more painful subjects, and this gave the whole interview a rather strained and unreal character. Nevertheless, Kashkin sensed in him a profound though carefully concealed feeling of despair. This man obviously had been desperately hurt.

It is perhaps because of the compassion and sympathy displayed by his Moscow friends in these difficult times that Balakirev was always to feel more kindly toward them than toward his St. Petersburg comrades.

CHAPTER THIRTEEN

THE DECLINE
(Mussorgsky after "Boris")

*"Farewell, a long farewell to
all my greatness."*

SHAKESPEARE

I

Maybe it was inevitable; maybe it was merely the result
of fortuitous circumstances: the fact is that Balakirev's withdrawal caused irreparable damage to his "gang." Like a flock
forsaken by its shepherd, the latter now started to split up
and scatter.

The more sensitive members had begun to notice this
early. Already in July 1872, Mussorgsky had written to Liudmila Ivanovna Shestakova: "The past of the group is bright;
its present is overcast: gloomy days have set in. I am not
accusing any of its members, for there is no malice in my
heart; but being a good-natured humorist at heart, I cannot
help characterizing the group with a quotation from Gri-
boyedov: 'some have dropped out; others, see, are slaugh-
tered.'... Try as I may to drive away the tiresome fly which
keeps importuning me with the expression 'fallen apart,' the
fly stays right there, buzzing away, as though there were
laughter, evil laughter in that buzzing. It is up to you, my
little dove, to gather together again the remnants of the shattered, scared host!" And yet, two years after these lines were
written, Mussorgsky was dedicating his *Boris Godunov* to the
members of the very group he claimed had "fallen apart."
It is apparently easier to diagnose the symptoms of decay
than to part, once and for all, with something that is dear and
close to one's heart!

Strangely enough, it was only after the "Balakirev Gang" had begun to decline that its existence came to be realized, not only in Russia itself but also abroad. In the West, Liszt had been the first to point to them as a new phenomenon in music. He had always been unusually receptive to, and inquisitive about anything that was new in art. The works of the German composers with which his music stands were littered, no longer gave him satisfaction,—with the one exception, of course, of the great Richard. He had seen the score of Borodin's *First Symphony*. The publisher Bessel had also sent him copies of Mussorgsky's *Nursery* and Rimsky-Korsakov's *Antar*. Liszt was a man of impeccable taste; moreover, all these young Russians were pupils of his old friend Glinka, besides being ardent admirers of Liszt himself. He was soon quite won over.

Their own recognition of the Master had come slowly; now it became enthusiastic. Mussorgsky especially was thrilled when Bessel's brother, who had visited Liszt in Weimar, told him that the great man was quite taken by his *Nursery,* that he wished to make a piano transcription of one number and to dedicate to its author one of his own little pieces, a trifle, *"une bluette"*! One of Liszt's lady admirers by the name of Adelaide von Schorn, who performed the functions of a secretary, described in detail, in a letter to Bessel, the Master's reaction to the piece: Liszt was moved and even overwhelmed, although he was shocked by Mussorgsky's lack of taste and contempt of form . . . "How new!" he kept repeating, "How ingenious!" Having finished playing it, she wrote, Liszt "pounced like a lion upon his pen and then and there wrote Mr. Mussorgsky a letter, describing his feelings and impressions. I mailed the letter myself." Alas, the letter never reached its destination. Neither did Liszt make the promised piano transcription or dedicate a *"bluette"* to the young Russian composer. Mussorgsky was, nevertheless, elated. "If this is true," he wrote Stassov, "if he was not simply carried away by his own enthusiasm, then Liszt's wide range amazes me, it is incredible! I may be a fool in music, but in the *Nursery,* I think I was *not* a fool, for my understanding of children and my concept of them as people living in a small world of their own and not merely as entertaining dolls, is certainly not a sign of foolishness on the author's part. Be this as it may: I never expected that Liszt who, with very few exceptions, likes to choose gigantic themes, would understand and appreciate my *Nursery* and even be enthusiastic about it; after all, the kids in it are Russian kids, with powerful native undertones. I wonder what Liszt will say or think when he sees *Boris,* even if only in its piano transcription! Lucky are the Russian musicians to obtain recognition from such an ace as Liszt!" And he added: "God grant him many more years of life, and perhaps, when it becomes possible, I will go over to Europe to see him and entertain him with the latest news, but only together with you, generalissimus, not otherwise! For the present, however, I am condemned to wither away and grow sour among the Chaldeans."

Stassov was quite carried away by this idea of visiting Liszt and didn't wish to put it off. He even offered to pay for Mussorgsky's expenses. But the latter wouldn't hear of it; he claimed that he had too much work at the office; that he couldn't "intrigue against his own chief," who was allegedly suffering from some eye disease. "When you see Liszt," he said to Stassov in another letter, "I would like to ask you, my dear, to hand him a little note, but then this may look bad; for one thing, what shall I say to him in that note? Besides, have I the right to act like this? Silence! Silence, as if I were some sort of a Trappist monk! However, I believe in my star; it cannot be that I shall never cast eyes on the men of Europe. But if I don't—we will endure that, too, just as we are doing now." And all of a sudden he voices admiration for Europe; a surprising thing on the part of a Russian nationalist: "If in Petrograd, on a soil built up of decayed human corpses, there glimmers from time to time a sensible thought, if something boils over inside and the dozing All-

Russian creative spirit awakens, I wonder what the aspect
of Europe may be?" And he goes on to claim that "the mystical picture of the *Dance of Death* could only have been conceived by a Liszt" and that "this daring European has proven
the kinship of piano and orchestra. Just as the colossal *Te
Deum* (which compares to Beethoven's enormous second
mass as St. Peter's in Rome compares to our own cathedral
of St. Isaac) could only have been conceived in the mind of
that other daring European: Berlioz."

II

Liszt's recognition meant a great deal to the "Balakirev
Gang" (they even sent him an enthusiastic collective telegram
on the occasion of his sixtieth birthday), but more important,
even in Russia the new composers were beginning to attract
notice, however hostile.

One of the first to honor them with his unfriendly attention was the great novelist Ivan Sergheyevich Turgenev. The
latter visited Russia but rarely; whenever he returned there
from his voluntary exile abroad, however, he deemed it his
duty to study and take note of "the latest trends." He
regarded himself as an expert and a connoisseur of music;
indeed, due to his intimate friendship with Pauline Viardot,
he associated a good deal with musical circles. He now proceeded to sum up the musical situation in Russia. He had
from the outset been prejudiced against the "Mighty Handful," be it only because it was Vladimir Stassov's "baby." For
he considered Stassov a pleasant and even talented, but unin-
telligent man, who epitomized that hated Slavophile pride
in the field of art. Turgenev even wrote a "poem in prose,"
in which he said that one could do anything in the world
except argue with Vladimir Stassov. This statement did not
prevent him from arguing with Stassov, in his high falsetto
voice, for hours on end. During one of these arguments, he

fell suddenly silent, whereupon Stassov exclaimed joyfully: "There, Ivan Sergheyevich, you see? You yourself agree with me!" Turgenev replied: "If ever you catch me agreeing with you, open the window and call the police, for it will mean that I have gone crazy!"

In his novel *Smoke,* one can find echoes of these arguments in the words of Potughin: "Not only Meyerbeer, but the last German flutist, modestly piping his tune in the most humble German orchestra, has twenty times more ideas than all your Russian so-called self-made 'talents'." Turgenev claimed that Mussorgsky and "those other 'Handful' Boys" would be "more thoroughly forgotten fifteen years hence, then the Egyptian pharaoh Rameses XXIX." Who could have foretold that barely half a century later, the fame of these "Handful Boys" would exceed his own, and this in his beloved Western Europe, of all places! However, as he was a highly conscientious writer, he expressed the desire to make the "Rameses'" acquaintance. The meeting was to take place in Dimitri Stassov's apartment, but the Group's feelings had been hurt by Turgenev and they never showed up.

The great satirist Saltykov-Shchedrin also deemed it appropriate to take note of this novel phenomenon. In a bitter and rude little sketch, he pictured Stassov as the critic Neuvazhai-Koryto (which, translated literally, means "A rut lacking respect"). The latter was, in Saltykov-Shchedrin's words, not a musician but "an instigator, a firebrand and a receiver of stolen goods." Mussorgsky was referred to as "Vassili Ivanovich," who never appears in person in the sketch, but merely sits next door, playing the piano against the background of Neuvazhai-Koryto's enthusiastic exclamations: "Vassili Ivanovich drums something on the bass notes and then suddenly hits the trebles. 'That's the children's nanny!'—Neuvazhai-Koryto whispers, 'she's arguing with Nadenka . . . Ah! And there's Nastenka!'—'How do you know it is Nastenka?'—'How do I know? Why, because

Nastenka's tonality in in E major, while Nadenka's is in F
major!'" All this, though quite witty, was unworthy of
Saltykov-Shchedrin.

III

About this time, also, fate put the musicians of the "Handful" in touch with one who, in the history of Russian music
has come into his own as their most successful rival: Piotr
Iliich Tchaikovsky, Professor at the Moscow Conservatory.
Tchaikovsky had long been hostile to Balakirev and his
"eaglets"; their music and their ideology were all too alien
to this former pupil of Anton Rubinstein's and present friend
and colleague of Anton's brother Nikolai. Moreover, Tchaikovsky suffered from a curious trait: He always suspected new
acquaintances of personal hostility toward him and his art
and hated them, as it were, in advance; though he had only
to get to know these newcomers a little better and to convince himself that his first suspicions were unjustified, for
his attitude to soften and his hatred to change to sympathy.
In this particular case, his suspicion that Balakirev and
his group hated and despised him were not completely un-
unfounded. With his usual lack of critical intuition, Cui had
on one occasion even labeled Tchaikovsky a "musical non-
entity"! The tense situation showed when Balakirev asked
for the dances from his opera, *The Voyevoda* for a concert
of the Imperial Musical Society, and Tchaikovsky reacted
coldly and demanded an official request from the Society's
Board of Directors. But when the request came, he softened,
agreed to lend his piece for the performance and even
begged Balakirev for "encouragement." The latter answered
him with his usual curtness: Only a tenderfoot needed encouragement, he said, not mature artists like Tchaikovsky
who, on the contrary, needed severe criticism. Whereupon
Tchaikovsky's heart melted.
This was the starting point of a friendship which was to

grow over the years, but which was nevertheless always to bear that touch of strain which characterizes the relationship between two hostile commanding generals during a truce. Balakirev fell literally in love with Tchaikovsky. He suspected that this young, subtle, sad and elegant young man was immensely talented (unlike Cui, Balakirev was rarely mistaken). He was also, perhaps, attracted toward him because of Tchaikovsky's notorious perversity. (In Mili, these same tendencies had remained *in statu nascendi*.) There may even have been involved some tactical considerations: Tchaikovsky looked as soft and as malleable as wax; how wonderful, indeed what a triumph it would be if he could succeed in molding this wax according to his own fancy, in making a disciple of Tchaikovsky, in getting him to join the "Balakirev Gang"!

And yet in this "romance" it was Balakirev who was to be the more loving, the more devoted of the two partners. Tchaikovsky was of course grateful to Mili for his recognition, his appreciation, his kindness. He valued highly Mili's intelligence and talent, even though he regarded him as "the originator of all the bizarre theories of this strange group." But he never really loved him. Tchaikovsky was, to say the least, eclectic in the choice of friends. These included for instance, the critic Hermann Laroche (whose intolerance in terms of musical taste and whose violence were worthy of the "Gang") as well as the despotic Nikolai Rubinstein and the half-wit Bochkariov. Yet, something in Balakirev irritated and indeed repelled him. "He is a most kind-hearted man and seems well-disposed toward me," Tchaikovsky wrote his younger brother Anatoli, "but for some reason I do not seem able to put my life and soul into our friendship. He demands that I spend the whole day in his company and that bores me. Neither can I say that I like the exclusiveness of his opinions on music or the violence of his expressions."

However, for several years Tchaikovsky was, or seemed to have become, one of Balakirev's pupils. It was Balakirev who

gave him the idea of writing an overture on the subject of
Romeo and Juliet. Mili didn't know too much about literature, but what he knew, he knew well; he rightly guessed
(as in the case of his own "eaglets") that Tchaikovsky would
find inspiration in this story (as he was to be inspired, later
on, by another Balakirev "find"—*Manfred*). Tchaikovsky
even turned to Stassov for a subject for a symphony and the
latter recommended Shakespeare's *Tempest*. In his criticism
of Tchaikovsky's work, however, Balakirev was as severe and
as objective as he was with all his friends, but Tchaikovsky
understood that this was the criticism of a friend and therefore endured it with patience. Balakirev was particularly
merciless about Tchaikovsky's symphonic poem *Fatum*. He
called it a "ragged blanket" and claimed that it had been a
flop with the public (though he himself had conducted it)
because the composer was ignorant of the contemporary
music of Liszt, Berlioz and the others. To which Tchaikovsky
answered meekly: "I admit that I wasn't elated by your comments, but I wasn't in the least hurt and I pay tribute,
mentally, to the sincerity and candor which are among the
most attractive traits of your musical personality."

By now Tchaikovsky had made his peace with the other
members of the "Balakirev Gang"—"that Jacobin Group"
(as he called it). He regarded Rimsky-Korsakov as a serious
and erudite musician. Borodin he also liked very much
though more as a human being than as a composer. He was
inclined to despise Cui, despite the latter's good points. Only
one member of the group genuinely disturbed him, both as
a person and in terms of art, namely Mussorgsky.

Tchaikovsky was under the impression that because of an
innate boorishness, Modest took pleasure in "wallowing in
dirt," in art as in his everyday life. The man, admittedly,
had talent, but his was a brutish, lowly talent. Mussorgsky
was in a word a sort of musical Caliban. Hence whenever they
met, they clashed.

One day, Mussorgsky happened upon Tchaikovsky at the

music editor Bessel's. "Beauty," Tchaikovsky began, "unmistakable, unqualified musical beauty! Everything should
be sacrificed to that demand! One should continue to study,
to perfect the form; one should study the classics and especially the divine Mozart. Dilettantism bodes no good!"
Which was not very tactful; most of his new friends realized
only too well that this was a stone cast in their direction. But
Mussorgsky was just as passionate and violent; speaking,
allegedly, of Saint-Saëns (though it was pretty obvious that
he was actually referring to Tchaikovsky himself) he countered: "I despise those votaries of absolute beauty who utilize
miniature chamber orchestras in order to dress up puny little
thoughts in rich orchestral robes. It's not merely music that
we need, or words, or palette or chisel, no! Give us live
thoughts, live conversation! You can't get away with nothing
but pretty little sounds!"

Even physically they were in complete contrast. Though
they were of the same age and came from the same *milieu*;
though both of them looked older than their young years
and showed a tendency toward stoutness, there was about
Tchaikovsky's features, indeed about his whole appearance,
something ever so elegant, a trifle melancholic even. His
manner was simple and full of charm, he was delightfully
polite. Whereas Modest (although his manners were still
good) seemed truly to take pride in talking with marked
affectation and brutal irony.

And yet, both of them should have realized that they were,
fundamentally, "birds of a feather," that among contemporary Russian composers, they alone resembled one another;
that they had merely been fooled by their habits, their environment, their past. But then how could Tchaikovsky
admit that of all the musicians of this "strange group" (as he
called them), he himself was closest, not to the musical
"gourmet" Rimsky-Korsakov with his marvellous Oriental-
Russian embroidered carpets; nor to the epic Borodin, but
to this slightly ridiculous, ever viperous, eternal student

Mussorgsky, with his puns and mannerisms. And how could Mussorgsky admit that the highly polished Tchaikovsky would one day overwhelm Russian—and not only Russian—audiences, not with his elegant, melancholic *Autumn Songs,* but with terrifying, *Boris*-like sounds, wrenched from the depths of an anguished soul.

These sounds, beneath which could be sensed "the stirrings of chaos," were quite alien to the other Russian musicians of the day. Only these two men—so different, so hostile to one another—knew their meaning.

IV

Upon completing *Boris,* Mussorgsky did not rest on his laurels. Stassov immediately suggested that he write another historical opera and pointed to the beginnings of the reign of Peter the Great as a fateful moment in Russian history when the country—under the tyrant's leadership—broke with revolutionary ardor with its past. Those were indeed picturesque, terrible, bloody times. One of its most colorful episodes was the mutiny of the *Streltzi* (the Czar's praetorian guard of musketeers) under Prince Khovansky in favor of the young Czar's sister Sofia, a mutiny which was suppressed amidst terrible reprisals. The spiritual force behind this mutiny was provided by the so-called Old Believers, a dissident orthodox sect, which claimed to uphold "the true faith" against "Peter the Antichrist." Following their defeat, many thousands of them burnt themselves alive rather than submit to the victorious young Czar. Stassov provided his friend with a whole pile of books on seventeenth-century Russia.

Mussorgsky was immediately carried away by the subject. He sensed that these past events were not completely dead, that certain features were still alive even now, in the Russia of his day, and he set down his thoughts in a remarkable letter to Stassov: "The power of the *chernoziom* (the Russian black earth) will soon become manifest, as long as you plow it up from the very bottom. This was done at the end of the seventeenth century, with implements made of alien materials. Mother Russia did not immediately realize what these were and that the *chernoziom* had opened up and begun to breathe." Mussorgsky felt that the very same thing was happening in contemporary nineteenth-century Russia, that the Russian people "were groaning and so as not to groan, were drinking themselves silly, only to groan the more," for "officialdom is alive as ever and the search is continuing; except that times have changed: the 'actual' and 'secret' councilors' are preventing the *chernoziom* from breathing."

As he plunged into the reading of the sources, of the "grass roots" (as he called it) he discovered many a gem, which he noted down in a copybook dedicated to "Vladimir Vassilievich Stassov, whose love inspired this humble work." The first page carried the heading: *Khovanshchina, a people's musical drama in five parts.*

Actually, there was as yet no opera to dedicate; it was all still a dream, and this bothered him somewhat. But his doubts were soon dispelled. "It is of no concern to me, it need be of no concern to me," he wrote, "if there exist no precedents for the dedication of an as yet nonexistent work" and he found a clever way out of his predicament: he would dedicate to Stassov not the work, but its author, i.e. himself. "I dedicate to you that period of my life which will be devoted to writing *Khovanshchina*; there will be nothing peculiar if I say: 'I dedicate to you both myself and my life for this period . . . For a new work, *your* work is about to be started, I'm already beginning to live it . . .'"

The reason for this haste in dedicating a nonexistent piece may also have been that deep down in his heart he knew that the culminating point in his life had been reached, that he had topped the crest, that he was walking toward the sunset and would, maybe, never finish this new opera. He was only 33 years old; he had, it would seem, many more years of work ahead of him; but in fact his strength was ebbing.

It was Stassov who planned *Khovanshchina's* libretto. The action was to revolve around an imaginary old hermit, Diosifei (formerly Prince Sitzky), a leader of the Old Believers and a man of extraordinary spiritual strength who was to be modeled after the celebrated Archpriest Avvakum. Diosifei it was who inspired the two Princes Khovansky to rebel. These Princes Khovansky—father and son—were typical representatives of the darker, more unpredictable forces at play in ancient Muscovy. Both of them were rather unpleasant characters, the father an arrogant and petty tyrant, while the son was perverse and insignificant. In contrast to them, Mussorgsky proposed to depict yet another prominent personality of the period, Prince Golitzin, the lover of Czar Peter's sister Sofia and a partisan of reform. The action was to take place in the so-called "German" or foreign settlement in Moscow, on the Khovansky country estate and in the forest, among the fugitive Old Believers. Stassov sketched also two feminine roles, those of Marfa and Suzanna, who are both in love with young Andrei Khovansky and therefore jealous of one another. The opera was to end after the mutiny's failure with the mass self-cremation of the Old Believers, led by Diosifei.

Modest went to work with a will. But although he claimed that *Khovanshchina* was "cooking" just as *Boris* had "cooked" before, in fact his progress was slow. Not that his talent had failed; far from it. In fact, all he now wrote showed that it was as great as ever. Moreover, there was now none of the frightened tension which had characterized his work on *Boris*. Mussorgsky had assigned himself this time a different task; and he was solving it differently. If the over-all picture was perhaps not as impressionistically bright, the colors, for their part, were purer and deeper. Besides, its whole rhythm was different: it was more classical, the melodies were better rounded off, the contours were softened. But the extraordinary vigor of human passions and personality traits, the amazing mastery of the historical brush-work, were as great as ever. Mussorgsky's weariness showed itself more in the pace of his work than in the quality.

And yet by the summer of 1873 already, his new opera had assumed concrete form (if not on paper, then at least in his head). "The introduction," he wrote to Stassov, "the dawn in Moscow, the matins at cockcrow, the patrol of the Bailiff's men, and the removal of the street chains as well as the opening bars of the action are ready, though not written . . . There's also another good device, bearing some resemblance to the truth: the Old-Believer girl, being madly in love with young Andrei Khovansky, exorcises him in her forest retreat with the spell of the 'wild wind' . . . Sensing that the time has come to prepare herself for death, her voice pierces through the stage action and the orchestra with the desperate cry: 'Death is coming!' The Old Believers, dressed in shrouds and holding green tapers in their hands, come out of the forest, ready for self-cremation . . ."

In another letter to Stassov, he gives further details: "The Old-Believer girl, your favorite, is so good, ai! ai! ai! . . . No matter to whom I show the burial scene, their eyes pop, it is such an unprecedented thing; it's the death sentence of a loving, deserted woman . . . The Old-Believer girl taunts Andrei claiming that the German girl (Susanna) does not love him and, chanting *Alleluia*, she circles about him, a green taper in her hand . . . On the love theme of the incantation, she sings to him: *Your mortal hour has come, dear one; embrace me for the last time; you are beloved by me unto the very grave; to die with you is like to sweetly sleep, Alleluia!*"

His listeners' eyes had good reason to pop, for this incantation scene in *Khovanshchina* is indeed conceived with faultless dramatic intuition. Then, by way of contrast to ancient, pre-reform, Old-Believer Russia, and as a symbol of victory of Peter's New Russia, Mussorgsky brought onto

the stage a squad of *Preobrazhensky* Foot Guards who had
come to arrest the Old Believers and their march music, or—
as Mussorgsky himself called it—"Peter's theme," effectively
cuts in on the Old-Believers' wailing.

Meanwhile, the seventeenth-century atmosphere in which
he lived was beginning to tell even on his conversation and
his style of writing. Already before that, because of his
natural tendency toward a highfalutin and ornate manner
of speech, he liked to use a pseudo-folksy Russian language,
like that of the medieval chronicles. His association with old
Professor Nikolsky, had taught him the use of fanciful slav-
isms. Now he kept reverting to the gauche terminology of
ancient Muscovy.

Not only in his letters, but in Mussorgsky's whole behavior
one could note a change. New friends appeared. Closest to
him now was a young poet, Count Arseni Arkadievich
Golenishchev-Kutuzov who was quite a gifted man, but
whose talent Mussorgsky greatly exaggerated. He even hoped
that Stassov would agree to add Kutuzov to his famed "trio,"
claiming that there hadn't been such a poet in Russia since
the deaths of Pushkin and Lermontov. "Here is no synthetic
poet like Nekrasov," he wrote Stassov, "neither does he suffer
in his production from the labor pains of a (Lev) Mey.
Kutuzov's personality can be compared to the freshness of a
warm summer morning. Besides, he has an incomparable
technique." He praised in Kutuzov the latter's "aristocratic
mind," his severity toward himself, the fact that there was
a "built-in critic" as Balakirev used to call it. All these
exaggerations made the soundness of Mussorgsky's critical
judgment questionable.

V

Besides his artistic triumphs and disasters, Mussorgsky had
suffered during these years much personal sorrow. First sudden death had come to one of his closest friends, the architect

and water color painter Victor Hartmann. His passing was
the first real personal loss since the death of his mother.

Hartmann lived in Moscow and was only an occasional
visitor in St. Petersburg. Both Mussorgsky and Stassov had
always greatly exaggerated his significance as an artist. Besides their feeling of friendship for him, they had appreciated
the fact that Hartmann, though a Jew, was as much a Slavophil at heart as they were themselves. Actually, in formu-
lating Hartmann's alleged esthetical objectives, Mussorgsky
voiced sound views on architecture which, however, had little
in common with the sugary art of his late friend: "Pictorial
art," he said, "should not evoke merely beauty; a building
is only good when, in addition to its handsome façade, it is
solid and well-planned; when you can sense the purpose for
which it was built and perceive the artist's aim." With these
words, he anticipated the theories of the modern French
school of architecture by nearly half a century.

Modest didn't react to this death right away. Only a year
later, on the occasion of a memorial exhibition of Hartmann's water colors (which were, as indicated, of a rather
doubtful quality) he felt a sudden, magic, blinding flash of
inspiration: He would honor the dead artist's memory by
composing a series of musical evocations of his paintings.
This intuition became his now famous *Pictures at an Exhibition*.

He thus reverted, once again, to his concept of a realistic
figurative music for the piano, a medium less well adapted
to such experiments than, say, vocal music. The solving of
this problem was made somewhat easier by the fact that
Hartmann's water colors had both movement and rhythm, in
other words they possessed those elements which are most
easy to evoke in music. Some of them had children playing,
in others birds chirped, in others still a cart creaked by . . .
The exhibition was held in January 1874, but for some reason Mussorgsky started work only in June. His progress,
however, was unusually rapid. "Hartmann is 'cooking' just

as *Boris* used to 'cook,' " he wrote Stassov. "Sounds and thoughts hang suspended in mid-air, I swallow, I dine, I find barely enough time to scribble away on the paper." This time, fortunately, the "cooking" was not a mere verbal exaggeration as in the case of *Khovanshchina*. The work was dedicated to his "dear generalissimus" Stassov, who had organized the exhibition.

The first picture evokes the composer himself as he walks about the galleries and is entitled *Promenade*. This theme also serves as an interlude, connecting the various other pictures: Mussorgsky wanders about from room to room, now slowing down as he approaches a particular exhibit or reminisces about his late friend, then again hastening his steps. This changing rhythm is delightfully effective. In the second picture, entitled *The Gnome*, there is an evocation of movement but it is not the leisurely walk of the composer, but the rapid, hoppity-skip of some sort of fantastic, fairy-tale creature. This too, is a very successful scene. The third episode, *Le Jardin du Luxembourg* evokes by means of whimsical and changing rhythms the playing and squabbling of children. There is a charming ballet scene of unhatched chicks, followed by the exceptionally poetical scene with the farm cart, where the basses evoke the slowly creeping wheels and the driver cuts in with his merry song. Then there is the amusing scene of two Jews arguing, one of them wealthy and pompous and barking away like a bulldog, the other poor and cringing before him in a plaintive treble. In fact, nearly all of these *Pictures at an Exhibition* are good and they have remained popular with pianists to this day.

The text which accompanied the composition seemed to echo that "mystical strain" which Balakirev had noted in him in much earlier years, but which had seemed long dead. Quoting (not without errors) the Latin saying *de mortuis in lingua mortua,* he added: "The late Hartmann's creative spirit guides me; it evokes the vision of skulls and the skulls light up quietly."

He had barely completed this composition *in memoriam,* when he suffered yet another loss. Nadiezhda Petrovna Opochinina died in June 1874. His comment upon her death took the form of a poem in prose, which he planned as an epitaph. It began with the words: "Oh cruel death!" but broke off almost immediately afterwards: "No, I haven't the strength to continue!"

From that moment was to date his growing interest in the subject of death. It was then that he conceived those weird, frightening, wonderful *Songs and Dances of Death* to words of Golenishchev-Kutuzov, which will probably never lose anything of their eery power.

The first number of this cycle, entitled *The Forgotten One,* was inspired by a picture he had seen at an exhibition of Vereschaghin's paintings: A woman sits and rocks her baby in its crib and sings to it quietly about how the father—who is away at the wars—will come back presently and she will bake a cake for him. But the father has died long ago and is lying "alone . . . forgotten . . ."

While he was writing these *Songs and Dances of Death,* he worked on still another cycle of songs, also rooted in the innermost mystical sanctuaries of his soul. These songs went virtually unnoticed by the public and disappointed even his friends. To them, Mussorgsky's personality was uncomplicated and clear: he was a realist who sang about the poor and the destitute of this world. They did not realize that there existed yet another Mussorgsky, the lyrical singer of the night, of abandonment, of solitude. They shrugged their shoulders in irritation and passed by that other Mussorgsky; even Stassov, who claimed to know him so well, even Borodin.

This cycle of five songs, written again to Golenishchev-Kutuzov's words and which he entitled *Of the Shadows,* stands as a thing apart from Mussorgsky's other works, both because of its depth of feeling and of the brilliant cleverness of its harmony. The words are of no great interest, but they probably suited the composer's mood of the moment, for he made them sound so tragic, that they evoke the image of an aging Rembrandt or that of an already insane Van Gogh and perhaps also, the sorrow and grief that was haunting his distinguished-looking and melancholic contemporary—Piotr Iliich Tchaikovsky.

CHAPTER FOURTEEN

THE END OF MUSSORGSKY

*"Tel qu'en lui-même enfin
l'éternité le change."*

*(Only in eternity did he be-
come, at last, himself.)*

MALLARMÉ

I

Life had done something cruel—it had turned a musician
of genius into an inveterate drunkard.

This cannot be imputed exclusively to Mussorgsky's weakness of character. For though he was not a strong-willed
man, he was steadfast in his loyalty to his ideals and tireless
in his efforts on their behalf. There must therefore be another explanation for this disease which seems to have
plagued so many Russian men of talent. Perhaps it was a sort
of a "non-acceptance" of life. Having set themselves the un-
attainable as an objective, having sought oblivion and illusory happiness, they eventually awakened to the futility
of their dreams and destroyed themselves.

Within the few years that followed *Boris,* Mussorgsky
changed even physically. He grew stouter and more ungainly;
his voice thickened and his nose was now the color of a ripe
plum. His elocution became more elaborate and confused.
As long as he was sober, he retained his natural elegance of
manner, but as soon as he lapsed into one of his "spells" he
became cantankerous and arrogant, got into brawls in public
places, quarrelled with servants and waiters for preferential
treatment and was obnoxious to a high degree.

Shunning solitude and craving company, he had taken a
liking to suburban wine-gardens, night-spots and pubs. His
favorite haunt was at the sign of *Malo-Yaroslavetz* on Greater

Morskaya street, where everyone knew him and where he always could find a crony to listen to his soliloquies on art, interjected with the usual battle-cries: "Forward!" "Dare!" "Onward to uncharted shores!" Here, the landlord and waiters treated him with respectful familiarity, whispering into the ears of newcomers: "Yes-SIR . . . A MOST celebrated composer! . . . His opera is being played at the Mariinsky Theatre! . . ." Here he was able, literally, to souse himself in brandy in the congenial company of part-time bit players, circus "artists," bookies and jockeys. Occasionally people of a more exalted rank would drop in—the celebrated raconteur Gorbunov; Maksimov, the author of a classical study on the penal settlements of Siberia, or the brothers Zhemchuzhnikov. But the "select" crowd drank no less than the others and time and again Mussorgsky could be found in their midst, completely intoxicated.

Had his spells of drunkenness been more frequent, life with him would have become quite impossible. But as it was, even the somewhat foppish Golenishchev-Kutuzov was able to put up with him. First they shared the same boarding-house, later they moved into the Count's own apartment —all in all they roomed together for three years.

Mussorgsky loved him as he loved few people in his life, and when Kutuzov decided to get married, he flew into a jealous rage and sought consolation for this "affront" (as he termed it) from Stassov: "The poor boy has gotten all mixed up!" he spluttered "He wants to get married! And this is not just a passing fancy, no! The real thing, with all the trimmings! There's another fool for you! I really gave him a piece of my mind!" Like Stassov, Mussorgsky was opposed to marriage for artists, on principle; he claimed that were it ever to be learned that he too was contemplating such a step, this would mean that he had gone crazy. He soon reconciled himself to the situation however, and even became a friend of the young Countess. In fact, not the poet's marriage, but something much less important put an end to their life under the same roof.

One evening in August 1876, Mussorgsky returned home late to find the entrance door locked with no one to answer the bell—Kutuzov having gone away on a trip and absent-mindedly taken the key with him. At first Mussorgsky roamed the waterfront of the Neva for hours; then, like Pushkin's Evgheni Onieghin, he sat down to rest on one of the stone lions guarding the entrance of a nobleman's mansion and here, all of a sudden, a happy thought struck him; just across the river, on Vassilievsky Island, there lived one of his oldest and dearest friends, Pavel Naumov; he would go and visit him!

There are not many houses that are prepared to open their doors to chance guests at all hours of the night. But Naumov's was one of them. However late the hour, you could "head for his beacon," as the Russian saying goes, and stand a fair chance of finding him up and about, sipping a glass of wine with a friend. And if he happened to be already asleep—you just woke him up.

Mussorgsky was not mistaken. Despite the late hour he was warmly welcomed; an emergency bed was made up for him on a little red parlor couch and this, although he had originally come to spend only one night, became his home for years.

Naumov was a witty and merry man who, though considered an artist, wielded his brush but rarely, and whose kinship with the artistic world was due, no doubt, primarily to his marked preference for the bohemian way of life. In his own words, he was a "good-for-nothing" who enjoyed the good things of life and knew how to go about it. He had already expended two fortunes, his own and his wife's, as well as the considerable wealth of a sister-in-law with whom, upon parting with his wife, he now lived maritally. A grown-up son, *"Sergushok,"* lived with them. The whole family treated Mussorgsky with loving respect, took good care of him and

Modest was certainly thoroughly happy in their midst. Moreover, he liked Vassilievsky Island with its masses of green foliage, the garden about the house, the broad avenues, the proximity of the Neva—all of which was almost as nice as living in the country.

The Naumovs spent the summers in Czarskoye-Selo, where their guest usually accompanied them. "Country life," he wrote from there, "is wonderful . . . The trees come up to your windows and their branches whisper things—what? I know not, but it must be something good . . . If the body holds out and, God willing, the mind is at rest, my opera *Khovanshchina* may well not refuse me its favors much longer. Last night I hardly slept a wink from the novelty of it all. The utter quietness, broken only by the occasional bugle of the signal-man down at the railroad crossing as he operates his switches or by the dutiful barking of watchdogs. And then, like the *glissando* of a harp, the drowsy rustling of the leaves . . . The moon comes stealing up through the foliage to your pillow ever so quietly, ever so tenderly . . . If God wills it I may, in the midst of all these kind and good friends, be able to do all that I am so very eager to do . . ."

What a poetical description for one who was wont to be so stingy in his musical evocations of nature. As for his "kind and good friends," despite this pastoral picture they were able apparently, to provide him with anything but quietness and tranquility, which is what a composer needs most. All around him life throbbed, merry, noisy or in his own words: "visitors, endless talks, occasionally music and every type of news, rumor, gossip . . . We live, we breathe, we work!"

His former friends viewed the new ones with suspicion, fearing their bad influence. But these fears were uncalled-for. At least they couldn't be accused of encouraging his drunkenness, for neither the Naumovs themselves nor their friends drank much. For his part, Mussorgsky did his best to dispel the old friends' hostility by playing on their weaknesses. Thus to Mrs. Shestakova, Glinka's sister, he hastened

to describe Naumov's enthusiasm while listening to her letters which Mussorgsky had read aloud to him: Naumov kept
pacing back and forth and exclaiming: "But how good she
is! But how kind she is!" Stassov, on the other hand, he tried
to placate by stressing the interest which Naumov took in the
latter's beloved Public Library. Modest even begged Stassov
to show "the building of Minerva" as he cryptically called it,
to "the family which has taken this sinner to its bosom." But
their suspicions and hostility were not easily lulled.

Actually, of all his former friends, only Stassov's and Mrs.
Shestakova's opinions were by now of any importance to him.
With them he still felt good, for he sensed their warm devotion to him. But for all her kindness, even Glinka's sister
found it difficult, at times, to associate with him.

At first, as is the case with so many inveterate drunkards,
Modest carefully concealed his weakness and when dining
with friends, would stubbornly refuse their offers of wine,
only to disappear suddenly with some innocuous alibi which
everybody recognized as meaning that he was off again on
one of his binges. Then this bashful phase passed and another
took its place. He would turn up at Stassov's or Mrs. Shestakova's in the naive belief, so characteristic of drunkards, that
he had only to sober up a trifle and chew a mint-drop or two
in order to successfully conceal his condition. On several days
in succession he came to the latter in such a "terrible state,"
as she said, that the poor lady quite lost her head. Finally,
summoning up her courage, she asked her "Mussinka" not
to come to her when he happened to be in what he himself
diffidently described as a "state of nervous irritation." Mussorgsky promised solemnly and, on the very next day, re-
appeared subdued and quiet. With her, as a rule, even when
he was "naughty" and despite the inevitable outbursts of
drunken rage and cantankerousness, he retained his inherent
gentleness of manner. She thought the world of him and he
remained her "beloved Mussinka" all through the ups and
downs of his life.

But toward the friends of his early days, his fellow composers, his relationship cooled noticeably. Whenever they
chanced to run into one another, they would try to do as if
nothing had happened and repeat: "We *must* meet again,
we must *absolutely* meet again," but they never made any
effort to do so.

On one occasion, after a prolonged separation, Mussorgsky met Rimsky-Korsakov in the street. Though they were
driving in opposite directions, they jumped out of their cabs
and warmly embraced. Standing on the sidewalk, Rimsky-
Korsakov hastened to tell him that he had hardly composed
anything lately, except 16 fugues, each more intricate than
the other. Mussorgsky said nothing. What could he say? But
later he complained to Stassov: "When on earth will those
fellows stop busying themselves with fugues? That isn't what
modern man expects of art! Let them start reading genuine
books, let them talk to live people! Whatever the nature of
life, however bitter it may be at times, let them be sincere
at all cost! Let them talk to people straight from the heart—
that is my recipe!"

He was inclined to consider Mrs. Rimsky-Korsakov's "arid
hissing and whisperings" responsible for her husband's passionate interest in dry formalism and for his "betrayal" of the
"Balakirev Gang." His profound resentment made him behave oddly in Cui's and Rimsky's presence, and talk in
mysterious and meaningful insinuations or else remain silent
altogether, which was perhaps even wiser since conversation
could so easily turn into argument which could, in turn, get
so easily out of hand.

After one such encounter at Mrs. Shestakova's, he described
to her the attitude of his former associates as "an insolent
betrayal of the best, of the most lively, of the most powerful
concepts of art. And where is this betrayal being perpetrated?
In the very same hospitable house where once upon a time
life throbbed and where the new objectives of art used to be
discussed and evaluated! . . ."

Behind their backs he spoke about Cui and Korsakov with incredible violence. He called them "talmudists," "pundits of art," "gravediggers." The traditions which they invoked, he said, were nothing but decayed scholasticism. "Only jackals," he said, "and hyenas relish carrion. Human beings like fresh nourishment!" Though Rimsky-Korsakov, of course, knew nothing of these comments, he somehow sensed that Mussorgsky regarded him with what he called "suspicion." "He seems to look upon me," he wrote, "as he would on a professor of scholastics out to catch him in the act of writing consecutive fifths."

Mussorgsky attributed this "betrayal" also to the fact that Balakirev had ceased to be their foster-parent, their guardian. To a friend he wrote: "When Balakirev first seized hold of them in his iron gauntlet, in mid-air, as it were—they breathed through his powerful lungs . . . But then the gauntlet relaxed its grip and all of a sudden they felt tired, they felt that they needed a rest . . ."

Actually he could have said the same of Borodin, but of "that chemical gentleman," he spoke always in much milder terms. What he accused Borodin of was not treason but indifference, oriental quietism. "Oh!" he muttered, "If only Borodin could get real mad!" But more often than not, he would merely remark in a tone of good-humored irony: "I wonder where he is sipping tea now . . ." This "tea-sipping" became in Mussorgsky's eyes a sort of ironical theme-song for Borodin, a symbol of the latter's laziness and passivity. He used to say to Stassov: "If only one could with your help drag him out of his teacup, or rather out of that samovar!" To Borodin, however, he addressed sterner summons: "For God's sake, dear friend, explode! Explode like live people explode! Show them whether you have claws or seal's flippers, whether you are a beast or just a tame pet, neither fish nor fowl!" However, Borodin's music continued to thrill him.

And then, all of a sudden—oh miracle!—the leader of the Gang himself began to show signs of "thawing." After five years of absence, Balakirev began occasionally to attend the gatherings at Mrs. Shestakova's or Stassov's. On the occasion of Stassov's birthday, Balakirev even revived one of their old traditions and, taking advantage of his friendship with the piano manufacturer Becker, sent him a grand piano with he himself had carefully selected. Later that evening, he sat down at the piano without even being begged and announced in his stentorian voice: "Today I will play you this and that . . ." He played, as usual, first a Beethoven and then a Schumann sonata, later on something by Chopin, then something of his own and finally something by Liszt. After which he gulped down a cup of tea and departed early. And now again as in the olden days, he would argue passionately about music and his favorite tonalities and at such moments he seemed just like the Mili Balakirev they had always known.

This "thawing-out" process was partly due to the fact that Mrs. Shestakova had suggested that he should, together with Rimsky-Korsakov and young Liadov, undertake the editing of Glinka's collected works. Balakirev was unable to eschew what he regarded as a moral obligation. He was not an easy person to work with, he was too capricious and Rimsky-Korsakov had a very hard time. Besides, his editing technique was far from faultless. But this assignment offered Mili a renewed opportunity to convince himself of Glinka's genius and to become ecstatic over Glinka's harmonies, his translucently ethereal orchestrations, his limpid depth of vision, all of which helped to heal his wounds and gradually bring him back to music. Glinka thus rendered his pupil a last and invaluable service. Balakirev even brought to light his own old manuscripts and started again, slowly as was his wont, with endless corrections, to work over them.

And yet this was no longer the Balakirev of old. He had, as it were, frozen in his tracks; his taste, his methods of composition, instead of progressing, had become static. The years of crisis had left their mark on him. His "clericalism," so rare in their set, was also assuming alarming proportions.

Not content with being now himself an ardent churchgoer, he was constantly trying to persuade his avowedly unbelieving friends to do the same. He kept imploring them in urging tones: "But why not? Just for my sake! . . ." He no longer ate meat and even stopped wearing a fur coat "out of respect for the animals," going about in bitterly cold weather in a cloth coat, his neck and beard swathed in a scarf. His house became a sort of refuge for animals of every type. He treated dogs with Christian humility, and when one of his wards bit him so nastily in the finger that his hand swelled up and it was feared that he might never be able to play the piano again, he did not seem to mind. When walking his beloved dog "Chummy," he would guard it jealously against all potential flirtations and, if need be, pick it up and carry it out of harm's way. He regarded it as a crime to kill even the meanest insect and when he happened to catch a cockroach or a bedbug, he would carefully release it with the words: "Go, little one, and God speed!" All this was most irritating to his friends. "Balakirev with his pussy-cats, his doggy-woggies and ikon-lamps . . . ," grumbled Liadov.

He had always been especially severe with Mussorgsky. Moreover, the rumor had reached him that his former pupil had become even more self-important and arrogant. However, one day, at Mrs. Shestakova's, they met again and talked as old friends and Mili was struck by Modest's humility and modesty. He admitted later to Stassov: "I was pleasantly surprised by our Modinka. There was absolutely no sign of bragging or conceit. On the contrary, he was modest, he listened carefully to what I said and did not argue when I stressed the need to know the rules of harmony. He didn't even object when I suggested that he start taking harmony lessons with Korsinka. I was pleasantly surprised, very pleasantly surprised, indeed. For the time being and until the autumn, I have urged him to do something useful and he has taken back his *St. John's Night* to correct and revise. It contains such powerful passages that it would be a pity to leave it in its present disorderly condition."

This enthusiasm was mutual. And of course the fact that Mussorgsky voiced unqualified praise for Balakirev's latest composition, his tone poem *Tamar* which was already well advanced, was further balm to Mili's heart.

But for all his alleged readiness to study harmony with Rimsky-Korsakov, Mussorgsky stuck to his guns, emulating in this the sectarian fanaticism of the hermit Diosifei from his opera *Khovanshchina*. Though he no longer trod his path with the giants' strides of yore, he could not depart from it, either. He worked slowly nowadays. Considering that *Khovanshchina* had first been conceived way back in 1872, when *Boris Godunov* even had not yet been produced, the decline of his creative powers becomes all to evident. At that time this decline was only noticeable in the volume of his output since everything he wrote for *Khovanshchina* was still superb. The first act was completed in 1875. Thereafter he would compose every now and then additional excerpts which, in Stassov's words, were "quite wonderful." But unlike *Boris,* the orchestration no longer followed apace. The latter required a stubborn effort of which he was becoming increasingly incapable. He kept postponing it and was only too glad when Rimsky-Korsakov, having selected his *Dance of the Persian Maidens* for a concert of the Free School of Music, proceeded to orchestrate it himself.

Without completing even half of *Khovanshchina,* Mussorgsky started off on a new opera, this time on a comic Ukrainian theme borrowed from Gogol's story, *The Fair at Sorochintzi.* He may possibly have done this for the sake of his old friend "Grandfather" Petrov, who had been one of the great singers of his day and who now, in his declining years, longed to sing something relating to his native folklore. Mussorgsky regarded it as a sort of "breather" after *Khovanshchina.* He had moments of doubt that he, a Great Russian, could succeed in evoking all the subtle musical intonations of the Little Russian dialect; he would start work on *The Fair* and then give it up again. But his misgivings were without foundation: the opera contains many a genuinely comical feature.

In another field of composition, however, namely in his songs, the decline of his creative powers showed itself also in the quality of his work. None of his more recent songs could vie with their predecessors. And yet these later, inferior works were published with greater ease than the earlier ones that had immortalized his name. Bessel paid him as much as 20 rubles apiece which, of course, was not very much, but then Bessel never did pay regularly. All in all in his lifetime, Mussorgsky received from him 701 rubles and 50 kopecks (the equivalent of half as many gold dollars) and these included his fee for the piano rights of *Boris Godunov*. Apart from the box-office returns from this opera, this paltry sum was all that this great composer ever earned for his work!

And yet his compositions were played quite often now at public concerts. This was not merely because they gave singers an opportunity to display their dramatic talent, but also because many of these singers were his personal friends. Besides, they loved to sing to his own accompaniment. He could play at sight and could switch from one key to another at will; the singers could thus be sure that they would never be "let down." Furthermore, he never charged anything for these services so that he was soon in great demand at charity and benefit performances. He held his own even when "a trifle above par." On one occasion, when he was due to accompany an Italian singer at a students' charity ball, one of the young organizers dropped in to take him to a rehearsal. He found to his horror the composer drunk and when he admonished him, Mussorgsky merely muttered incoherently in French: *"Pas possible, pas possible . . . Le soir je serai exact . . ."* The student had serious doubts that he would ever turn up, but to his surprise Mussorgsky arrived on time and though the singer had a sore throat and asked to sing in a lower key, he was able to adapt the accompaniment accordingly. The Italian kept exclaiming enthusiastically: *"Che artista! Che artista!"*

His success as an accompanist even went somewhat to his head. Realizing that he would be unable to hold on to his job and being justly concerned about his future, Mussorgsky hoped that he might be able to earn a living as a concert pianist. With some pride he told Stassov: "If it were necessary to earn one's daily bread by pounding the keyboard—we'd manage!" Alas, he little realized that there was a considerable difference between accompanying free of charge at a benefit concert and "pounding the keyboard" as a professional pianist.

Although, by some miracle of subconscious will-power, he was always able to sober up and turn up at his office at the Ministry when required to do so, he was nevertheless becoming increasingly incapable of systematic work. For a long time this was tolerated. He even received his promotions when these were due, but the last one was already merely by way of a consolation prize: his early retirement was a foregone conclusion and he knew it. He was threatened with starvation. He could talk his head off about being able to "pound the keyboard"—deep down in his heart he himself didn't believe it. Once, in a fit of despair, he complained to Leonova, the celebrated *contralto*, that he would soon find himself thrown out into the street, that he simply didn't know what to do. Leonova, an old friend and admirer of his, did her best to reassure him. She told him that she was about to start her own singing classes, that they could run them jointly, that in any case she would never forsake him. What were friends there for, she added, if not to help one another in an hour of need? Her words and her kind velvety voice soothed him. His eyes lost their expression of a hunted animal, and he became again his usual gentle self.

Although Stassov was himself beset by countless problems and worries, he was deeply concerned about his friend's fate.

Appealing to Balakirev's "fatherly and benevolent feelings," he implored him to save "poor old Mussorgsky" who, he said, was about to lose his job and might then, quite possibly, drink himself to death. But Balakirev was skeptical: "Mussorgsky is physically too much of a wreck," he replied, "he will never change." Nevertheless, he introduced him to his friend Filippov.

A prominent *Slavophil* and an expert connoisseur and collector of Russian folk songs in his own right, Filippov had always admired Mussorgsky's work. Now, upon meeting, they took an instant liking to one another. Sobered up and dressed in his best suit of clothes, Mussorgsky looked "almost a gentleman." Filippov, for his part, had about him an air of devout and slightly sanctimonious fastidiousness which struck Modest with awe. The holy ikons on every wall, the indescribable fragrance of incense, ikon-lamp oil and eucalyptus which hung in the air—all this imbued his sumptuous apartment with an atmosphere reminiscent of the residence of the abbot of a prosperous monastery. In due course Filippov introduced Mussorgsky to other high-ranking persons, including even a Grand Duke (though one couldn't be too sure, for Mussorgsky spoke about this in his usual tone of self-importance). Better still, Filippov gave him a job in his own Ministry of State Control. This job was of course a sinecure. Modest was expected to turn up from time to time only for the sake of appearances. Yet even this was becoming increasingly difficult.

At the end of 1878, he heard a performance of *Boris* for the last time. He had attended a rehearsal and had behaved most strangely: First he had strained his ear and listened with an air of rapt intentness, then he had let his head drop to his chest only to lift it up again, shake his mane and point his hand dramatically to heaven. As usual, Napravnik, the conductor, noticed every slip. He had a very sharp ear and musical memory and led his orchestra like a skipper piloting his craft: "Hey!" he would call out all of a sudden, "the second French horn over there—a half-tone lower, if you please!" The meticulous and rigid Czech was capable of warm feelings. Moreover he had always regarded his Russian colleague with sympathy, even though much in Mussorgsky's music made him wince. But he refused to even consider *Khovanshchina*. "One revolutionary opera," he said, "is enough!" At this particular performance of *Boris* the public had somehow learned that the composer was in the house, and he was called out several times. The artists sang with considerable feeling. But this was an expurgated version of *Boris*. The scene *Before the Walls of Khromy* had been dropped, and Napravnik had made other cuts which took away much of Mussorgsky's joy.

II

That autumn of 1878 he had his first seizure. Whether an epileptic fit or simply a stroke, it was anyhow something very serious. It happened at one of Leonova's parties. The hostess took excellent care of him. A doctor was summoned, who happened to be familiar with the patient's constitution. He gave the latter but a couple of hours to live, but fortunately he was wrong. Mussorgsky recovered, and his illness seemed to have left no traces. Indeed, at this late juncture, life graced him with something resembling a smile, a wry smile, almost a grimace. Leonova suggested that he accompany her on a concert tour through Russia.

Though Daria Mikhailovna Leonova had long ago forsaken the Imperial Stage, she had not given up her singing career. Her voice, that wonderful velvety contralto which in olden days had fascinated both Glinka and Meyerbeer, was of course no longer what it used to be. But her technique, her artistic mastery, her temperament had survived. She was, moreover, both courageous and enterprising. By way of Siberia, the Russian "Wild West" of those days, she travelled to China, giving concerts at every whistle-stop and reaping the enthusiastic acclaim of the hospitable Siberians. From China she proceeded to Japan, where she was probably the first European visiting artist. Via the U.S.A. she returned with fresh laurels, countless basically true but exaggerated stories about her triumphs, a roomful of Japanese furniture and knick-knacks of sometimes doubtful authenticity and the nickname of "Leonova the Jap." Taking advantage of the resulting publicity, she then gave a series of concerts in Russia, in the two capitals—St. Petersburg and Moscow— and in the provinces. Now she was planning a new major tour.

This was easier said than done, for the Russian provincial audiences were still largely unappreciative of classical music. The programs had to be both varied and not difficult. Moreover, it was necessary to take along an accompanist, as one could not rely on local talent. Leonova and Grindin, her common-law husband who acted as her manager, had a lucky inspiration: Why not invite Mussorgsky? He could perform both as an accompanist and as a soloist and, besides, the mention of his name on the program might enhance her appeal.

Their motives in promoting this plan differed. Although she naturally viewed with some pride the prospect of having their names posted side by side in the programs, Leonova sincerely hoped that a change of air would do Mussorgsky good. Grindin, however, was a harsh and grasping man. His main concern was that the accompanist be inexpensive and that the over-all risks involved in the whole venture be reduced to a minimum.

Mussorgsky welcomed the invitation with joy and just a little bit of nervousness. There was also a formal objection: he would have to obtain leave of absence from the Ministry of State Control. But Filippov was all for the trip: What good could it do a Russian artist to sit around eternally in cold, "Teutonic" St. Petersburg? Let him travel around Mother Russia for a while! With his backing, all formalities were easily overcome, particularly since Filippov realized that his protégé's days at the office were counted anyhow.

Stassov emphatically opposed the trip. He felt that Modest was degrading himself, that by agreeing to become the accompanist of a "voiceless aging opera diva," he was compromising the whole "new school" of Russian music. Mussorgsky's claim that he would make 1.000 rubles during this trip—he considered illusory. Balakirev's reaction was even more violent: "What a terrible thing is happening to Modest," he complained to Mrs. Shestakova. "You would be well advised to hinder this trip with Leonova. On the one hand, you would save him from playing this shameful role and on the other—both Modest and Leonova are taking a terrible risk. What'll happen if he suddenly has one of those haemorrhages like the one he had in your house? Do you think that she'd enjoy taking care of him? For you can be sure that she will be only too glad to make him drink—after all it's cheaper that way!"

But the matter was already settled and in July 1879, Leonova, Grindin and Mussorgsky left for the South.

Modest was terribly agitated. It had been so long since he had last left St. Petersburg. He knew so little of Russia. And now, after all the bustle and excitement and last-minute preparations, here he was on the train, with Daria Mikhailovna, her husband and her maid.

The tour took them first to Poltava, then to Elizavetgrad, Nikolaiev, Kherson, Odessa, Sebastopol, the Crimea and by way of Rostov, Novocherkassk, Voronezh and Tambov, back to St. Petersburg where they arrived late in October.

Despite the generally enthusiastic tone of Mussorgsky's letters, there crept into them time and again a note of disappointment because of the ignorance and lack of musical appreciation on the part of many of their provincial listeners. The artistic success of the trip, nevertheless, seems to have been greater than its material returns. Perhaps their programs were too high-brow. Modest assured Mrs. Shestakova in one of his letters, that at long last her brother Glinka's music "had really resounded throughout the towns of Russia they had visited." Their repertory, he said, included primarily the works of Glinka, Liszt, Dargomyzhsky, Serov, Balakirev, Cui, Borodin, Rimsky-Korsakov, Schubert, Chopin and Schumann. "With such levers," he added, "you could challenge the whole world." He refrained from mentioning that there had been other "levers" besides, namely Gounod and Meyerbeer. For, if like every sectarian, he was from time to time obliged to associate with the "untouchables," there was no need to write about it.

As for Mussorgsky's own contribution, though he was certainly not the virtuoso he might have become in his youth, he performed like a real artist. But his participation was, generally speaking, purely incidental. The press spoke almost exclusively about Leonova.

His more enthusiastic letters reveal a state of advanced spiritual deterioration. For he must have had many a painful experience during this trip. After one unsuccessful concert to an empty house in Yalta, Stassov's daughter, with whom they were staying, came upon him in the dressing-room, where he sat distraught and pale, his head buried in his hands. For even in his condition he must have realized that Russia was not yet ripe to appreciate art. At times he may have recalled his own words, spoken many years earlier: "Russia is producing fruit which she does not appreciate because she has no need for it. There is a certain amount of artistry in Russia, but art itself is a luxury item, which nobody really needs."

The result of this venture was twofold. On the one hand, Mussorgsky enjoyed himself, he felt cheered though tired. He got to know more of Russia and was inspired to write a few piano pieces. But he had also been torn away from his main vocation—the writing of operas.

III

In St. Petersburg he found himself worse off than before his departure. What he had always feared had now come to pass: his career as a government official was over. Leonova's singing classes had also come off to a bad start; pupils were scarce, though Mussorgsky did his best, devising new methods of instruction, writing duos, trios, quartets (so that he must have had at least four pupils!) and Leonova was pleased with him. And yet even now the doom which he had always feared more than anything else did not materialize.

For a long time his friends had been bracing themselves for just such a contingency. Stassov had sounded the alarm early and had explored every possible solution. Balakirev had suggested a benefit concert in Mussorgsky's honor. But the limited returns from such a venture would soon have been expended and Modest would then have found himself again in trouble. The poet Zhemchuzhnikov (one of the co-authors of the popular satyrical skit "Kuzma Prutkov") who was a friend both of Mussorgsky and of the Naumovs, then advanced a different suggestion which, thanks to Filippov, was presently implemented.

Filippov got together a group of friends who undertook to pay the composer a monthly allowance of 100 rubles (approximately $50). To spare Mussorgsky's feelings, this allowance was to be presented to him as an advance installment payment for *Khovanshchina*. In this manner, the money would also serve as an incentive for its early completion. But this was not all. Another group of friends and admirers (who remained anonymous and kept the terms of their "deal" secret) had also gotten together, meanwhile, and had agreed to pay him 80 rubles ($40) a month for his *Fair at Sorochintzi,* against a commitment on the part of Mussorgsky to complete the opera by November 1879.

There thus began an odd competition between the two

groups responsible for Mussorgsky's support and, consequently also between the two operas—a competition, moreover, which did not favor *Khovanshchina* since no deadline
had been set for *its* completion. (Mussorgsky hoped to finish
it during the following year.)

Upon learning about these plans from Stassov, Mussorgsky replied: "I have never suffered and do not now suffer
from pusillanimity. If Providence wills it that I broaden the
well-trodden path that leads to the very life-purpose of art—
I will be grateful and rejoice. What art demands of its
votaries today is so tremendous that it can well engulf man
in his entirety..."

In any event, this twofold "deal" was to be Mussorgsky's
salvation since he had no longer to worry about his daily
bread. But he continued to lead a bohemian life and, unfortunately, he went from bad to worse.

In May 1880, Rimsky-Korsakov received from Stassov a
letter with a foreign postmark, which included a timid suggestion: "Why don't you look up our poor old Mussorgsky?"
(Stassov must have guessed that the reaction to such a request
would be at best half-hearted.) As it happened, Rimsky-Korsakov had meant to do so anyhow but as is so often the case,
he kept putting it off. Finally, having talked the matter over
with his wife, he decided to try and get Mussorgsky to come
out and stay with them in the country.

The official pretext for his visit to Modest was to select
some excerpts from *The Fair at Sorochintzi* for a forthcoming concert of the Free School, which he now conducted in
Balakirev's stead. He arrived around noon and found Mussorgsky sprawled out on a Persian divan barely covered with
sheets of doubtful cleanliness. He had just awakened, his hair
was tousled, his eyes bleary and his face all puffy. Rimsky-
Korsakov started leafing through a pile of sheet-music. There
was little new. At first Mussorgsky wouldn't hear about going
to the country. He claimed that he was busy, that he had
already accepted an invitation to Leonova's. Then he seemed

about to give in. Korsakov gazed at his friend sadly. He had little faith in his promises. Besides, he couldn't help feeling that for all his wife's sense of duty and although she would consent to any sacrifice in order to help a childhood friend in need, it would be no easy thing for her, with her passion for order and cleanliness, to put up with Mussorgsky as a houseguest.

In the end, of course, Modest never did visit the Rimsky-Korsakovs in the country. What would he have done there? He would have felt like a fish out of water in their well-kept home. He was far happier at Leonova's "Japanese bungalow" in Oranienbaum. Although she herself was by no means easy-going, the very familiarity with which she treated him denoted in her a mixed feeling of pity and respect. Because of that, he was prepared to endure both her capricious whims and Grindin's boorishness and even his own somewhat ambiguous status in that household. Because of that also, he was prepared to run her errands, go marketing and putter about the kitchen. But more than anything else he loved to garden.

An observant little boy, who happened to be living in the same house at the time and who was to become years later a well-known professor in his own right, remembers seeing him many a time armed with a pair of gardening shears and a watering can, pruning here, watering there. He never forgot the composer's face, he says, which had such an uncanny likeness to Repin's celebrated portrait. In the evening guests would assemble, for Leonova kept open house. His threadbare clothes, his very appearance singled Mussorgsky out. For years now he had never worn anything but second-hand clothes off a friend's back, or purchased from a dubious source. It was all very gay and noisy. Modest kept shuttling busily between the dining-room and the kitchen, uncorking countless bottles and with such a loud pop that every time the little boy was startled. He took good care of the guests, he also did not forget himself and as the evening wore on, he became steadily paler and more excited.

At the head of the table, Daria Mikhailovna Leonova reigned supreme as she reminisced about her life, about her past triumphs, about Glinka. "I simply *adored* him," she exclaimed, "and—why lie?—he too was not indifferent to me. One day, as I was waiting for him to give me a lesson, he came in with a friend, they were both tipsy and they decided they wanted to play cards. Only there happened to be no card-table, so do you know what he said? He said to me: 'Dashenka, my dear, may we play on your back?'—'You're very welcome, I'm sure, Mikhail Ivanovich!' I said, and would you believe it? They did, although in those days my back was not as ample as it is now!" She addressed all her guests, however important, with the same tone of bantering familiarity, and when she stopped talking, there was sometimes a second of silence. "She's communing with God..." a young whippersnapper snickered one day. "Yes," was the thundering rebuff, "with God and not with you, you fool!" Whereupon everyone roared with laughter.

Here, because of the relative quietness and wonderful sea air, and despite the nightly revels, Mussorgsky resumed work on *Khovanshchina*. Early in May 1880 he completed Act III and then in August the fourth. He was in a terrible hurry and kept cutting from the libretto everything that to him seemed superfluous which did not always improve matters. Stassov would protest, but in vain. The composer may have sensed that his strength was waning and therefore have sought to speed up his work. At the end of August he wrote to Stassov: "As for the poor old sinner Mussorgsky, I can only say that he has just, at this very minute, concocted the scene at the fair from *Sorochintzi—Khovanshchina* is all set. As regards the orchestration—Ye Gods! If only there were more time!"

But time was now running out. And yet *Khovanshchina* was not even orchestrated and the *Fair at Sorochintzi* was a complete mess. Some fragments had already appeared in print and were now being performed, but most of the first and second acts were not even tied together in a logical sequence and the third act had not been written.

On January 28, 1881 Dostoyevsky died. A memorial concert was given early in February. Here, for the last time, Mussorgsky performed not only as an accompanist but also as a solo pianist and he made an overwhelming impression on his audience. For he depicted the pealing of the bells this time not triumphantly, as in *Boris'* coronation scene, but in the form of a muffled funeral lament, that was extraordinarily moving.

On February 3 the orchestra of the Free School, playing under Rimsky-Korsakov's baton, performed Mussorgsky's *Route of Senacherib* in the author's presence. The conductor was dissatisfied with both orchestra and choir, but the piece was a success. On the 14th, the same orchestra was scheduled to perform Parassia's meditation scene from *The Fair at Sorochintzi* but Mussorgsky was not destined to attend.

He kept feeling steadily worse, both mentally and physically. He visited Leonova nearly every day now, either to accompany her, or to help with her classes, or because he could think of nowhere else to go. On February 11, he burst in on her, his face twisted with pain and fear and started again to bemoan his fate. His situation was hopeless, he said, he would soon find himself out in the street. Leonova knew that these fears were by now merely the product of his own diseased imagination and she was presently able to reassure him.

Next day, February 12, he again turned up. He looked rested and nothing foreshadowed what was about to follow. Leonova had been invited to the birthday party of one of her pupils and Mussorgsky went along with her. When they arrived, the party was in full swing, the young lady of the house dutifully sang a few pieces and then Daria Mikhailovna herself performed. She sang, as usual, with much dramatic feeling and the guests were charmed and delighted. Suddenly Mussorgsky, who had been standing near the dining table, crashed to the floor. His host's son rushed up; one of the guests happened to be a doctor; presently Modest regained consciousness. There could be no question of his going home alone in this condition and Leonova, kind and helpful as always, drove him back to her flat.

Here he seemed to recover, but he was afraid of remaining alone and shuddered at the very idea of being sent home. Leonova comforted him and told him that he could stay overnight. The maid made up a bed for him in a small parlor and Daria Mikhailovna instructed her to get up from time to time to see whether he needed anything, and if necessary, to awaken her. But all was quiet that night. Next morning, as Leonova was having her breakfast, Mussorgsky walked in dressed and cheerful and when she asked him how he had spent the night, he replied that he had sat up all night dozing in an armchair, but that now he felt fine. He had hardly spoken when he swung slowly around to the right and crashed again full length to the floor. If he hadn't been turned over onto his back, he would have suffocated. That day he had two further seizures and lost consciousness.

When, in answer to her summons, Stassov and Filippov arrived, it was decided to remove him to a hospital. But this was more easily said than done. Private nursing homes were expensive, the municipal hospitals were overcrowded. One of the Emperor's private physicians—a Dr. Bertenson—found him an unoccupied ward in the *Nikolayevsky* Military Hospital where, in order to sidestep the formal ban on civilian patients in military hospitals, the composer was signed in under a false identity: he became Dr. Bertenson's "volunteer batman."

The room was clean, airy and had spotless white-washed walls, but it was an ordinary public ward in which there stood a number of empty beds. When Mussorgsky first caught sight of these stark walls and especially of the vacant beds, he became frightened. A screen was brought in and set up to conceal them, but he was not easily reassured. When this was reported to Balakirev, the latter found nothing better to say than that this wasn't so bad, after all, from the point of view of the salvation of Mussorgsky's soul, since it would serve to remind him of the vanity of all material things! But despite these pious though harsh words, he hastened to visit him.

In general, as is often the case when the irrevocable happens, even those friends who had so long snubbed him, took alarm, at last, overwhelming him with kindness and solicitude. Balakirev, the two Stassov brothers, Repin, Rimsky-Korsakov, Golenishchev-Kutuzov, Grindin came practically every day to see him. They brought him linen and a few books, including Berlioz's *Traité de l' instrumentation* which he proposed to study before proceeding to the orchestration of his latest operas. As he didn't even possess a dressing-gown and so that he shouldn't have to wear the drab robe supplied by the hospital, Cui made him a present of a fine grey robe with scarlet collar, cuffs and piping.

Mrs. Rimsky-Korsakov, Mrs. Cui and Dimitri Stassov's wife also visited him frequently. Thanks to the strict hospital regime his condition soon improved and when he had lady-guests, he would have himself moved into an armchair, would put on his "sumptuous" robe, speak to them in French and become again his former courteous self. Alone of the ladies, Liudmila Ivanova Shestakova, his oldest and truest friend, never got around to seeing him. She was old now, her health was failing; she was moreover, perhaps, just a trifle scared of seeing her "Mussinka" in hospital in this condition. Presently she received a letter through the mail in which he begged her not to be alarmed, for he hoped to soon visit her himself. And because she was frail or because she was also a little selfish, she took him at his word.

But this improvement was merely an illusion. Although the doctors differed about the exact diagnosis, some claiming that he had had a stroke, while others asserted that it had been an epileptic seizure, they all agreed as to the prognosis: Whether he lived a year or only a day, one thing was certain —he would never recover.

He remained at all times fully conscious; he recognized everybody; he rejoiced at everything, but he talked completely at random as if he were a little out of his mind. Perhaps he *was* a little out of his mind. And yet however sad it was to listen to his wanderings, it was harder still during his moments of lucidity when he would cheerfully and hopefully discuss his plans, how he would visit the Crimea and Constantinople, how he would compose this and that . . .

He dreamt of writing a new opera for which he had already begun collecting material. One day it was to be called the *Empress' Bodyguard* (in Russian *Leibkompantzi*) and was to tell the story of Catherine I's *Coup d'Etat* of 1715, the next day it would bear the name of *The Pugachev Rising,* after the dread peasant *Jacquerie* in Catherine the Great's reign. As always, he was especially attracted by moments of national crisis and popular ferment. He wanted Golenishchev-Kutuzov to write the libretto and kept repeating to him his pet theories about how one should go about writing a historical drama: "You must read everything," he would say, "ferret out everything, explore every hidden nook and cranny and then think it over again and again, not once, not twice but a hundred times, if need be. Roll up your sleeves, Arseni, let's talk it over!" and he added: "I'd like to work on your creative ideas . . ." And when he said this, he seemed so lucid and reasonable that his friends had to turn away to hide their tears.

Ilia Repin, the celebrated painter, had just arrived in St. Petersburg for the opening of the yearly exhibition of the Itinerant group. Stassov now decided that he should paint the portrait of their dying friend. Repin agreed gladly.

Those were alarming and hectic days. On March 1, Czar

Alexander II was killed by a bomb. The town was racked with fear, hope, rumor and expectation.

Amidst all this excitement, Mussorgsky sat for his portrait three times—on March 3rd, 4th and 5th. The sittings tired him. From time to time, Repin would interrupt his work to read the papers to him and he seemed to follow the political news with interest. While the artist painted, Mussorgsky slouched in his armchair, dressed in Cui's dressing-gown, the scarlet collar and lapels shining brightly as the cold March sun reflected from the white-washed walls. There was so little space that Repin could use no easel and had to prop up his drawing board on an unpainted wooden hospital table. The portrait was never finished. The artist had to go away for a few days and by the time he got back, Mussorgsky's condition had suddenly deteriorated.

It hangs nowadays in the Tretiakov Gallery in Moscow. No photograph can give an adequate idea of its tremendous impact and power. There is about it something of the self-portraits of the aged Rembrandt. For these two men had much in common. Both were inspired and yet at the same time realistic and human, with an avid craving for life. Repin's portrait sums up a whole existence. It pictures with the forcefulness of a Rembrandt both the destruction wrought by years of struggle and the stubborn spirit which had withstood that destruction. In both cases this resistance is focused in the eyes. Rembrandt's eyes shine with an all-observing, shrewd intelligence. Mussorgsky's are of a more dreamy quality, they are more contemplative. And if at times in real life they seemed to lack expression, here in this portrait they are filled with introspection, patience and pain.

Another visitor to St. Petersburg these days was Mussorgsky's brother Filaret. Upon leaving the hospital, one day, he made a fatal mistake—he gave Modest a little money. The latter was about to celebrate his birthday. One of the hospital attendants—the human heart is frail—let himself be talked into buying him a bottle of brandy, to toast the event. This was apparently too much for the patient's weakened condition. An erisypelatous rash broke out on his leg and his condition took a sharp turn for the worse.

The last two days of his life he suffered much. Fortunately, he was unconscious most of the time. When his state became quite desperate, his friends decided to safeguard his musical heritage from getting into his brother's possession; they drew up a notarial deed bequeathing everything to Filippov, but the patient was already unable to sign it and Kutuzov signed for him.

Mussorgsky died on March 16, 1881. His last night on earth was peaceful. Shortly before dawn, the attendants on duty heard him moan and cry out. When they entered the ward he was already dead. The time was 5 a.m. He was 42 years old.

He was buried on the 18th of March, in the Writer's Corner of the St. Alexander-Nevsky monastery. Only a few people attended the funeral. Stassov, naturally, took care of all the arrangements. His sister-in-law, Dimitri's wife, pronounced a brief eulogy. Stassov himself said nothing. He felt too much bitterness in his heart. And yet even he, the unbeliever, couldn't help being moved and stirred by the inspired words of the funeral service, so pregnant with divine hope and truth. On first thought, what could be more deceptive, standing at the edge of this yawning tomb, than the words of the ritual invocation: "Grant him eternal peace, oh Lord! in his blessed passing . . ." Nevertheless, they filled his heart with tenderness and compassion. The choir intoned the wonderful last prayer: "Eternal memory . . ." Those too, were no empty words, surely. So long as Russia existed, so long as the Russian language was spoken and Russian songs sung, Modest Mussorgsky would live on in the memory of his people. He was one of those to whom monuments are raised. He had been, and always would be one of the great glories of Russia and yet in his lifetime Russia had spurned him. As Stassov watched the coffin being lowered into its final resting place, all that had been superficial, comical, odd about Mussorgsky seemed to fade from his memory. What he remembered now was only the image of a great musician— Glinka's peer, and the admirable qualities of the fighter who all his life had battled for his beliefs and his faith.

CHAPTER FIFTEEN

THE "CHEMICAL GENTLEMAN"

*"O vous, soyez témoins que j'ai
fait mon devoir
Comme un parfait chimiste et comme
une âme sainte."*

BAUDELAIRE

I

Throughout the spring and the autumn and sometimes even part of the winter, while his wife, Ekaterina Sergheyevna, lived with her family in Moscow and he himself led the existence of a "married bachelor" (as he ruefully put it) Borodin was in the habit of writing her long daily letters. These, in diary form, covered every detail of his life; they told her what he had done, where he had been, whom he had seen, as well as his own reactions to and thoughts about everything he did. About music, however, or about the books he had been reading, or even his chemistry work he spoke to her but rarely. Indeed, it would hardly be possible, re-reading them now, to tell that they were written by a scientist, still less a composer. And yet they provide invaluable material for a better understanding of one who remains one of the most attractive, and at the same time most elusive members of the "Mighty Handful."

Borodin would usually start each letter with one of the countless endearing names which he had devised for his wife. Often they made no sense; in fact they did not even sound always very endearing. He would invariably begin and end them using the formal addressing rather than the informal. When he switched to the informal one, it usually meant that he was about to speak of something fairly prosaic. He would also sometimes use children's language or refer to himself in the plural. And instead of a signature, he would write simply: "Me"!

The letters would start with the moment he got up in the morning. He had remained true to his student days' habit of rising early. The maid would light the samovar, he would drink a cup of tea, after which he would go off, to a lecture or to his laboratory. He suffered from certain peculiarities, or "bad habits" (as his wife chose to call them). Thus, as he was extremely sensitive to light and sounds, he would at night pull a heavy cloth drape across the window and cover up his eyes with a small pillow or dark silk handkerchief. Also, and despite her protests, he loved to wash stark naked. As he roamed about the apartment, dressing, or later, along the corridors of the Academy, he would sing in a loud voice senseless songs, preferably in French, such as: *On aime son petit picot striculé*! The main attraction seemed to consist in the rapid and sudden alternation of intonations and sounds. He had also other, esthetically more unattractive habits, which his wife fought even more persistently and with just as little success. In one of his letters, for instance, he informs her proudly: "I no longer scratch my head in public, but then neither have I cut my hair or my nails (except the pigtail that had begun to dangle down my back: a professor can't very well go about with a pigtail). My good behavior is due, perhaps, to the fact that there's no one there to reprove me!"

This habit of describing everything in such meticulous detail to his wife was to lead to well-nigh tragic consequences.

II

It all began in the country, one summer, when the Borodins were staying with the Kalinin family at the latter's estate in the Government of Tver. Without, at first, their realizing it, their hostess, young Mrs. Kalinina, *"Anka"* (as she was known to her friends) fell in love with him. And so long as they remained unaware of it, they were happy. She was then only twenty-one years of age. Her brother, the rather talented amateur-composer Nikolai Lodyzhensky was close to the Balakirev group, indeed he had been largely instrumental in arranging for the acceptance by the Direction of Imperial Theatres of Mussorgsky's *Boris Godunov*. She herself was also musical; moreover she was interested in science and claimed to wish to study chemistry too (though this may have been merely a pose). She had beautiful, luminous eyes which grew even more so when she smiled. Actually, it was Ekaterina Sergheyevna who first discovered her and later, when the crisis came, Borodin would remind his wife that he had first learned to see Anka in a different light "through her eyes."

He was, naturally, flattered that this lovely young woman should look at him with an air of adoration, laugh delightedly at all his jokes (because of which he now joked more than ever) and echo his every word. He wasn't even unduly embarrassed when one day, in the presence of his wife and another acquaintance, she suddenly seized his hand and kissed it. But presently, Ekaterina Sergheyevna began to be jealous of her and through her carelessness Anka soon provided a motive for this jealousy. Shortly before departing on a trip abroad, she told a friend that she was leaving Russia "for Ekaterina Sergheyevna's sake," because she wished her no ill, because she had no further claims, etc. This tone of condescension was bad enough. But Anka added that she would remain abroad and wait patiently until Borodin was free! All this was of course repeated to his wife and she was, quite naturally, furious. True, she *was* in poor health. But to cynically speculate on her possible death was really going too far. To make matters worse, Borodin himself was no doubt not sufficiently attentive to her or sensitive at the time, so that when they parted in the fall—he to return to St. Petersburg, and she to spend the winter in Moscow—relations between them were somewhat strained. Nevertheless,

he continued to write to her almost daily, and it is then that
he committed a near fatal slip.

For Anka did not stay long abroad. She was not feeling
well, she kept squabbling with her rather boorish husband;
moreover they had not been able to afford a prolonged trip.
Actually, the main reason for her return to St. Petersburg
was, probably, that she simply couldn't live without Borodin.
Yet, though they belonged to more or less the same "set,"
they did not immediately meet again. Borodin knew that
his wife would resent his seeing her and he avoided her, and
when they eventually met after all, they were both studiously
cool and aloof. And then, one cold autumn day, she came
to see him at his home. She was wearing a light spring dress
and no jacket; she was cold and shivering, having probably
roamed the streets for a long time without daring to enter.
He noticed immediately how thin and sad she looked despite her happiness at seeing him again. He led her into his
study and offered her a cup of tea. She began to talk, dis-
jointedly, incoherently, about her sufferings, her difficult
relations with her husband. After which he, in turn, began
to talk. He had long pondered what he would say if and when
things came to a head. What he said was full of sound sense,
too full, perhaps. He said that he couldn't, that he dared not
break up his wife's life, that their relation should be that
of brother and sister. He spoke quietly, calmly, but his head
was burning, his hands were cold as ice, there were tears
in his eyes. "What's the matter?" she cried out anxiously,
"are you ill? Have you fever?" But he went on in the same
vein. Suddenly, she interrupted him: "For God's sake stop!
Why do you say such things? I know myself that this is so!
What do I care whether I am a sister to you, or a daughter?
I know only that I am happy with you, and that I am
unhappy without you. I'm not asking anything of you, I can't
hope for anything . . ." And then she smiled, adding: "You're
my sweet one, that's what you are!" and quickly kissed his
hand. Laughingly he lent her one of his wife's jackets and

they went out, and together they roamed about town for hours. She informed him that her husband had gone for a few days to Moscow on business; again she spoke about her unhappiness and then, with uncalled-for frankness, she began to speak of certain intimate ailments from which she was suffering. For some reason, they dropped in to see her sister at the latter's hotel and not finding her at home, stayed to lunch at the hotel restaurant. Next day, he arranged for her to see a gynecologist, after which they went to call on his mother. Anka wanted to see the house in which he had lived and grown up. She insisted on being shown every room and his old mother became quite sentimental and started to kiss her, so that the atmosphere was soon very cozy, even patriarchal. Suddenly, the old lady mentioned the name of Kalinin, Anka's husband, whereupon Anka burst into tears and implored her not to spoil one of the few happy days in her life . . .

Borodin described all this in detail to his wife. Why? For the sake of truthfulness? So that she shouldn't think that anything worse had happened? Or because she knew or guessed anyhow? True, he added that she had been constantly present in his thoughts that day, that nothing of this would have happened had she been there, and he begged her to return to St. Petersburg. And in the end she agreed to do so, insisting only that he put her up in a hotel "so that she shouldn't be in his way"!

For a little while he kept insisting in his letters to his wife that he couldn't forsake Anka, that he was her only friend, her only mainstay in life, that without him she would be lost. And then, all of a sudden, it was over. Only a short while ago he had suffered deeply, hopelessly, for the first time in his life, hardly sleeping, roaming the streets at night, pacing back and forth in his apartment. Now, suddenly, he began to notice all of Anka's human frailties which, up to then, he had ignored: her occasional pettiness and vulgarity, her lack of culture. He realized, at present, that however much she might bicker and quarrel with her husband and suffer because of it, yet she wouldn't dream of leaving him; indeed she probably couldn't do without this bickering and quarrelling. It dawned on him that both she and her husband were people of another world, that they simply didn't fit into his own—neither the world of science or the world of music. And as if a further act of contrition were needed on his part, he now began to speak about Anka to his wife in the rudest, indeed cruelest terms. "Anka," he wrote, "is a slut . . . The Kalinins are cooling toward me, thank God!" And he added: "Oh! How ashamed I am of the past. Pardon me . . . Forgive me . . . It was just an accident!"

But as a result of this episode, that sense of normalcy, of balance and composure, which had been so characteristic a trait in his earlier days and which had distinguished him from most of the other members of the "Mighty Handful," was now gone.

III

As was the case with many a Russian intellectual of his day, there was much in Borodin's life in those years that was genuinely pleasant and comfortable, but also much that was unattractive. Although his pay from the Academy of Medicine and Surgery, as well as that from the Academy of Forestry and Higher Women's Courses (at both of which he also taught chemistry) came in regularly, he was constantly short of money, largely because he and his wife kept open house and the servants robbed them shamelessly. They were always in debt and though Borodin had by now reached general's rank, he continued to travel third class and had great difficulty in persuading his wife, because of her poor health, to travel in second. Sometimes, to make ends meet, he would speculate on the stock exchange, though mostly without success. Finally he decided, for safety's sake, to take out a life insurance policy at the value of 10.000 rubles (although, in view of his wife's condition, there was a fair chance that he would outlive her). To make things worse, her own large family were also constantly in need, while his two younger brothers, handicapped by a poor education, were often without a job, so that he would sometimes have to help them, too. True, the apartments provided by the authorities to the teaching staff of the Academy were spacious, but maintenance was poor, the pipes were always leaking, and there was often an unbearable stench throughout the building. The heating too was inadequate and occasionally they would have to vacate the premises while a periodic invasion of bedbugs were exterminated with lavender-oil.

Even during the rare months she spent with him, his wife would hardly contribute much comfort or orderliness to his "bachelor's existence." As she suffered from insomnia, she would retire late, preferring to spend her days on a sofa, smoking and reading. She was easily carried away by people, especially lonely intellectual women and was constantly surrounded, therefore, by various female hangers-on, so that their apartment often resembled a boardinghouse. People slept everywhere, in all the rooms, on various couches, even on chairs joined end to end. Sometimes, these occasional boarders would even invade the sanctum of his study. They were of every type and origin: Moscow friends and relatives of Ekaterina Sergheyevna visiting the capital, his own friends and acquaintances, who happened to be without an abode, a pupil or two (and their respective sweethearts—male or female, as the case might be). All of them were welcomed and fed and begged to remain long after they had outstayed their welcome. And besides these transient or semi-transient guests, there was also a constant flow of occasional visitors: students come to ask for advice; colleagues from the Academy or Higher Women's Courses; musician friends. And this continued in his wife's absence.

The fact that Borodin could work at all under such extraordinary conditions testifies to the stern discipline he

imposed upon himself and which enabled him to remain
more or less undisturbed by the chaos all about him. His
work continued along three parallel lines. Firstly and mainly
—his scientific studies in which, even though his talent was
not up to the level of his musical gifts, he rightly saw his
vocation. The second field of endeavor to which he devoted
much time was, alas, again not that of music either. It consisted of his civic duties; his charities, his philanthropic
activities—all of which were virtually a *must* for a Russian
intellectual of those days. Even during the summer, when
the other activities ceased, he was not always able to devote
all of his time to music, as they sometimes rented a summer
house sight unseen, without bothering to ascertain whether
it contained a piano. The house would often be situated in
some God-forsaken spot, far removed from civilization, where
Ekaterina Sergheyevna (who believed in natural therapy)
could go about barefoot all summer. Often there wasn't even
a decent stove.

And yet music remained an integral part of his life. Indeed,
he probably preferred his friends, the "musikuses" (as he
called them) to his other friends, the "chemikuses." But he
felt about them and about music generally somewhat as one
might feel about a holiday, a pastime hobby. The humdrum
prose of everyday life focused around his friends of the Academy. From time to time, of course, it was ever so pleasant
to meet with Korsinka, with Mussorgsky, with Stassov, to
perform for their benefit one of his compositions and listen
to their critical remarks. It was somewhat less pleasant when
they ventured to enquire about his progress with *Prince Igor.*
The Purgold sisters even made him a present of a little
golden locket in the shape of a tortoise—a subtle reminder
of the agonizing slowness of his creative efforts. Stassov and
Mussorgsky were less diplomatic about it and would poke fun
at him cruelly. Long ago, Korsinka had given him a pile of
blank sheet-music with the letterhead in bold print: "*Prince
Igor,* an Opera in Four Acts by A. P. Borodin," which con-

tinued to lie on the window sill, gathering dust. His *Second Symphony* was equally slow in coming—he took six years to write it!—but finally it was ready ("the elephant and its droppings," joked Stassov). In 1876, Napravnik conducted it at a concert of the I.M.S. But it was not a success. *Igor,* meanwhile, did not budge, despite the composer's determination to resume work on it some day. Ekaterina Sergheyevna had all along been hostile to this opera. In this age of positivism and realism, it seemed silly to her that he should revert to a semi-mythical story about Russia's earliest days. Couldn't he find a more contemporary subject? Indeed, he himself may partly have shared these views. Strangely enough, it was not one of his musician friends who convinced him of the need to resume work on his masterpiece, but one of his colleagues at the Academy, his favorite disciple, the chemist Shonorov, who regarded *Igor* as "a work of genius." His opinion settled the matter. And yet even now, it was still too early to rejoice.

For ever since the Anka Kalinina episode he had been suffering from a feeling of despondency. He felt that there was something useless, transitory, short-lived about human existence. Writing to a friend, the singer Karmalina, he complained that "when I discuss him (i.e., *Igor*) I feel somewhat ridiculous. I find myself resembling (Glinka's) Finn in *Ruslan.* Just as he, dreaming away his dreams about his love for Naina, kept forgetting that time, meanwhile, was flying and finally solved the problem only after both he and Naina had become old and grey—I too continue to cherish a perennial dream, that of writing a Russian epic opera. And meanwhile time is flying with the speed of an express-train; the days, weeks, months and winters go by and conditions continue such that I find it simply impossible to think seriously about music . . . It is impossible to wave away the swarm of daily worries and thoughts that have no relation to music and that continue to plague me. I find no time to pause to think, to re-tune myself according to a musical key, without

which no major effort, such as writing an opera, is possible."
And this realization filled him with an odd feeling of sorrow,
such as he had not known before. It was as if he were the
prey of a recurring nightmare in which something infinitely
dear to him was ever escaping his grasp, as if life itself were
eluding him.

IV

In June 1877, Borodin departed on one of his periodic
trips abroad. The purpose of this particular voyage was to
arrange for two of his favorite pupils at the Academy to take
their doctor's degree at the University of Iena. Before leaving, he had mentioned to his wife that it might be a good
idea for him to take advantage of this opportunity to visit
Franz Liszt, who lived nearby, in Weimar. At this time
there was no brighter musical star than Liszt. His fame was
unequalled; his popularity unmatched; a veritable cult had
grown up around him. From Cui, from the publisher Bessel,
Borodin had now learned that the Master had seen his First
Symphony and, what was more, had liked it. What greater
praise could there be? But Ekaterina Sergheyevna knew her
husband and she therefore doubted very much that the visit
would ever materialize.

Presently, however, she received from him a letter in which
he retraced step by step, *ab ovo* as he put it, his meetings
with the great man. "We were sitting in our hotel, on June
30," he began, "and glancing through a paper, when we
suddenly read, that there was to be on July 3 in the Cathedral
of Iena a concert of church music, mostly new things, including four pieces by Liszt: his *Benedictus* for violin, piano and
organ; his *Ave Maria Stella* for male choir and organ, his
Ave Maria for organ and his *Cantico del Sole* for baritone,
choir, organ and piano, plus (how this got on a programme
of church music, I don't know!) Chopin's *Marche Funèbre*
in Liszt's arrangement for cello, piano and organ. Naturally,

we hastened to book seats. At the same time we learned that
Liszt might be coming himself to Iena . . . I must mention
here that I had wanted to pay him a visit anyhow, but had
somehow never summoned up enough courage to do so.
Now, however, I decided to go to see him the very next day.
The distance between Weimar and Iena is about ¾ hour
by train . . . Arriving in Weimar, I decided that Liszt, like
everyone in Germany, must lunch around 1 o'clock and that
I had better, therefore, have lunch myself first and go in
search of him afterwards. It appeared, however, that nobody
knew where he lived. Finally, at an antique-dealer's shop I
learned his address: Marienstrasse 1-17, on the outskirts of
the town, close to the park. The two-storied house in which
he lives stands at the corner of the street. Tiny, built of
stone, it is covered with climbing wild vine. The small wicket-
gate in the iron fence opens into a small, spotlessly neat,
attractive garden . . . Two ladies were seated in the garden
when I arrived, one of them very attractive and clearly not
German. *'Ist Herr Doktor zu sprechen?'* I ask in my best
German.—*'Oh jawohl! Oben, eine Treppe!'* she replies.
Thank God! I say to myself and climb a flight of stairs.
I had hardly reached the top and handed over my card
when there appeared before me, as if he had arisen out of
the ground, a tall figure in a long black coat, with a long
nose and long white hair. *'Vous avez fait une belle symphonie!'* the figure barked and stretched out a long hand.
'Soyez le bienvenu!' he went on, *'Je suis ravi, il n'y a que
deux jours que je l'ai joué chez le Grand-Duc qui en est
charmé!'* The first movement is delightful, the *andante* a
masterpiece, the *scherzo* delightful, and then this, this is
clever . . .' and his long fingers proceed to give an accurate
imitation of the part you know so well. *'C'est d'une originalité
et d'une beauté!'* And so on and so forth! He seized my hand
and pulled me down to a seat on the sofa at his side. I now
wanted merely to thank him and bow my way out. But he
kept talking to me, questioning me, partly in French, partly

in German, jumping from one language to the other. When I told him that I was, actually, a mere *Sonntagsmusiker,* he chuckled and remarked: *'Ja, aber Sonntag ist immer ein Feiertag,* and you have every reason to *feiern!'* He questioned me then about the symphony's success, about the critics' reactions, etc. When I said that I was perfectly aware of its shortcomings and of the need for alterations, that I am, for instance, often clumsy, that I modulate too often (which has often been reproached me) . . . Liszt kept interrupting me: *'Dieu préserve!', 'N'y touchez rien!', 'Ne changez pas!', 'Vous ne modulez jamais ni trop ni mal!', 'Sie sind wohl sehr weit gegangen and das ist eben Ihr Verdienst. Sie haben aber nie gefehlt.* Do not listen, I beg of you, to those who would hold you back from the path you have chosen to follow; you are treading the right path, you have so much artistic instinct that you do not have to fear being too original; remember, the very same advice was given, in their day, to Beethoven, to Mozart and the rest of them and that they would never have become great masters had they followed it.' He questioned me about Korsinka, whom he holds in very great esteem. *'Mr. Rimsky est un très grand talent!'* He related what a dismal failure *Sadko* had been in Vienna, how Anton Rubinstein, who conducted it, came to show him the score and remarked: 'This thing was a failure with me, but you will probably like it.' Which was indeed the case. He ranks *Sadko* very high. He questioned me about Balakirev, about Cui . . . 'You know,' he said, 'the Grand-Duke knows your music very well and likes it very much. Here in Germany it is of course not much appreciated. Do you know Germany? They write an awful lot of music; I am flooded with it, but ye Gods! how flat it all is! Not a live thought! Whereas in your veins there is a live stream; sooner or later (later—more likely as not—than sooner!) it will fight its way through, even here . . . Judging by your card,' he went on, 'you seem to be a master of chemistry. When, how and where did you manage to acquire such a vast musical technique? Where did you study? Surely not in Germany?' And when I told him that I had not attended the Conservatory, he chuckled: '*C'est votre bonheur, mon cher Monsieur! Travaillez! Travaillez toujours!* Even if your music were to encounter no sympathy whatsoever, even were it never to be played in public— believe me, one day it will come into its own! Yours is a tremendous, an unusual talent! Don't listen to anyone, *travaillez à votre manière!*' And when I thanked him for his kindness, he interrupted me angrily: 'But I'm not complimenting you; I'm so old that I cannot afford to say anything but the truth to anyone!' Then upon hearing that I lived not in Weimar, but in Iena, he added: 'Fine! This means that we will meet again tomorrow. *Où logez-vous?*' I naturally wouldn't think of allowing him to bother to return my visit. '*Alors je vous invite demain pour dîner dans le "Bären"* . . . *Sie sind also morgens mein Gast, vergessen Sie es nicht!*' I did not dare ask him to play for me, that would have been too cheeky on my part."

Borodin then went on to describe to his wife how the next morning he had planned to drop by the *Gasthof zum Bären* to beg the *Maestro* to forgive him if he could not dine with him, he had only travel clothes with him, but that on his way there he had dropped into the Cathedral where they were just about to begin to rehearse the afternoon concert. Suddenly, he had heard a whisper: "*Der Meister kommt!*" and he had seen Liszt approaching down the aisle on the arm of the lady Borodin had talked to in his garden, in Weimar (this, he learned later, was Baroness Meyendorf, the widow of a former Russian ambassador to the Grand-Ducal court of Weimar) and followed by a merry crowd of young people —his pupils. As he took his place in a pew, Liszt noticed that one of the girls was poorly seated; he beckoned to her to come and sit down at his side. Then, shading his eyes with his long, thin and beautiful hand, he settled down to listen to the music. Soon, however, he was back on his feet and taking the conductor's place, he went on to conduct the

orchestra himself, calmly, serenely, with hardly a gesture or
an exclamation. Later, he sat down at the piano and played
his arrangement of Chopin's *Marche Funèbre*. As he was
leaving, the young girl he had beckoned to his side ran up
to Borodin and introduced herself. She turned out to be a
compatriot, Vera Timanova, who had heard much about him
from the *Maestro*. When he confided to her his intention of
declining Liszt's invitation to dinner, she begged him to do
nothing of the kind, that the old man would be terribly hurt.
Thus the luncheon took place after all.

Liszt sat at the head of the table, Baroness von Meyendorf
to his right hand, Borodin to his left. The Baroness informed
Borodin that it was she who had played with Liszt his symphony at the Grand-Ducal palace. She seemed better informed than the *Maestro* about musical developments in
Russia. Liszt himself now questioned him about Serov (whom
he did not seem to hold in very high esteem). Serov, apparently, had wanted to stage his *Judith* abroad, but Liszt
had warned him quite frankly that it was doomed to failure
outside of Russia, whereupon the composer seemed to have
been quite distressed. "But I told him the truth as I saw
it," the old man said, "for there is not much creative imagination in that opera!" And Borodin concluded his letter with
the words: "All this is to me like a dream. It's as if I were
in the *Venusberg* in *Tannhäuser,* only here it is Liszt who
plays the part of Venus . . ."

Shortly thereafter, Liszt invited Borodin to a *matinée,* a
traditional Sunday event in his Weimar house. Borodin was
not able to leave Iena that afternoon, however, but went to
Weimar the following day. Upon his arrival, he learned that
the *Maestro* was studying with his pupils. He decided to try
and attend this lesson. As a rule, Liszt did not allow strangers
to be present at his lessons but he welcomed Borodin with
his usual kindness: "There you are, at last! Why didn't you
come yesterday? I missed you. I would have shown you that I
am still able to play quite nicely Chopin's *Sonata for Piano*

and Cello!" And pointing to his class, he exclaimed: "These are all famous pianists, if not right now, then they will be in the future!" The whole atmosphere of the class, Borodin found, was delightfully casual and cozy. Occasionally, Liszt would interrupt one of his pupils, explain a passage, play it over himself or comment on their playing with gentle humor, so that they shouldn't feel hurt: "Try now and play this *à la* Vera!" he would say. (Vera being the girl Borodin had met in the Cathedral of Iena the day of the concert.) Though she had tiny hands, he now heard her play the most difficult passages of Liszt's own compositions with amazing ease, thanks to certain "tricks" which, it appears, the author himself had taught her. She was clearly his favorite. After she had finished playing his *Fourth Rhapsody,* Liszt himself sat down at the piano and repeated a few passages. "It must sound as solemn as a triumphant cortege!" he exclaimed, and jumping up again and taking Vera's arm, he started to march her around the room, humming the theme of the rhapsody. He praised her playing so warmly (*"Sie ist ein famoser Kerl, die kleine Vera!"*) that the girl had tears in her eyes. And he was just as kind with his other pupils, especially the girls. When the lesson was over, he saw them out onto the landing, helped them with their coats and bestowed a kiss on each one's forehead, while they kissed his hand. Borodin was both touched and amused. After all, he couldn't help remembering that Liszt was a monk!

That evening, Borodin had tea at Baroness Meyendorf's house. Liszt was already there when he arrived. The butler announced that tea was served. Liszt offered his arm to his hostess and they proceeded to the dining-room, where, this time, Borodin sat at her right hand and Liszt at her left. After tea, the Baroness slyly begged the old man to show her how a certain passage of one of his rhapsodies should be played. Liszt burst out laughing. "You wish me to play the whole rhapsody?" he asked. "Gladly! Only first I would like to play M. Borodin's symphony at four hands, together with the composer. Which part would you rather play, Sir, *primo* or *secundo*?" But Borodin wouldn't hear of it and finally the Baroness took his place and he had the rare and wonderful experience of listening to one of his own works being played by one of the greatest pianists of all times.

But Liszt was as stubborn as he was kind. "I would still like to play this together with you," he insisted. "It cannot be that you do not know how to play it. You are so clever at arranging things for the piano that I simply cannot believe that you don't play the piano yourself!"—"*Jouez! Jouez donc!*" the Baroness whispered, "*Autrement Liszt vous en voudra, je le connais, moi!*" They started with the *finale*, then played the *scherzo*, then the first movement and thus the whole symphony. Though Borodin kept fumbling over some passages and leaving others unfinished, Liszt insisted that they play through each movement: "Why skip anything? This is so good, there are few such masterpieces in music!" Then Borodin was invited to sing some excerpts from *Prince Igor,* after which Liszt agreed at last to play his symphony. Before leaving, they made him promise to come to Weimar again the following Sunday in order to show them his *Second* Symphony. As he and Liszt walked back to the station (the *Maestro* had, despite Borodin's protests, insisted on accompanying him) Borodin felt quite dizzy with pride and happiness.

On the following Sunday, Borodin went to Weimar as he had promised. First he stopped to pick up Vera Timanova, after which they proceeded together to Liszt's house. "*Eh bien! Vera, tranchez-nous la question orientale à votre manière!*" Liszt exclaimed as they entered. Whereupon Vera sat down at the piano and played, beautifully, Balakirev's excruciatingly difficult *Islamey*. Then Liszt himself began to play the scene of the dances from Rubinstein's *Diemon,* while Borodin and the girl sat on either side of him and turned the pages. Something about Liszt, about his manner of playing and improvising reminded Borodin of the early

Balakirev. Like Balakirev, Liszt also kept re-arranging and adding to the pieces he played, so that his listeners had the impression, each time, of listening to something new, something often more significant than that which he was meant to be playing.

That evening, the Baroness had a surprise in store for Borodin: The Grand Duke of Sachsen-Weimar had asked to meet him and had agreed to come to her house. In vain Borodin tried to explain that he was not properly dressed for such an occasion. "The Grand Duke is interested in you," she replied, "not in your clothes!" And although Borodin, like many a Russian intellectual of his day, was inclined to be prejudiced against Royalty in general, he soon had to admit that the Grand Duke was not just another German princeling, the son of a Russian grand duchess and the grandson of a Russian Czar, but that he was a worthy descendant of Grand Duke Karl-August, the friend and benefactor of Goethe as well as of many other great artists of his day. He turned out to be a modest and pleasant-mannered man, who talked to him about Russian literature (which he knew well), about the works of his friends Rimsky-Korsakov and Cui (whom he referred to as *"Monsieur Coui"*). He said that he was happy to meet yet another representative of their group, whose work he himself deeply appreciated, etc. etc. Then Liszt sat down at the piano together with a young Polish pianist by the name of Zarembski and performed Borodin's symphony. The Grand Duke was quite enthusiastic and promised to include this work in the program of the coming concert season.

Borodin attended yet another *matinée* at Liszt's before returning to Russia. This time he received a gift of an autographed photograph and a manuscript. As he departed, he felt all of a sudden that all that to which he was now returning: his chemistry, his students, his charity events, far from being the "only genuine life," was something needlessly hectic, indeed perhaps even futile.

CHAPTER SIXTEEN

THE "HERR PROFESSOR OF MUSIC"

"Con tanta servitu, con tanto studio."
MICHELANGELO
(With so much patience, so much effort.)

I

After his marriage to Nadia Purgold, Rimsky-Korsakov began to see less and less of his friends of the "Gang." This estrangement was gradual and was at first barely noticeable, for Nadiezhda Nikolayevna was too tactful and intelligent a woman to allow a sudden disruption in their relations. And yet, although she had but recently been herself an enthusiastic supporter of the Balakirev group, she wished at present not to be part of it. For now that she was married to *"Korsinka,"* she resented the fact that his friends and even Balakirev himself regarded her husband's talent, or rather his "genius" (for she refused to refer to it in any other terms) as something of his, Balakirev's, creation. As is sometimes the case with a loving woman, she now began, in her turn, to suffer from wounds of pride which in him had healed long ago, and under her influence Rimsky-Korsakov was at times inclined to forget the tenderness and care with which Balakirev had fostered his young talent and that, despite his paternalistic tyranny, he had not allowed his powerful personality to crush his younger friend's budding musical talent.

Upon being appointed to the post of professor at the Conservatory, Rimsky-Korsakov had in the beginning been also its most diligent student. For he felt that he had to start from scratch, to re-learn musical theory systematically and, like Salieri, to verify the rules of harmony with the aid of algebra. As a result, his pupils would to their amazement find their own professor attending, copybook in hand, the classes of his colleague Iohansen.

Success, like disaster seldom comes alone: After his appointment to the Conservatory, after the triumph of his *Fair Maid of Pskov,* he was now also given the opportunity to cast aside his naval uniform and to become a civilian employee of the Navy Department, with functions which he himself seems to have drafted and which were quite in line with his personal requirements at the time. The Grand Duke Constantine, head of the Navy Department, had recently taken over the function of President of the Imperial Musical Society (which, until her death, had been held by the Grand Duchess Elena Pavlovna). There was thus, at their respective highest levels, a sort of "union" between the Navy Department and the IMS. To further consolidate this union, the Grand Duke now gladly acquiesced in the appointment of his young subordinate to the post of "Inspector of Naval Bands" which (since he earned at the Conservatory only 100 rubles a month) became, thereafter, Rimsky-Korsakov's main means of support. In addition, the Navy Department set up within the Conservatory a special section "for the training of military band musicians" for which scholarships were granted and of which Rimsky-Korsakov was also put in charge.

He could now, at last, devote his entire time to music. He performed his new functions with zeal: Travelling around in Russia, checking the repertoires of the various military bands, verifying the quality and condition of their instruments, looking into the qualifications of the bandmasters. At first he was strict, criticizing both repertoire and performances and even dismissing an aged conductor (for which action he later on bitterly reproached himself). But before long he realized that this merely caused unnecessary hardship to his subordinates and thereafter he did what had been expected of him in the first place, that is he praised and congratulated, rewarded and encouraged. But because, though not yet thirty, he was already "somebody," as it behooves a "somebody," even his praise was wont to be somewhat perfunctory.

These functions turned out to be useful to him for still another reason: they enabled him to study the nature and possibilities of the wood-wind and brass instruments. Conscientious as ever, he started to study the clarinet, the flute and the trombone (for which he showed a special aptitude) and his study was soon cluttered up with instruments of every type and species. He even won over Borodin to this new hobby and they would spend hours together, discussing the possibilities of the various instruments and other problems of orchestration. He also—though without success, for this was unfeasible—attempted to draw up a systematically classified list of all the wind instruments. Then, with a view to improving the average repertoire of the navy bands, he rearranged for them a considerable number of classical and contemporary pieces. And lastly, he began to explore yet another field of musical endeavor which for a long time he had regarded as the private sanctum of such "Gods" as Berlioz or Balakirev: In February 1873, he conducted his first concert.

He chose for the program Mussorgsky's *Rout of Senacherib* and his own *Symphony No. 1*. Though he was able to conceal this from the musicians, he was terribly nervous before the performance and was all the more touched to receive a letter of encouragement from Balakirev (who was still going through his period of retreat). The concert was a success and that autumn (perhaps at Balakirev's own suggestion) the administration of the rather inactive Free School of Music requested Rimsky-Korsakov to take over the symphonic concerts, the resumption of which was now being planned.

The programs he chose for the first two concerts amazed friend and foe alike. They consisted exclusively of the classics: Palestrina, Allegri, Haendel. . . The most modern of them all was, in fact, Haydn! To Stassov, Cui and Mussorgsky, this was a clear proof of betrayal on his part; he was in their eyes now virtually an outcast. Actually, the main reason for this choice was that the Free School had a good choir and that in order to present an interesting choral program, you could hardly avoid turning to the classics.

Subsequent concerts were somewhat more modern in the choice of program, nor did Rimsky-Korsakov forget to include samples of the Russian school. From now on, he was never to cease conducting. Though this had not been his original vocation, he came to love it, but though he showed great knowledge and good taste, he was never able to achieve with his orchestra the subtle rendering and daring sound effects which characterize as a rule the leadership of a *virtuoso*.

Thanks to his extraordinary capacity for hard work, even during these years of continuous and varied activity he never stopped composing. True, his products were still somewhat clumsy, as though he had not yet learned to put to use his accumulated theoretical knowledge. He wrote a quatuor, a quintet with piano, a string sextet—all of them replete with contrapuntal subtleties. But his favorite pastime during these years was to write fugues and canons. Stassov stated that Rimsky-Korsakov wrote 61 fugues and a rough dozen canons during a single summer, and added sadly: *"De mortuis!"* This type of music was so much to his liking that he wrote *Four Variations and a Fuguette* on Russian folk-song themes and even re-orchestrated his *Fair Maid of Pskov* according to all the newly learned rules of the art, thereby killing much of its colorfulness and fire! It seemed as if one could justly apply to him Berlioz's well-known pun that "the fugue is a form of music in which one melody runs on ahead, far outdistanced by the listeners." His *Third Symphony* was a failure; it pleased neither the public, nor his friends, nor the critics (with the single exception of Cui). Even Borodin's approval was qualified: "It's a good symphony," he joked, "but I keep feeling that this is the work of a German *Herr Professor* who has put on his glasses and is about to write *Eine grosse Symphonie in C.*"

II

He was indeed becoming a *Herr Professor*. He would himself at times voice surprise at his proneness to "dry formalism." On one occasion, when two of the most talented pupils of the Conservatory, Liadov and Dütsch, "went Bohemian" and ceased to attend classes and, generally, to work and therefore were expelled, he even displayed cruelty. The two culprits begged him to intercede in their behalf, they promised to behave properly and to work harder than ever. But he refused to do anything for them; eventually, they were taken back without his intervention. Liadov later on became one of his closest friends in spite of this incident. "You have to study," he would say, "which means that you must not neglect harmony and counterpoint. You must acquire a good technique and see to it that the various voices ring clear. We all, i.e., I myself, Borodin, Balakirev, but especially Cui and Mussorgsky, were wont to ignore this need. Because of this lack of technique, Balakirev composes rarely, Borodin at great pains, Cui sloppily and Mussorgsky messily and often absurdly." Though he did not deny them talent, a talent perhaps even superior to his own, he claimed that he "did not envy them."

And yet the fruit of his own "soul-searching" was pretty meager. True, his former opponents were now welcoming him back to the fold like an errant son, who has at last seen the light (though the critic Laroche—whom he, incidentally, detested—shrewdly doubted the sincerity of his "conversion"). And also true: Tchaikovsky's attitude toward him was very positive. "All these innumerable counterpoints," Tchaikovsky said to him, "these 60 fugues are such an exploit on the part of one who, only eight years ago, wrote *Sadko,* that

I would like to proclaim far and wide how tiny, pitiful, naive and smug I find myself in comparison! With your enormous talent, one can expect you to produce things that will leave far behind anything yet composed in Russia." But this praise was projected into the future. The present provided less reasons for satisfaction so that at times even he would wonder whether his would be the life of a creative artist, or merely that of a useful artisan in music. Were his *Antar,* his *Sadko,* his *Fair Maid of Pskov* merely a childhood slip, the whim of an inexperienced youth?

Fortunately, this was not so. A long path of glory lay ahead. He had merely to find his way to integrate his knowledge of theory with the free flow of his fantasy, and technique would become the servant of his inspiration; method would be transformed into the guardian of freedom and the *Herr Professor* become a wizard, a sorcerer, a teller of merry, colorful fairy-tales.

Two events contributed to this revival of his creative talent and both were related to Balakirev. In the first place, Mili enrolled him as a member of the team that was editing Glinka's work and this daily communion with Glinka's lucid, limpid and delightful music, this initiation into the late master's musical world, which had already healed many of Balakirev's own wounds, now had the effect of a powerful stimulant also on Rimsky-Korsakov. Then, Balakirev introduced him to Tertzi Filippov (Mussorgsky's friend and benefactor) who, though he knew countless Russian folksongs from memory, was unable to put them to music. Rimsky-Korsakov now proceeded to take them down and to harmonize them, after which Filippov had them published. Upon completing this first anthology, he continued to collect folksongs and eventually he put out an anthology of his own, entitled: *One hundred Russian songs,* some of which had been taught him by Borodin's old maid (whose contribution he acknowledged in the dedication). He was especially interested in the more ancient songs and specifically in those

pertaining to the cult of *Yarilo*, the sun-god of the ancient
Slavs. As usual, he prepared the ground carefully, studying
all existing material and documentation on the Slavs' religious
customs. Far from obstructing his inspiration, this meticulous
spade-work seems to have made it easier for him to give free
rein to his artistic inventiveness.

The first subject to inspire him to write another opera was
Gogol's *May Night*. He had been reading this fairy tale to
Nadia Purgold the day he proposed to her and was, therefore,
particularly devoted to it. The opera retained all the poetic
quality and unsophisticated humor of the original story and
showed clearly that the fantastic world of the fairy-tale was
one in which he excelled. He played it to Borodin and
Stassov and even the latter had to admit that it was delightful
and that he had never expected anything like it from "that
dried-up old Roman" (*Rim*—the first syllable of his name—
being the Russian word for Rome).

But *May Night* was merely a beginning, a precursor of his
most important operatic work, *The Snow Maiden* (in Russian: *Sniegurochka*). He had come by accident across a transcription in verse of this fairy tale by the famed Russian
dramatist Ostrovsky. He had read it once before, but the
positivistic and realistic views professed by their group at the
time were strong in him too, and he had failed to appreciate
its poetic merits. Now, however, he was enthusiastic; what
could be better and more charming than the Kingdom of
Berendey, or more profound and poetic than the cult of the
sun-god *Yarilo*, or more deeply moving than the story of the
Snowmaiden, whose cold heart had become suddenly in-
flamed with human love. Having obtained the author's permission to do so, he now proceeded to write the libretto
himself.

He spent the summer of 1880, not as he usually did in one
of the innumerable villas or *dachas* with which the countryside around St. Petersburg was dotted, but in genuinely rural
surroundings, the estate of *Stelovo*, near the town of Luga.

Here everything charmed him: the fields of barley, buck-wheat, oats and flax; the woods and coppices; the fruit-garden in the back of the mansion; the tiny river flowing through the estate in which they bathed; the lake overgrown with rushes and water lilies and the names of the neighboring villages which suggested their ancient Slavic origin. As he read and re-read Ostrovsky's poem, he found himself gradually trans-ported into a world where reality and fantasy were inter-twined, where every moss-grown tree-stump was transformed into a wood-goblin, where the smallest wood grew into an enchanted forest, while the bare hillock at the bottom of the garden became the mountain abode of *Yarilo* the sun-god, and the threefold echo which could be heard from the second-floor balcony was multiplied to symbolize the sounds uttered by all the countless strange denizens of the forest. The summer happened to be particularly hot and stormy, practically no day went by without a thunderstorm and it was against this background of continuous thunder and light-ning that his opera progressed with unprecedented speed. In order to go faster still, he did not orchestrate while compos-ing (as he used to in the past) but wrote the music straight for piano and voices. His piano, incidentally, was out of tune. He called it jokingly his "piano in B." By the middle of August, *The Snow Maiden* was finished.

He himself always loved this opera. He even dubbed it his "Ninth Symphony." He considered it not only his best opera, but the best opera that had ever been written. It was accepted by the Mariinsky Theatre and Napravnik began to study it with his usual conscientiousness. But the music was not to his taste; moreover, he still bore Rimsky-Korsakov a grudge for the latter's ill-considered attack on his own opera in the press; he requested cuts and when Rimsky-Korsakov mentioned shyly that even long operas were sometimes staged with suc-cess, as for instance Meyerbeer's *The Huguenots,* the usually polite and reserved Czech flared up and coldly staring at him, replied: "Yes, but *The Huguenots* is a *live* opera, whereas yours is as dead as a doormouse!" The public, nevertheless, liked it; only the critics were, as usual, sour.

On an earlier occasion, Rimsky-Korsakov had commented upon the strange conflict that existed within him between the man and the artist. The man in him, he said, was rationalistic, up-to-date with current events, he refused to believe in the supernatural, in the "not-of-this-world" and felt somewhat uncomfortable at funerals. Whereas the artist in him loved all that was most fantastic, fairy-tale-like; regarded ancient pagan pantheism as the best of all religions and strove to put to music the ancient religious rites and dances. And he had accordingly come to the conclusion that art was merely an enchanting delusion, a stroke of magic. But throughout that summer of 1880 the artist in him reigned supreme over the man. And it is because of that, perhaps, that more than any other of his operas, *The Snow Maiden* conveys such an impression of genuine human truthfulness.

III

It is to the extent that he believes or does not believe in the metaphysical function of art, that the artist may be aligned with one of the three main schools of artistic thought —the classical, the realistic and the romantic. Some artists regard art as the supreme truth, possessing the power to transform life and these, even though they might call themselves classicists or realists, are in fact romantics. For it is in the nature of the romantic school to blend life with art. Art should not only reflect life, it should also transform it. At the same time, the romantics are drawn beyond the bounds of both art and life, toward something limitless, infinite, eternal. "I seek that which does not exist on earth"; these oft-derided words of a decadent lady-poet could well serve as their motto. The superhuman, the titanic, the mystical—these are the worlds with which they are concerned, even though this blending of life with art may not be successful, even though it may bring hardship, insanity and even destruction in its wake. And as a result, Byron dies of cholera at Missolonghi, Lermontov is killed in a duel, Mussorgsky drinks himself to death, Gogol starves himself to death, Balakirev gives up music for years, etc. etc. In their youth, all artists are romantics; all of them yearn for love, for sanctity, for eternity; and fortunate is he, who early recovers his senses and realizes the need for self-containment and moderation, the need to keep art and life apart. Alone the biographer is genuinely attracted to the romantics. For it is in the nature of the biographer to seek the point of contact between the two concepts of life and art, as a source of fantastic, wonderful sparks. Conversely, the biographer is apt to be bored with the sober specialists and professionals.

Rimsky-Korsakov was one of those professionals who had learned to separate art from life. He had decided early to forego the unusual, to forego perhaps even dreaming about the unusual. Instead he had chosen to live the habitual routine life of an ordinary human being, with its everyday routine joys and sorrows—though these, incidentally, need not necessarily be any less profound than the more flamboyant emotions of the romantics!—a life based on method, system, hard work. The best in him, however, served art, not life, so that a biographer can find but little to relate about him. To understand him, to explore his innermost soul, therefore, it is necessary to study his works, not his life.

And yet, meanwhile, life too was following its course. Children were born to him, the first four—children of his youth —healthy, strong, capable; the last three—children of his old age—more frail (two of them died). His work at the Conservatory continued apace. Only his friends and acquaintances changed, and occasionally also his home. At one time, the Rimsky-Korsakovs and the Borodins lived as neighbors, so that it was even agreed that every time Rimsky-Korsakov signalled out of his window, Borodin would give up his chemical experiments and turn to music! In the summer, the whole family would leave town, occasionally travelling abroad. Toward the end of his life, Rimsky-Korsakov took a special liking for his estate *Vechasha,* where he found it particularly easy to work. Shortly before his death, he bought still another estate, situated nearby, *Lubensk,* which had a magnificent fruit garden. It is there that he died.

IV

The early eighties witnessed two events which were to be of equally great significance for the history of Russian art and music generally, and for Rimsky-Korsakov in particular. They were, to some extent, inter-related. The first was the discovery of a new "genius," a new hope for the Russian school of music. The other was the beginning of Rimsky-Korsakov's friendship with the millionaire Beliayev.

This "genius" (which was the way the ever-enthusiastic Stassov, of course, referred to him) or at any rate this major talent was a young high-school boy by the name of Aleksander, or *"Sasha"* Glazunov, whose father was a well-known and successful publisher and whose mother was a musician in her own right, who had studied music with Balakirev. Young Glazunov had taken his first lessons with Balakirev too, after which the latter had passed both him and his mother on to Rimsky-Korsakov. Despite their difference in age, the two men soon became close friends, regarding each other virtually as equals. For Glazunov's progress was so incredibly rapid that he had soon learned all there was to learn and by the age of sixteen had already written his first symphony and first quartet. This symphony was so unusual, so mature, that Balakirev promptly included it in the program of a concert of the Free School where it scored a considerable success. Considering the composer's age, all this seemed so unbelievable, that the rumor immediately spread that the boy's parents (who could afford to do so) had commissioned the symphony to be written by his teachers. Actually, apart from a few minor corrections, it was entirely his own work.

Sasha Glazunov was soon the idol of his older friends, partly because they recognized their youthful selves in his image, partly because they chose to see in him that which they most wished to see: Stassov—the continuer of the Glinka tradition in the Russian school of music and the cornerstone of a new "Mighty Handful"; Balakirev—another pupil, another disciple; Rimsky-Korsakov—a real, serious professional musician who, unlike himself, unlike most of the "Balakirev Gang," had been fortunate enough to find his footing right away, without prolonged fumbling in the dark. Still more enthusiastic and passionate, however, was the recognition accorded to young Glazunov by Mitrofan Petrovich Beliayev, a lumber millionaire who was just then acquiring a growing influence in St. Petersburg musical circles.

Czarist Russia seems to have been quite a unique breeding-ground for this type of person. A merchant with the soul of an artist, himself an artist *manqué,* very good-looking in a rugged masculine sort of way, with hair down to his shoulders, a large head set on a somewhat bullish neck and a powerful torso, Beliayev had, in his young days, himself dreamt of becoming a musician. Having lacked the courage, however, to give up the family business, he had had to be content to play (pretty poorly) the *alto,* to participate in amateur chamber-music recitals and to throw fabulous parties for all his musician friends. He also played, occasionally, with the orchestra which, under Liadov's direction, performed at the German Club. Liadov was thus the first composer he befriended. But his was too capricious, too effeminate, too unbalanced a temperament for Beliayev's taste. Presently, he met also Stassov (who greatly impressed him) and Rimsky-Korsakov (whom he recognized as a sincere, earnest, "100% man"). But although he appreciated and respected them all, nothing could compare with the passionate devotion he displayed toward Glazunov. This feeling may have been prompted, to some extent, by the social and ideological kinship that existed between them. For unlike the other members of the "Balakirev Gang," Glazunov came from the same world as Beliayev, the merchant world, and in Russia this had been, since times immemorial, a very special world indeed, somewhat like that of the Parsees of India. Even their religion often distinguished the wealthy merchants from the rest of Russian society, for many of them were "Old Believers" (a sect that had broken away from the main body of the Russian Orthodox Church in the seventeenth century). Beliayev may also have recognized in Glazunov the artist that he himself might have become, in his early days, had he possessed more talent and a greater determination. And as a result, that which he may not have done for others (though they might really have needed it) he was now gladly, enthusiastically prepared to do for Glazunov, who did not need his help, being himself wealthy. First he founded in Leipzig a publishing house to publish Glazunov's music; then he organized the so-called "Russian Symphony Concerts" to perform Glazunov's symphonies; then he created prizes to reward him and encourage him. Finally, he took Glazunov on trips abroad, to entertain him and round out his education. There was just nothing he would not have done for him. Not that Beliayev was a complete altruist. Indeed, he could also be rude as well as brutal. One day, when Serov's widow came to see him about the publication of her late husband's opera, he refused to receive her even though she came, she said, on Rimsky-Korsakov's recommendation. "*They* are not dressed yet," she was informed.—"That's all right, I'll wait."—"*They* don't wish to talk."—"In general, or only with me?"—"*They* don't wish to talk with *you*."

Everything Beliayev did was done on a large scale. The publishing house bought only those compositions which it regarded as first class, paying top prices for them and printing them at the best printing establishments, the operas being printed simultaneously in the complete orchestral score, in the *Klavierauszug* and in the individual part scores. The composers were required to check the galley-proofs twice over; they were not paid until this was done. The direction of this publishing house was in the hands of Rimsky-Korsakov, Stassov and Liadov. Liadov and Rimsky-Korsakov also directed his "Russian Symphony Concerts," Beliayev acting only in an advisory capacity which, however, carried considerable weight. His music prizes (the "Glinka Prize" and others) for chamber and symphonic compositions were distributed anonymously, through Stassov. Not content to subsidize these operations during his lifetime (the value of his awards alone was estimated for that period at some 60.000 rubles) Beliayev saw to it that they were well endowed after his death, through a bequest of a further 600.000 rubles. This endowment fund was to be administered by Rimsky-Korsakov, Glazunov and Liadov and, after their death, by their appointed successors. This set-up operated so smoothly that it survived up to the Revolution. But already during his lifetime, the publishing house kept buying the works of minor composers, a scheme which eventually became a heavy burden. Also, the prizes were not always given to the most worthy. Shortly before his death, Rimsky-Korsakov himself received an award of 1.700 rubles for which he was mercilessly teased by his friends.

Beliayev's house became, naturally, a gathering place for many musicians. His "musical Fridays" had long been a regular feature of the St. Petersburg season, the cult of the arts pleasantly alternating with the carousing and merry-making traditional in the pre-Revolution merchant world. These gatherings would begin with a concert of chamber music; this was followed by a sumptuous supper of caviar in huge silver bowls and bottle upon bottle of expensive wines and champagne, after which the guests would sit down to a game of cards that lasted until dawn. How little this resembled the modest gatherings at Balakirev's or the Purgolds'!

Presently, Beliayev's "musical Fridays" began to be frequented also by less desirable elements (in Rimsky-Korsakov's view). Thus, Tchaikovsky introduced to his host the critic Hermann Laroche who, despite Rimsky-Korsakov's undisguised hostility, was soon *persona grata* there. Tchaikovsky himself, whenever he happened to be in St. Petersburg, always attended them and his charm was, as usual, irresistible. Gradually the cult of Tchaikovsky grew until it was firmly established in the Beliayev circle. While Rimsky-Korsakov was prepared to reconcile himself to this trend, he could not abide the presence of "that fat pig Laroche" (as he called him). The latter sought to gain admittance to his house too; on one occasion, he was even so bold as to come there uninvited, but encountered such an icy welcome on the part of Nadiezhda Nikolayevna that he withdrew in confusion. Neither she, nor her husband could forgive him his persecution of Mussorgsky and his mocking of all that constituted the essence of the Russian school of music.

Besides, the latter's leader himself was not in Beliayev's good graces. He refused to publish Balakirev's works or to help finance the concerts of the Free School which, in his opinion could in no way benefit Russian music. Balakirev, for his part, was inclined to look upon Beliayev's Symphony Concerts merely as well-financed competitors and he was indignant that Rimsky-Korsakov should have consented to "enter that shopkeeper's service" as he put it. He referred to Beliayev invariably in such biting terms that Rimsky-Korsakov eventually had to request him to refrain from doing so in his presence.

Rimsky-Korsakov realized, of course, full well how much the Beliayev circle differed from the Balakirev group of his young days. But then the times of storm and stress were now over. Russian music had come into its own. There was no longer any need for a revolutionary group of musical innovators. The Beliayev circle could afford to be moderately progressive; not too hot, not too cold; eclectic; tolerant;

routine-like. Its members had no longer any call to be narrow-minded; they need not reject either Wagner, or the classics; and they adored technique and theory. In other words, the Beliayev circle reflected faithfully the opinions and tastes of its guiding spirit—Rimsky-Korsakov.

Curiously enough, although Beliayev was an ardent opponent of those he called contemptuously "illiterate decadents" and even forbade his executors in his will to encourage them, one of his last and most dearly beloved protégés was, of all people, Scriabin (though the latter was in those days still an imitator of Chopin). "Write just as you think and feel," he would say to him, "however much I may scold you for it." And this close friendship between the nervous, over-sensitive, over-refined and egocentric composer, who was destined to become, in a way, the leader of the world "decadent" movement and the somewhat uncouth, all-of-one-piece Maecenas, lasted until the latter's death.

V

Mussorgsky's death was a painful loss to Rimsky-Korsakov. Although they had not been close for years and hardly ever saw each other any more, he could never forget that Modest had once been his closest friend and that they had started off together in life and in their work. It meant, moreover, an additional burden of work for him.

For the deceased's musical heritage was in a state of great disorder. Though Modest regarded *Khovanshchina* as completed, only a few excerpts had actually been published; furthermore, with the exception of the few pieces which Rimsky-Korsakov had himself scored with the author's consent in the latter's lifetime, most of it was not even orchestrated. Mussorgsky himself had scored only three pieces: *Martha's Song,* the *Choir of the Streltzi* and *Shaklovity's Aria* (which had been, incidentally, mislaid). In addition, the whole opera was full, in Rimsky-Korsakov's opinion, of gross technical mistakes. Even the existing orchestrations had to be corrected. He had now to become in effect a sort of second author of *Khovanshchina*. He plunged into this work with his usual conscientiousness and entered into the spirit of the opera with such complete self-negation that he could rightly joke that: "I feel, at times, that I *am* Mussorgsky, that my name is Modest Petrovich!" But as usual, he took it upon himself to make many cuts (including the scene where the people destroy the scribe's stand) and also to change some of the tonalities, to shorten some of the parts, or even to re-do them altogether. For this, however, he always made a point of using the composer's original notes and drafts. One cannot say exactly, therefore, what was the author's original contribution and what was his own share. One thing is certain, Rimsky-Korsakov's merit in saving *Khovanshchina* was great.

The situation with *Boris Godunov* was somewhat more complex. The opera had been completed already in Mussorgsky's lifetime. There existed (in Bessel's edition) a *Klavierauszug,* as well as a full orchestral score which had never been printed, but had served for staging it for a number of years. Rimsky, personally, always had mixed feelings about *Boris*. "I worship this opera," he would say, "and yet at the same time I hate it! I worship it for its unusual power, its daring, its originality. And I hate it because it is unfinished, because of its harmonic crudeness, and—in certain parts—complete musical incongruity." His decision to correct *Boris* has been explained, therefore, by his desire to make it easier to stage and thus to render it more accessible to the public. Rimsky-Korsakov's cuts certainly made it more "digestible" and his sumptuous and yet delightful re-orchestrations smoothed down the rough edges of Mussorgsky's recitatives, softened the puritanical harshness of his harmonies and tempered his revolutionary innovations.

But this tremendous work of editing was not dictated solely by technical considerations. Rimsky-Korsakov was also prompted by deep-rooted personal convictions. He was not out merely to correct the slips of a pupil. He was, in fact, continuing his perennial struggle against that "teaching of ignorance" for which he had begun to reproach both Balakirev and Mussorgsky more than ten years earlier. Indeed, had he now allowed these errors to pass, had he left untouched this reckless, dilettantish, musical hodge-podge, he would thereby have denied all that he himself had so long stood for; he would have acknowledged that he had been wrong all along and that he had studied and worked in vain. Though he sincerely believed that he was serving his friend's memory and though the sumptuous raiments in which he "dressed" *Boris* were eventually to astound the world, it is doubtful whether Mussorgsky himself would now have recognized his own work.

Actually, Rimsky-Korsakov had himself some misgivings about the propriety of his action. "What right have I," he wrote, "to change that which has already once been submitted to the verdict of the public? The composer completed his work as best he could, as best he knew. For good or for evil, it is done." He rightly surmised that he would be "ostracized" for these changes; indeed even "beaten up." The objection came, in the first place, as he expected, from Stassov, his own sister-in-law, Sasha Molass, and all the other "Old Believers" of the Russian school. Later, these were joined by the "decadents" and the "innovators," and this was for some reason even more unpleasant to him. And yet his sense of duty and his conscience overruled even the fear of being "ostracized." It was not his fault that his late friend, for all his creative talent, suffered from an "unpardonable sloppiness and ignorance," indeed if he had simply a "poor ear" (sic!). Oddly enough, Rimsky-Korsakov was himself extremely sensitive to any criticism of his own compositions. For safety's sake, he would even preface the edited scores of his operas with the warning that he would tolerate no cuts and on one occasion, when it was pointed out to him that *Sadko* was too long for the tastes of a Parisian audience, he came up with the

somewhat naive suggestion that it be staged in two installments. And yet Mussorgsky's operas could, in his opinion, be
cut as he saw fit.

VI

Borodin's sudden death meant to Rimsky-Korsakov the
loss not only of one to whom he was linked by childhood
memories, but that of a dear friend whom he had never
stopped seeing and to whom he had remained deeply devoted. True, in recent years, Borodin had changed much,
both physically and spiritually. Following a bout of cholera,
he had lost all his earlier stamina and vitality while his oriental indifference and lethargy increased at the same time.
Musically he had become completely sterile. But nothing
heralded an imminent end. Then, on February 15, 1887, at
a pre-Lenten ball, where Borodin dressed in a Russian silk-
shirt, danced around and joked, he suddenly crashed to the
floor, dead. All his life the spoilt child of fate, Borodin had
thus been granted one last favor, that of dying instantane-
ously, not knowing how near his end was.

Rimsky-Korsakov had done all in his power to ensure that
Prince Igor be completed. He had even offered to serve as
Borodin's "musical secretary" and had implored him to allow
him to orchestrate the opera, promising that this would be
done in his, the author's spirit, and following his instructions. But Borodin reacted with little enthusiasm to this
suggestion and gave him only one scene to "put in order,"
and when his friend became too insistent, he would seek to
put him off by promising to do anything he asked. But when
the latter then enquired: "Well, have you written anything?"
he would reply, very seriously: "Sure I have written something!" (by which he merely meant that he had written a
letter) and when Rimsky-Korsakov pressed him: "Have you
re-arranged anything?" he would answer in the same spirit:
"Of course!" (meaning that he had shifted his note-music

from the table to the piano). The opera made somewhat more rapid progress only when Rimsky-Korsakov succeeded in obtaining certain excerpts for his symphonic concerts, for in such cases Borodin was obliged to score the selections he had chosen. And yet even then he could not always be relied upon to finish the assignment on time. On one such occasion, the program had already been printed and posted, there was little time left for rehearsals, and the scoring had still not been completed. Borodin, Rimsky-Korsakov and young Liadov had to sit up all night to meet the deadline. To speed things up, they wrote in pencil; the score-sheets were then fixed by Borodin with a layer of gelatine, after which they were hung up to dry on clothes-lines which had been strung across Rimsky-Korsakov's study, like laundry.

Rimsky-Korsakov had always known that if he outlived Borodin, it would be up to him to complete what had always seemed to him a "marvellous opera," but that, conversely, were he the first to go, *Igor* would never see the light of day. All night long, following his friend's death, he remained awake, trying to recall those parts which had so often been played in his presence, but had never been written down. When dawn came, he had made up his mind. The opera would be completed, whatever the cost. And he found some consolation in this thought.

Together with young Glazunov, whom he had enrolled for this new assignment, he now proceeded to go through Borodin's files. Fortunately, they had so often listened to their friend as he played to them his various compositions, that they had thoroughly penetrated his musical world. Much of *Igor*, however, had either never been written down, or had merely been jotted down on odd scraps of paper which they now had to find, identify, decipher and consolidate. Glazunov had fortunately an exceptional musical memory and he was thus able to reconstrue many a missing part.

Slowly, laboriously, their work progressed. They discov-

ered, for instance, that the opera had never had an overture.
But Glazunov recalled the scenes and specific themes which
Borodin had meant to use for this purpose, some of which
he had even noted down. The overture, as we now know it,
is therefore actually the work of Glazunov. The prologue
and first scene of Act I were left as they were, but already in
the second scene, Rimsky-Korsakov was obliged to add a
short passage linking up the exit of Prince Vladimir Galitzky
with the arrival of the *boyars* (the Princess' recitative: *"I am
all a'trembling"*). Borodin had written a brief sketch of the
Tocsin, to which Rimsky-Korsakov made certain additions.
Act II gave them no less trouble. They had constantly
to add a couple of bars here, a recitative there, an entire choir
number elsewhere. Thus, the *Russian Choir* was re-written
by Glazunov from memory in its entirety, though he could
not vouch for its complete accuracy. Even worse was the
situation with Act III, for which Borodin had not even prepared a scenario. This was now done by Rimsky-Korsakov.
The march of the *Polovetzki* warriors had not been orchestrated, etc. etc. Some of their additions were based on random
themes, found scattered among Borodin's notes, without any
indication as to how they were to be used. All this was done,
of course, as far as possible in Borodin's spirit and according
to his personal technique, but in fact only Act IV was really
entirely his own.

They worked without remuneration: the rights for *Prince
Igor* (Borodin's widow having survived her late husband by
only a few months) were turned over to the Academy of
Medicine and Surgery for the purpose of setting up a scholarship fund in his memory.

VII

Rimsky-Korsakov's own creative work seemed, over the
years, subject to many ups and downs. At the age of sixteen,
he had astounded Balakirev with his first symphony. After

three years of silence he had, upon his return from the training cruise, offered an enthusiastic public his *Sadko* and *Antar*.
Then, for four long years he had written his delightful *Fair
Maid of Pskov*. After which his creative talent seemed to have
been exhausted. Six years were to elapse before it found a new
period of inspiration in Gogol's *May Night,* reaching a further
peak of perfection in *The Snow Maiden*. Then, seven more
years of drought, followed in the late eighties by a remarkable
new inspiration which led to his *Spanish Capriccio* (1887) and
his *Scheherezade* and *Sunday Overture* (1888). This was followed by a short spell (1888-1889) of Wagnerian influence,
after his erstwhile prejudices against his great German contemporary had been swept away overnight upon hearing at
St. Petersburg the first performance of the *Nibelungen*.
Though he had always regarded himself as a proficient master
of orchestration, he now realized how pale his own works
appeared when compared to this overwhelming, fresh, revolutionary torrent. Not that he liked all of Wagner's things.
Tristan and Isolde, for instance, depressed him. But he
studied Wagner as he had studied hardly any other composer,
even Bach.

This Wagnerian influence showed itself for the first time
in his opera-ballet *Mlada,* which many years ago had been the
theme of an unsuccessful joint effort of the whole "Balakirev
Gang" and for which he now wrote a new libretto. The
music, renewed and transformed in Wagner's spirit, turned
out to be both novel and enchanting. He felt an odd sort of
pain when writing this piece, as if it were his last composition, his swan's song. But though the Wagnerian influence
in *Mlada* was strong, there was in it, also, much of Liszt and
Balakirev. Its most Wagnerian feature was, perhaps, the
libretto, with its gods, its mythology, its rainbows and inun-
dations. Wagner, however, knew how to imbue his mytho-
logical dramas with grandiose metaphysical poetry. *Mlada's*
libretto, on the other hand, is just boring. For the first time,
also, he wrote for an enlarged "Wagnerian" orchestra and

he did it like a child discovering a new toy, with gusto
coupled with excitement. Like Wagner, he gave explicit
instructions as to how the work should be staged. For its
part, the Mariinsky Theatre—eager to become the Bayreuth
of "Russia's Wagner"—was very generous. And yet, despite the elaborate and costly sets and costumes and the
beauty of the music, *Mlada* was not a success with the public.
Nor is it likely to have a comeback. Less understandable is
its lack of success on the concert-stage, though this may be
due to the fact that in re-arranging, as was his habit, his opera
in symphonic form, Rimsky-Korsakov did not choose the best
passages.

Meanwhile, the composer's premonitions seemed about to
come true; he now suffered great personal grief: First his two
youngest children died one after the other, and then his wife
and other children fell seriously ill, so that he had to give
up his work altogether to look after them. At one time, he
thought that a change of climate, of atmosphere might be
the solution, that he should leave "tired, stagnant St. Petersburg," as he put it, and settle down in Moscow, which, he
thought, was "younger and more energetic, less cloudy, less
dark." The "cloudiness" and "darkness," however, were
really within himself. Then he engrossed himself in a field
that had hitherto been alien to him, that of philosophy and
esthetics, and he did so with such complete absorption that
the doctors soon forbade him to work at all. And then all of
a sudden, he recovered. It was as though he had crossed a
mysterious, hidden boundary line; as though his talent had
matured overnight and inspiration would, thereafter, never
again forsake him. And indeed, from then on and until his
death, he was to write one opera a year. Sometimes even one
opera, as he put it, would "jostle another" and he would
work on two of them simultaneously.

The first was again on a Gogol theme, *The Night Before
Christmas* (1894-1895); here he stressed the element of witch-
ery, a carry-over of paganism into Christian times. He empha-

sized elements which Gogol himself had mentioned only in passing, such as the night-flight of the demons and stars in the last act. Fourteen years had elapsed since his first Gogol opera, *May Night*, and yet the technique was the same. Only the inspiration seemed less powerful, the music had become more mental, more intellectual, less poetic, less humorous. When the time came to stage this work, there occurred a small tragi-comical incident. Under the then existing rules of censorship, it was forbidden to bring out onto the stage members of the ruling Romanov dynasty. What then was he to do with Catherine the Great who appears in the last scene? Rimsky-Korsakov went to see the Minister of the Court, who received him most courteously and agreed to suspend the rule in this particular case. Some of the rehearsals, however, were attended by a few elderly and stern members of the Imperial Family, who promptly demanded that their ancestor should not be impersonated on the stage. The ban was re-established.

He wrote his next opera during the summer of 1895, while staying at his favorite estate *Vechasha* (where he had also written *The Night Before Christmas*). This time he reverted to a subject which he had treated once before, many years ago, in the form of a symphonic poem, that of *Sadko,* the traveller from Novgorod who after a storm ends up in the underwater realm of the King of the Seas and is saved due to his love for the King's daughter. He wrote the libretto with the assistance of Stassov and of a new friend, one Bielsky, who was spending the summer in the neighborhood. This opera became one of his favorites and this time, fortunately, the public shared his preference. First staged at the millionaire-merchant Mamontov's private theatre, *Sadko* was to earn for itself, thereafter, a place in the Russian operatic repertoire.

A year later—a sudden odd tangent off his firmly chartered course—he wrote *Mozart and Salieri* in which, while respecting all of Pushkin's original text, he reverted to the declamatory recitatives so dear to Dargomyzhsky's and Mussorgsky's hearts. The opera was not much of a success, surviving only thanks to Shaliapin's performance in the role of Salieri.

In 1898 he wrote in the same style a short opera on the subject of Lev Mey's prologue to his own *Fair Maid of Pskov* —the very same prologue which he himself had chosen to leave out in writing the *Maid* 25 years earlier. He named it *The Boyarina Vera Sheloga.*

The following year he chose for a libretto another drama in verse by the same Lev Mey, *The Czar's Bride* (in Russian: *Tzarskaya Nevesta*), which Borodin had once also considered. This time he attempted to revert to Glinka's strictly vocal style, through a revival of Italian-type arias, duets and even (*horrible dictu!*) quartets and sextets. He had never had much melodic gift; his *forte* had always been the adaptation or imitation of folk themes and such a strictly vocal approach was bound, therefore, to be a failure, even though he himself was satisfied with the results. "Can my destiny be," he complained, "to depict only witchcraft, ghouls and monsters —terrestrian, aquatic and amphibious?"

His next work, *Czar Saltan* (1899-1900) was a real success. The libretto, based on a fable by Pushkin, was again done by Bielsky. *The Snow Maiden* and *May Night* had been based on "literary fables." Pushkin's stylized adaptations of genuine "folk fairy-tales" were somehow closer to his heart. Such folk-tales are in themselves a unique form of stylization, full of symbols and schematic implications. Their heroes are not live persons, but puppets with symbolic, uncomplicated feelings and emotions. Rimsky-Korsakov, who had always found difficulty in handling live people and their passions and in penetrating the human soul, was infinitely more successful in depicting the heroes of such fairy-tales. On one occasion he compared *Czar Saltan* to a "reproduction on squared paper" while *The Czar's Bride,* he claimed, was a "drawing off the cuff." The trouble was that these "squared-paper reproductions" succeeded with him far better than his "off-the-cuff drawings." They were more attuned to his talent, for he possessed a quite unique gift for putting into musical language the charm and originality of the Russian fairy-tale, its wise irony and that mysterious, bewitching "something" which is the essential attribute of a fairy-tale. And the result was invariably a sort of scintillating mosaic, an enamelled Persian-style miniature, loved by children and adult persons alike.

Then, following the less successful *Servilia* (1901-1902), *Skinny-Bones the Immortal* (in Russian: *"Koshtcheya"*) and *Pan Voyevoda* (1902-1903) he wrote his two last operas: *Kitezh* and *The Golden Cockerel* (in Russian: *Zolotoy Petushok.*)

Kitezh lends itself easily to a comparison with Wagner's *Parsifal.* But then the Germans are past masters at developing an idea through to its logical conclusion, in the Hegelian meaning of the word. Thus Wagner completed his creative cycle with a mystical drama which is a blend of Buddhist pessimism and Christian redemption. Though he was to live several more years after completing *Kitezh*, Rimsky-Korsakov's last work was to be not a mystical "idea opera," *à la Parsifal,* but the charming, provocative, engaging *Golden Cockerel.*

As *Parsifal* with Wagner, *Kitezh* was the high point, the summation of all that was most spiritual in Rimsky-Korsakov. And yet it is difficult to picture oneself anything that differed more from Wagner's ideas and ideals, than this cheerful, pantheistic, semi-pagan, semi-Christian mystery. For *Kitezh* is much closer to the spirit of St. Francis of Assisi, of Russia's Saint Serafim of Sarov and of Dostoyevsky's Father Zossima. The libretto was written by Bielsky in close cooperation with the composer. A man of many talents and interests, Bielsky created a dramatic poem of great beauty, irrespective of its musical quality. The legend of the invisible town of *Kitezh* is in itself full of mystical significance and charm. By now, the story is familiar: The Tartars advancing in their destructive march through Russia are about to besiege the ancient town of Kitezh, which lies on the shores of a wooded

lake called "Luminous Yar." But the prayers of the fair maid
Fevronia are hearkened to by the Virgin Mary, who saves
the town by immersing it at the bottom of the lake, where
it continues to live and prosper and from where one can
occasionally even hear the chimes of its countless bells.

Both librettist and composer were very successful in depicting the image of Fevronia, the fair Russian maid into
whose lips Bielsky placed words of Orthodox faith which
reflected Rimsky-Korsakov's own profound religious convictions:

> "Believe me, not that tear is holy
> Which starts to flow from grief.
> Only that tear is holy
> Which flows from God-given joy.
> And do not fear to sin, dear one,
> For each one will be loved for what he is . . .
> For in each soul there is a little of God's grace."

The music of *Kitezh* is also often beautiful and inspiring.
And yet it was slow in gaining the public's favor. The latter
found it too "intellectual," too devoid of deep, human
emotions.

VIII

Two circumstances, in particular, stimulated him and provided an incentive for his work. The first was that, apart
from the Imperial theatres (so far the only theatres in Russia), there existed now a number of private houses, the most
important and best organized of which was that of the Moscow millionaire and Maecenas Savva Mamontov. A railway
tycoon of great talent and violent temperament, Mamontov
regarded Rimsky-Korsakov's operas as works of genius and
opened the doors of his theatre wide to them. The painter
Vrubel's wife, Mrs. Zabello, was the first performer of the
heroines' roles, specializing in those of his more mysterious,
out-of-this-world characters, to which her small, but incredibly pure soprano was particularly well suited. Presently, the

composer and his star-singer began to correspond, and this exchange led eventually to a deep friendship between them, the only feminine friendship in his life . . . Besides this artist, a young musician of genius, the bass Feodor Shaliapin, was just beginning to gain world-wide fame, and thanks to him, the bass and baritone roles in Rimsky-Korsakov's operas glowed with unsurpassed light and colors. For his sake, the composer even revived (in a third version) his now long-forgotten *Fair Maid of Pskov,* and the triumph scored by Shaliapin in the role of Czar Ivan the Terrible far surpassed the purely musical success it had scored in its earlier versions.

Even more important, however, was the appearance in St. Petersburg of a rather large group of young people who greatly admired his work and who called themselves in jest "The Society of Unremunerated Cheer-Leaders." Thanks to them, it became easier for him to bear up with the utterances of anguish or despair of his critics and the public's cool reception of his latest works. Of these young admirers, the most vocal and sincere was one of his pupils, Yastrebtzov, a fanatic of music in general and of Rimsky-Korsakov's music in particular who, however, had never completed his studies at the Conservatory. With Yastrebtzov and his friends, Rimsky-Korsakov turned from a "dry stick of a Professor" into a warm-hearted and kind elderly friend, willing to devote to them much of his time and effort. He overwhelmed Yastrebtzov with manuscripts (which the young man frantically copied) and autographs and they were constantly together. Like Goethe's Eckermann, Yastrebtzov kept a diary in which he religiously noted down all that the composer said. Alas, Rimsky-Korsakov was no Goethe and when he was not talking about music, he would often say the most absurd things. He feared, for instance, that art faced a crisis. "In painting," he maintained, "Russia has surpassed Europe. But she has provided no new forms of art. It's always the same thing: genre and landscapes. Alright, you'll say that we don't have too many paintings of Siberia, or of the province of Viatka, but what with modern techniques we'll soon have them, too. What then?"

In music, however, he was far wiser, displaying an encyclopedic knowledge, vast understanding and faultless taste. And yet even here, he looked to the future with a certain pessimism. It seemed to him that before his very eyes and with his assistance, all possible new combinations of sound were being gradually explored and exhausted and that eventually music would become purely mechanical and a matter of routine. In this he remained true to his convictions—basically skeptical, a positivist incredulous of the inexhaustible power of the spirit.

He now proceeded to initiate Yastrebtzov into the most treasured secrets of his musical laboratory. For instance, he revealed to him one of his own accoustic peculiarities: He claimed that he saw all tonalities colored differently, like a visual spectrum. Thus E-major appeared to him stained dark-blue like a sapphire (the sea in the first part of *Scheherezade*), H-major a somewhat more steely blue, A-major rose-colored, B-major—green (a *Pastorale* green!). Moreover, these colors applied mostly to the sharp tones, the flat ones serving in the main to express moods and feelings. He considered that instrumentation did not consist merely of "embroidering" over a ready-made sketch, but that it was born simultaneously with melody and harmony and was closely linked to them. Passing then from questions of musical theory to the general meaning and significance of his own work, he stressed the religious, pantheistic character of his operas. This religiosity was of a somewhat peculiar type. Thus, he did not believe in immortality; indeed he considered the very belief in immortality to be intolerable to man. "What could be more terrifying," he said, "than eternal life!" Death to him was absolutely beautiful, the most admirable token of God's mercy. And all the while he kept warning his young admirer against becoming too carried away by his work, against the wanton use of the word "genius," pointing to the many different influences that permeated it: that of Balakirev, Berlioz, Liszt, Wagner. Sometimes he would talk of the importance of the "Oriental" element in his compositions and he would quote the lines of the popular rhymster Kuzma Prutkov: "In front there's the East, in the back too, and all around . . ." He had long explored this fantastic treasure-house of inspiration, which before him only Glinka, Balakirev and Borodin had visited. How powerful had been the impression made upon his young friends by the melodies which Balakirev had brought back from his first trip to the Caucasus and from which he was later to create *Tamar* and *Islamey*. Rimsky-Korsakov, for his part, had always preferred the Arab-Persian East from which he had learned to weave a delicate and intricate pattern of delightful melodies.

He would, occasionally, make the most unexpected statements. On one such occasion, he asserted that what was important in music was neither melody, nor harmony, nor of course orchestration, but . . . rhythm. This was actually an indirect condemnation of his own work. For if the prime factor in music had been color, he would have been the greatest composer that ever was. But to the hidden sanctum of rhythm he had never found an easy access. As he himself put it: "No artist can convey that which he really and personally feels. What distinguishes the creative artist from the ordinary mortal is merely his more differentiated receptiveness to the subtle, less intense human emotions." But then he had never feared to contradict his own past statements. At times, he would feel a sudden disgust with all that to which he had devoted his whole past life. "All that we hear nowadays," he confided to his wife, "seems to me dry, cold, unpleasant. Ah! Beethoven's quartets or symphonies—that's a different matter . . . Also Chopin, and Glinka, and the Italians with their octet from *Lucia,* their quartet from *Rigoletto* and their many melodies. *That* is life! *La Donna e mobile*—that's music; whereas Glazunov—that's only technique. I dare say that the whole Russian School of Music

is really not music at all, but cold brain-work." He realized
of course, that such a severe condemnation of the "Mighty
Handful" constituted also a condemnation of himself, but
he was prepared to draw the logical conclusion from his statement and even to cease to write music altogether. But fortunately, this too was merely a passing mood.

IX

Nowhere, would it seem, did these contradictions appear
so clearly as in his attitude toward the "Handful," who had
nurtured and fostered him. In a letter to the singer Karmalina written many years earlier, Borodin had admitted that:
"As long as we were all in the position of eggs under a sitting
hen (I am thinking in this connection of Balakirev) we were
all more or less alike. As soon as the fledglings broke out
of their shells, however, they grew feathers. Each such set of
feathers was of necessity different from the next, and when
their wings grew, each one took off wherever his nature
drew him. This lack of uniformity of direction, of aspiration,
of tastes, of creative power, etc. is in my opinion the good
and not at all the bad side of the whole matter." And this
was true in particular of Rimsky-Korsakov. There could be
of course no question of "betrayal" on his part. He had simply freed himself from the shackles of his mentor, Balakirev.
Outwardly, in terms of everyday life, they continued to see
each other. And Balakirev, for his part, despite his many disappointments, continued to love him and to associate him
with all his musical ventures, and even to care for him mate-
rially by finding him well-paid lessons. At the same time,
Mili kept poisoning his friend's existence with his capricious
and despotic whims and absurd demands. Thus, for instance,
having secured his election to the post of director of the Free
School, Balakirev went on to teach Rimsky-Korsakov in public how to conduct an orchestra, until the latter had finally
to abandon his post. The same thing happened when Balak-

irev, having been appointed to the influential position of
Kapellmeister of the Court Chapel (a post once held by
Glinka) engaged Rimsky-Korsakov as his assistant. Here
again, after much friction, Rimsky-Korsakov was obliged
to resign and thus to forfeit a good salary and an official
residence.

And yet, for all these trying experiences, he remained
throughout his life a "Balakirevite" at heart. In fact, he was
perhaps the purest embodiment of the Russian School of
Music, as Stassov and Balakirev himself had dreamt it up.
More than any of the others, he had shown himself able
to blend his own creative talent with the Russian folk-song,
until it could appear to the untrained ear that he had borrowed everything from this folk-music, whereas indeed many
of these songs were of his own invention. He turned the
Russian fairy-tale, the Russian saga, the Russian legend into
music and thus continued that which Glinka had begun,
passing the Great Master's tradition on to the younger generation, the Liadovs, the Igor Stravinskys. Even in regard
to the issue over which he had parted company with his
friends, that of "dilettantism" versus "theoretical prepared-
ness" he had now, after many years of pedagogical experience,
returned to much of that which the "Handful" used to propound. Thus, after teaching most of his adult life at the
Conservatory, he now shared Stassov's and Balakirev's opinion that for men of talent, the Conservatory was not needed.
Indeed, his views on the subject were a sort of synthesis
of those once upheld by Rubinstein on the one hand and by
Balakirev on the other, namely that conservatories served
the needs of musical artisans, not of artists, and that their programs should be redrafted accordingly. More than that,
he had even retained some of Balakirev's favorite teaching
methods; he would encourage his pupils to study Berlioz
and Liszt, or would make them compose a *scherzo* "taking
as model the *scherzo* in Beethoven's Fifth Symphony." And
prior to his final quarrel with Balakirev, when one of his

pupils produced something particularly interesting, he would take him to visit his old friend and sometimes even call upon Stassov to join them, and they would sit listening, the three of them, while the young man played his piece, as though they were back in the good old times.

But besides, Rimsky-Korsakov had remained true to his friends also because the bonds of childhood friendship are the hardest to break. Just as he would allow nobody but himself to criticize him, he protected the others from undue criticism. "They are spitting into the well from which they have all drunk!" he would say. He resented the fact that in Beliayev's circle it had become fashionable to scold the "Handful," that even Liadov did it, and Dütsch, and the others. Glazunov himself had been so bold as to assert that Mussorgsky was "a poor, a very poor composer." And at such moments he would feel solidarity with Modest, with Mili, with all of them, as though it were *his* past, *his* life's work which they were thus scolding and condemning.

X

Shortly before his death, fame once again favored him with a last smile. A young gentleman-dilettante by the name of Serghei Diaghilev, who was interested in all the arts and who was publishing a fashionable magazine called "The World of Art" (in Russian: *Mir Iskusstva*)—which Rimsky-Korsakov, incidentally, did not approve of—was about to undertake yet another of his countless ventures: the organization in Paris of a series of Russian historical concerts. There had been in the past many such ventures: Glinka's attempts; the music festivals given on the occasion of the Paris world fairs; the concerts of Tchaikovsky's works, well-subsidized by his faithful benefactress, Mrs. von Meck; the no less well-subsidized concerts of Beliayev—all of them had been costly, none of them had succeeded in arousing any enthusiasm in French musical circles. Rimsky-Korsakov had himself conducted the latter and was therefore inclined to be particularly skeptical, when Diaghilev now suggested that he also conduct this new series. Indeed his first impulse was to refuse outright.

But it was difficult to refuse a request from Diaghilev, for the young man had a will of iron and a way of overwhelming you, of stifling you until the request was granted. Moreover, when he needed something or someone, he could be disarmingly charming. In the end, Rimsky-Korsakov too succumbed. Actually, he enjoyed the trip.

When he first appeared in the pit of the Paris Grand Opera on May 3, 1907, he was met with a veritable roar of applause. Though his sparse, lean figure and professional head with the steel-rimmed spectacles and long goatee beard were by now familiar to most European musical circles, this ovation was directed, of course, not to his talent as a conductor—he conducted as usual, colorlessly—but to his contribution as a composer, to the author of *Sadko* and *Scheherezade*, because of the charming gaiety which he had helped them discover in Russian music. And when the great Arthur Nikisch performed his *Suite from Czar Saltan* and *The Underwater Scene* from *Sadko*, the dazzling colors of his music sparkled and glittered as never before.

The concerts were followed by receptions and tea-parties, at Saint-Saëns', at Chevillard's. Diaghilev had only to whisper in his ear: "We've got to go, Nikolai Andreyevich!" for him to follow, docilely. He refused only one invitation, that of an expatriate Grand Duke; a man of principles, he could not forget that he was a liberal and that in 1905 he had even resigned from the Conservatory in protest against the actions of the Czarist police. He was introduced to Richard Strauss, but they exchanged merely a few conventional courtesies. He had been informed of the latter's remark: "We are no longer children to dabble in paints" and had found such a judgment of Russian music quite unpardonable. The younger French composers, on the other hand, were exquisitely polite and full of respect. Debussy, who reminded him of a young bull, and the somewhat dry, elegant Ravel had long been eloquently enthusiastic over his music—an enthusiasm which he found himself unable to reciprocate with regard to their own works, though the young critic Calvacoressi tried hard to arouse his interest in it and though, for all his ironic distrust, he noted mentally a few "passable" passages. He was even persuaded to attend a performance of *Pelleas et Melisande,* but he left early, remarking half in jest: "I won't listen any more, I may get to like it!" And when he heard the French commenting ecstatically about Mussorgsky, he would smile and mutter: "You picked out everything in his work that stinks, piled it up on an altar and are now worshipping it!"

In the spring of 1908, shortly after his return to Russia, he suffered his first attack of *angina pectoris.* On June 8th, when staying at his farm at *Lubensk,* he suffered a second attack. This time he did not recover.

CHAPTER SEVENTEEN

EPILOGUE

I

Often, the greater part of the process of dying occurs while man still is physically alive. Gradually, he loses contact with a life his weakening fingers can no longer grasp; his eyesight begins to play tricks; the colors around him begin to pale; his hearing weakens and then sound itself turns into silence; his feelings, too, lose much of their intensity so that parting becomes less painful and the imagination ceases to conjure up frightening visions of nothingness; then his memory begins to fail him; forgetfulness is followed by oblivion, and the world departs from his soul earlier than he himself departs from this world. Even his outward appearance changes: his physical attractiveness diminishes, his eyes grow dim, the charm of his intellect loses its spell, and those he leaves behind find it less difficult to mourn that which is no more than a pale image, a poor substitute for the one they knew and loved.

Stassov retained to the very end both his manly good looks and his live interest in all that was new in the world of art. His critical vigilance, however, was no longer what it had been. The members of Diaghilev's "The World of Art" group, for instance, were looked upon by him with blind hatred; he called them "the syphilitic poison of art." And yet they were basically merely another "levy of talents," like those he had so passionately loved and so warmly welcomed in the past. As before, he spent the summer at his villa in Pargolovo, where he would sit all day working on the small, glass-encased, hot terrace of the house, dressed—as was now his habit—in a Russian shirt of scarlet or orange silk, on his feet a pair of soft Moroccan leather boots. He wore this dress everywhere—at the theatre, at concerts, at work in the Public Library—quite oblivious of the somewhat comic effect it produced. On Sundays, friends would come out to visit him—old friends, new ones. Young Shaliapin would sing to them, Maxim Gorky would read to them. Sometimes Balakirev would join them and, sitting down at the piano, would play with his usual fire, but no longer with the same power.

In one respect Stassov had remained eternally young: he had retained all his passionate temperament, his youthful ardor of feeling. He was past seventy when the lady who had been his companion of several decades, Praskovia Aleksandrovna Minkina, died. A letter has come down to us, which he wrote shortly after this tragic event to his sister-in-law, Dimitri Stassov's wife. It is an extraordinarily moving document: "Life with this team-mate was wonderful," he wrote, "incomparable, all of pure gold, radiance and joy." And he went on to relate how: "something idiotic, absurd, farcical even happened to me when, having driven up to a flower shop to put in an order for a wreath and having walked in, apparently, quite calm, after having been to the Telegraph Office, after having quite indifferently eaten three cakes at Dominic's, I now, upon entering the store, suddenly burst into tears and started to weep and to cry like a lunatic. The salesman and the shopkeeper stood there gaping, helpless, while I continued to sob like mad and to scream through my tears: 'Look at me! Look at this silly 70-year-old fool, standing and sobbing before you only because he has just lost an old woman. But don't laugh at me! Remember this horror can happen to anyone of you, even though you are now still young and dapper . . .' But still more awful," Stassov went on, "was that night—that first night of my new life . . . when the girls had finished sewing the death shrouds and though it was already 3 o'clock in the morning, my poor departed had to be dressed in them right away, because the body was beginning to stiffen and later the arms and legs would have ceased to bend. I said: 'Well, we'd better wash her and dress her.' And the women replied: 'Yes, yes of course, but for that we will have to call in some women.'— 'What? What women?' I shouted in fury and pain and turning to her niece who stood there, an orphan like my old grey self, I said: 'Will you do it with me? Just you and me, nobody else? . . .' And she replied bravely and willingly: 'Yes, yes, just you and I . . .' Whereupon, drawing off my jacket, I turned up my sleeves and called for a basin of warm water, then picking up a clean loofah I got down on my knees and smothered with kisses those poor, stiff legs, as cold as stone, and clung to them as though they were something holy— because I sought forgiveness for the years of unhappiness I had caused her, the long years of grief and sorrow and pain and jealousy, worse than which there cannot be, and kissed them again and again, after which I started to wash the poor, pale, disease-ridden body. What did I care if that which lay before me was just a naked old woman—what did I care, when tears were streaming down my cheeks and I was going mad from sorrow and pain . . ."

He himself survived another ten years, dying on October 10, 1906, aged eighty-two. He is buried within the writers' corner of the monastery of St. Aleksander Nevsky.

II

Balikirev lived four more years.

He had retained his creative powers virtually to the very end, continuing to compose though, as always, with agonizing slowness. In 1905, when he was already 68 years old, he published his first (and only) piano sonata. This piece is full of youthful power and glamor. He had completed his first symphony in 1898; his second, however, was finished only in 1908, less than two years before his death. True, parts of it had been drafted some thirty years before and yet it is impossible to distinguish the old from the new. Such a return to

the past was possible only because his creative talent, though
it had in no way diminished, had been laid up, so to speak,
had ceased to evolve. This was the same Balakirev, with the
same prejudices, the same nervous tics, the same qualities
and faults. While his spiritual twin, Liszt, continued to grow
and advance through life, Balakirev—for all his admiration
for Liszt—had stopped at the point Liszt had reached in the
sixties and his newest works seemed thus merely an echo of
the past.

The *First Symphony* was a success when it was performed
at a concert of the Free School. This was also his last performance as a conductor. There were, of course, the usual
wreaths, and speeches, after which the symphony was soon
forgotten (although it was to be performed again abroad,
in Paris and London). Gradually he lost contact with the
world. Presently the Free School, bereft of his loving guidance and energy, ceased to exist. In 1895 he resigned also
from the Court Chapel. He lost touch with many of his
friends. He could not forgive Rimsky-Korsakov, Stassov and
Glazunov their friendship with Beliayev. New people now
surrounded him, only one of whom had real talent—Serghei
Liapunov. It is upon him that the old man now concentrated
all his remaining loving attention, though he highly over-
rated Liapunov's talent. He also appointed him as executor
in his will.

The public and the critics did not find it difficult to forget
him. Contrary to the now accepted tradition, no one even
remembered in 1906 to celebrate the fiftieth anniversary of
his career as a musician. And when in 1909 an attempt was
made to give a concert of his works, the performance had
to be cancelled at the very last minute, not a single ticket
having been sold in advance.

Abroad, interest in him was somewhat greater. The young
French critic Calvacoressi corresponded with him regularly
and this gave Balakirev real pleasure for, over-rating Calvacoressi's influence, he hoped that the latter might help him

to propagandize Liapunov's work abroad. It also gave him pleasure to learn from Calvacoressi that the younger French composers—Ravel, Debussy, Ducas—appreciated his music. In contrast, Calvacoressi's attempt to arouse *his* interest in *their* work was not successful, indeed it could not be successful: he had long ago ceased to be a revolutionary in music, open to everything new. He was most pleased to learn that Calvacoressi himself was of Greek origin and of the orthodox faith, which meant that he was "one of the family." This "family" included, in his opinion, aside from all other Orthodox believers, the various Slavic people, even the Poles, and especially the Czechs, whom he had many years before castigated for having "succumbed spiritually" to Germanic influence but whose present struggle against Germanization he now commended enthusiastically. He had even overcome his hatred for Smetana and had performed the latter's works at concerts of the Free School.

His attitude toward Chopin had also changed. In his early days, he had both loved and criticized him. Now his love was unqualified. He took an active part in the erection of a memorial to Chopin at Jeliazovo Volia, near Warsaw, in 1894, and even performed personally as a pianist at the inaugural ceremony. Shortly before his death, he also participated in the celebration of the one hundredth anniversary of Chopin's birth. He was not able, however, to conduct personally the orchestral suite he had written for this occasion; this was done by Liapunov.—He had also the opportunity to take part in the celebrations in honor of yet another of his friends, Berlioz. On the one hundredth anniversary of Berlioz's birth, in 1903, he was invited to conduct in Paris a series of memorial concerts. He refused, however, partly because he feared the fatigue of a long trip, partly because he thought he might not be able to get the right food in Paris.

And he was right not to leave St. Petersburg, for he was now too old to change his habits, even temporarily. He belonged to this life, to this country, to this town. Here he

was well taken care of, by an old cook who catered to his
every whim and by an old valet, a bachelor like himself (when
the latter had thought of getting married, there was quite a
drama in the Balakirev household!). Here he was known by
every policeman on duty, here his neighbors greeted him
deferentially and called him "Your Excellency" while he, for
his part, knew every church and every church-warden and
how they prayed and sang and where. Here he occasionally
would give parties, when he would show himself to be such
a capricious host that to visit him became quite an ordeal.
Here he had spent his youth, full of high hopes and illusions. Here he now awaited death, seated by the window,
beneath his ikons. And here death came to him, on May 29,
1910. He was buried within the walls of the monastery of St.
Aleksander Nevsky, which also sheltered the last remains of
Glinka, who had foretold him such a brilliant future, of
Stassov, who had believed in him in the lonely years of his
youth, and of his once-timid pupils, Mussorgsky, Borodin
and Rimsky-Korsakov, whom he had trained and cared for
and who had then turned away from him and against him to
follow each his own individual path.

Cui survived longest, as though selfishness and coldness of
heart possesses a life-giving power of their own. He went on
composing. He was past eighty when he decided to complete
Mussorgsky's *Fair at Sorochintzi,* retaining untouched the
author's original scenario and merely adding the missing
music. In this version, the opera was staged in St. Petersburg
in 1917. He died a year later, on March 14, 1918, at the peak
of the Revolution. His death passed unnoticed. Russia had
no time for music or musicians.

III

The lives of those endowed with creative talent do not
always end with death but continue to influence those who
came after them. In Western Europe, Glinka is nowadays

merely a name. Even in Russia, the founder of the Russian School of Music is still a controversial figure. But whether he was a hero, a "semi-God," a powerful original genius or merely a major talent, of parochial importance only, who showed himself unable for all his good intentions to cast off the bonds of Italian influence, his importance in the history of Russian music is no longer open to question. Whether his music was that of a "genius," whether it was original or not, it possessed at any rate a powerful "seed-bearing" quality. Even such a "Westerner" as Tchaikovsky had to admit that "we all have our roots in Glinka's *Kamarinskaya*." And the composers of the Russian School were bound to him by a near-religious loyalty. One has only to listen to *Prince Igor* or *Sadko* to be immediately reminded of Act I in *Ruslan and Liudmila*. The ancient epic, heroic Russia is already there for all to see. And the "Orient" so dear to the hearts of the "Mighty Handful" is also there, in Glinka's *Persian Choir,* his *Aria of Ratmir* and his *Lezginka*. His technique of orchestration, his harmonies left their imprint on the work of all later Russian composers; they shared even his prejudices (such as his preference for certain types of wind instruments to others). All that which is most fascinating about the orchestrations of Rimsky-Korsakov and Balakirev existed already in embryo in Glinka's work. Such a lasting impact has no peer in the history of music.

Borodin's symphonies found their way to Europe already in his lifetime. A Belgian Maecenas, Countess Mercy d'Argenteau (a former mistress of Napoleon III) contributed greatly to their popularization. At her invitation, Borodin travelled to Bruxelles to reap his full harvest of praise, fame and laurels. Liszt also did much to make his work well known. Among the French musicians, Ravel was his greatest admirer. His *Polovetsky Dances,* after having been made famous throughout the world by the Diaghilev ballets, have become a favorite of the concert stage and even of radio, and his *Second Symphony* and *Second Quartet* are also extremely popular. *Prince Igor* holds a permanent place in the Russian opera repertoire and is also performed occasionally in the West. Its fame is due partly to Shaliapin's brilliant performance in the three roles of Igor, of Prince Vladimir Galitzky and of the Tartar *khan* Konchak. All music-lovers will cherish the memory of this dilettante of genius, who started his ascent to world fame by presenting to the doorman of the Moscow Maecenas Mamontov a snow-sodden bundle of sheet music.

Balakirev's posthumous fame suffered a more dire fate. His *Tamar* (which he had dedicated to Liszt) and his overture *Russ'* are occasionally still played, but his symphonies, his brilliant sonata and the difficult *Islamey* are virtually forgotten. True, his name, his legend continue to live on in the history of Russian music. For some mysterious reason, he was not able, in his lifetime, to give all that which in his beginnings he had seemed able to give. But that which he did give merited surely a better fate.

Rimsky-Korsakov is still alive, both in Russia and in the West. His controversial music retains all its charm and yet it is also a constant source of disappointment. It was not his fault if his talent was a little one-sided. At least he tried to, and succeeded in squeezing out of it every drop that it contained.

Mussorgsky's posthumous fate was more unusual. Only gradually did the West come to realize that there lived in Russia a strange, sickly genius, one of the greatest creative talents music has ever known. The first to speak his name in Paris was, strangely enough, one of Mussorgsky's pet bogeys, Camille Saint-Saëns. He brought back from his trip to Russia the recently published *Klavierauszug* of *Boris Godunov*. But he did not take the trouble to study his find, never suspecting that here was something explosive, even revolutionary. Jules de Brayer saw this piece at Saint-Saëns' and asked the latter to let him have it. De Brayer immediately realized that there was something amazingly powerful and novel about this opera, and he became Mussorgsky's first champion in France, though for a long time his was a voice crying out in the wilderness. In vain did he make the rounds of the theatres in the hope that one of them might wish to stage *Boris*. None of them possessed adequate facilities. Through de Brayer, the score reached Debussy. Though Debussy had himself visited Russia (where he had become a sort of "pet pianist" in the household of the von Meck family, Tchaikovsky's friends and benefactors) he probably had not heard much good about Mussorgsky there, and so for a long time the music lay on Debussy's piano unopened. But when he finally started to play it, his admiration knew no bounds. He realized suddenly that he had now found a powerful ally in his struggle against the hated German romanticism, against that Wagnerianism which had swamped the musical world with its churning, leaden waters. Mussorgsky's far-sighted "shot into the future" was to mark with his imprint all the work of Debussy and his friends. But for a long time he remained an esoteric "composer's composer," in fact until the appearance of two new admirers of his music: the Russian singer Olenina and her French husband Baron Pierre d'Alheim. The latter's sparkling lectures and his wife's performance of Mussorgsky's *Songs and Dances of Death, Nursery* and *Lovely Savishna* brought forth in France (although as yet only in certain limited circles) a veritable cult of Mussorgsky. This cult, however, would never have acquired the major, almost national proportions it eventually attained, but for Diaghilev. In 1907 already, his series of Russian historic concerts (under Rimsky-Korsakov's baton) had increased the public's interest in Mussorgsky's, Balakirev's, Glinka's and Rimsky-Korsakov's own works. The following year, Diaghilev decided to organize in Paris a recital of Russian operas. He hesitated long, relates Calvacoressi (who was associated with him at the time), between Tchaikovsky's *Evgheni Onieghin* (an old favorite of his) and Mussorgsky's *Boris,* the importance of which even he—like most

Russians—did not quite appreciate. His choice fell on *Boris,* partly under Calvacoressi's influence, partly because he wished to show up Shaliapin in an advantageous role. But once his mind was made up, Diaghilev spared neither means nor effort in order to show the object of his choice at its very best. Russia's most famous singers were assigned to the various parts. The choir of the Mariinsky Theatre was shipped to Paris in its entirety. The talented Sanin was appointed director and the admirable Felix Blumenthal— conductor. The result was unforgettable. *Le Tout Paris* literally gasped with admiration.

Since then, the recognition of Mussorgsky's genius has become virtually general and unquestioned. His works are now an integral part of all concert and opera repertoires, even though—despite the fact that the original versions are now in print—they are still performed in Rimsky-Korsakov's arrangements. In 1914, Diaghilev staged also his *Khovansh-china,* with Shaliapin, in Paris. His *Fair at Sorochintzi* has often been produced both in Europe and in the U.S.A., though not in Cui's but in Cherepnin's version, whereby the latter—unlike Cui—changed Mussorgsky's original scenario, adding, however, in the missing places not his own music but excerpts based on Mussorgsky's original notes.

Mussorgsky's fame is also still alive, of course, in his own country, in Russia. There too, the conviction is growing with the public as well as the critics, that in the person of this "ignorant dilettante," Russia possesses a genius who ranks with the very greatest.

APPENDIX

List of Illustrations

FIG. 2.

FIG. 1.

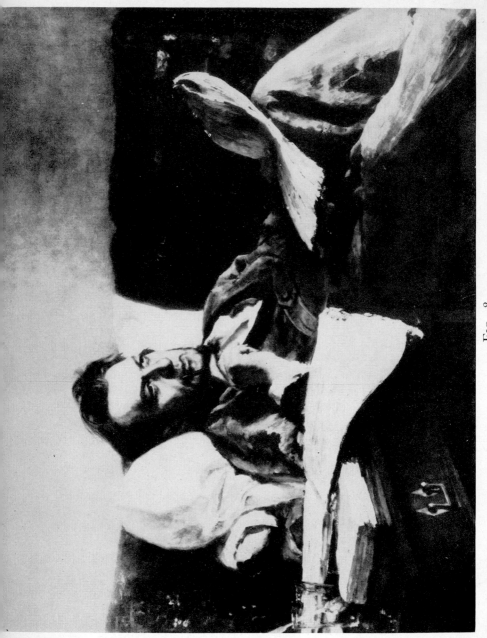

FIG. 3.

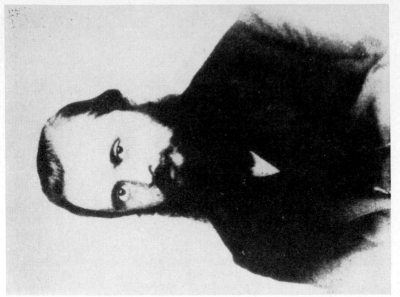

FIG. 5.

FIG. 4.

Fig. 6.

Fig. 7.

Fig. 9.

Fig. 8.

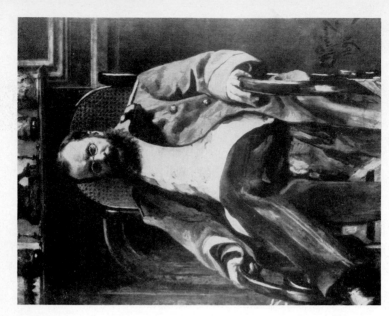

Fig. 11.

Fig. 10.

Fig. 13.

Fig. 12.